THE CAMBRIDGE COMPAN
ANDREW MARVELl

CW00552472

Andrew Marvell is one of the greatest lyric poets of
one of its leading polemicists. This *Companion* bring
perspectives to bear on the varied career and diverse writings of a remarkable
writer and elusive man. Drawing on important new editions of Marvell's poetry
and of his prose, scholars of both history and literature examine Marvell's work
in the contexts of Restoration politics and religion, and of the seventeenth-century
publishing world in both manuscript and print. The essays, individually and
collectively, address Marvell within his literary and cultural traditions and communities; his almost prescient sense of the economy and ecology of the country;
his interest in visual arts and architecture; his opaque political and spiritual
identities; his manners in controversy and polemic; the character of his erotic
and transgressive imagination, and his biography, still marked by intriguing gaps.

DEREK HIRST is William Eliot Smith Professor of History at Washington
University, St Louis.

STEVEN N. ZWICKER is Stanley Elkin Professor in the Humanities at Washington
University, St Louis.

A complete list of books in the series is at the back of this book

THE CAMBRIDGE
COMPANION TO
ANDREW MARVELL

EDITED BY
DEREK HIRST
AND
STEVEN N. ZWICKER
Washington University, St Louis

CAMBRIDGE
UNIVERSITY PRESS

CAMBRIDGE UNIVERSITY PRESS
Cambridge, New York, Melbourne, Madrid, Cape Town, Singapore,
São Paulo, Delhi, Dubai, Tokyo, Mexico City

Cambridge University Press
The Edinburgh Building, Cambridge CB2 8RU, UK

Published in the United States of America by Cambridge University Press, New York

www.cambridge.org
Information on this title: www.cambridge.org/9780521711166

© Cambridge University Press 2011

First published 2011

Printed in the United Kingdom at the University Press, Cambridge

A catalogue record for this publication is available from the British Library

ISBN 978-0-521-88417-4 Hardback
ISBN 978-0-521-71116-6 Paperback

CONTENTS

CONTENTS

CONTRIBUTORS

MATTHEW C. AUGUSTINE University of Oregon

PAUL DAVIS University College, University of London

DEREK HIRST Washington University, St Louis

JAMES LOXLEY University of Edinburgh

ANDREW McRAE University of Exeter

DIANE PURKISS Keble College, Oxford University

JOAD RAYMOND University of East Anglia

MICHAEL SCHOENFELDT University of Michigan

NIGEL SMITH Princeton University

JOHN SPURR Swansea University

NICHOLAS VON MALTZAHN University of Ottawa

PHIL WITHINGTON University of Cambridge

STEVEN N. ZWICKER Washington University, St Louis

1621	31 March	Andrew Marvell was born at Wynestead, near Hull, Yorkshire, son to the Reverend Andrew Marvell Sr, vicar of Wynestead, and his wife Anne (née Pease).
1624		Revd Andrew Marvell became Master of the Hull Charter House, a charitable foundation, and lecturer at Holy Trinity Church, Hull.
1629–33		Marvell appears to have attended Hull Grammar School.
1633		Marvell entered Trinity College, Cambridge, as a subsizar, or quasi-servant.
1637		Marvell's first published verse, in Latin and Greek, was printed in a Cambridge University celebratory volume, *Musarum Cantabrigiensium*, on the birth of the short-lived Princess Anne.
1638	April	Marvell was elected scholar at Trinity College, Cambridge; Marvell's mother died.
1639		Marvell took BA; may briefly have converted to Roman Catholicism.
1641	23 January	Revd Andrew Marvell drowned crossing the River Humber.
	September	Trinity College, Cambridge, moved to eject Marvell for non-performance of his college duties.

1642	22 August	Charles I raised his standard for civil war at Nottingham.
1642/3–7		Marvell travelled the Continent.
1645–6		In Rome, possibly with the young Duke of Buckingham and his brother Francis Villiers; Marvell visited Richard Flecknoe.
1647	12 November	Having returned to England, on this date Marvell sold inherited property outside Cambridge.
	November	Charles I attempted to escape from Parliamentary captivity at Carisbrooke Castle on the Isle of Wight.
1648–52		Until recently it was assumed that Marvell composed the majority of his lyrics over these years, after he had returned from the Continent some time before November 1647, and before the autumn of 1652 when he is likely to have left Nun Appleton. The assumption has been disputed.
1648	May to October	Second Civil War at its height.
	7 July	Lord Francis Villiers died; publication of Marvell's *Elegy upon the Death of My Lord Francis Villiers* presumably followed shortly thereafter.
	autumn	Probable composition of *To his Noble Friend Mr Richard Lovelace, upon his Poems*.
	5 December	Pride's Purge of Parliament, which ushered in the English Commonwealth, or republic.
1649	30 January	Execution of Charles I.
	24 June	Death of Henry Lord Hastings; publication of *Lachrymae Musarum*, including Marvell's *Upon the Death of Lord Hastings*, presumably followed shortly thereafter.

	August	Cromwell led army to Ireland.
	October	Parliament's *Resolves touching the Subscription to an Engagement* published, triggering the so-called Engagement Controversy.
1650	1 June	Cromwell returned from Ireland.
	20 June	The Commonwealth decided to invade Scotland.
	25 June	Lord Fairfax resigned his command and shortly afterwards travelled north to Nun Appleton.
	June–July	Probable period of composition of *An Horatian Ode upon Cromwell's Return from Ireland*.
	summer/autumn	Marvell joined the Fairfax household.
	late autumn	Composition of *To His Worthy Friend Doctor Witty upon His Translation of the Popular Errors*.
	November	Marvell likely to have written one version of *Tom May's Death*. May himself died on 13 November; Marvell may have written against him in 1647, and surely revised the poem after September 1661 when May was exhumed and cast out of Westminster Abbey.
1651	February	Marvell composed a Latin epigram on the embassy of Oliver St John to the Dutch.
	July–August	Marvell wrote *Upon Appleton House, To My Lord Fairfax*
	early August	The English army mustered within a few miles of Fairfax's estate to counter the threat of invasion from the north.
	3 September	Battle of Worcester, Cromwell's final defeat of the Scottish and royalist challenge.
1652	late	Marvell likely left Nun Appleton.

1653	21 February	Milton wrote on Marvell's behalf to John Bradshaw, President of the Council of State, recommending Marvell for government service.
	late February	Likely date of composition of first version of *The Character of Holland*, a poem revised in 1665 during the Second Dutch War.
	July	Marvell began his three-and-a-half-year tutorship of William Dutton, Cromwell's ward, within the household of John Oxenbridge at Eton College. Marvell's poem *Bermudas* was probably written in the following months; Oxenbridge was a Commissioner for the government of the Bermudas.
	16 December	Cromwell became Lord Protector under the Instrument of Government.
1654	February	Marvell sent the long Latin verse *Letter to Doctor Ingelo* to Dr Nathaniel Ingelo, chaplain to the Protector's embassy to Sweden.
1655	17 January	Anonymous publication of *The First Anniversary of the Government under His Highness the Lord Protector*.
	late autumn	Marvell travelled the Continent with William Dutton.
1656	spring	Marvell and Dutton at the Protestant Academy at Saumur.
	September	Marvell returned to England with the ailing Dutton.
1657	2 September	Marvell took government office as Latin Secretary.
1658	3 September	Death of Oliver Cromwell; sometime in the following months Marvell wrote *A Poem upon the Death of his Late Highness the Lord Protector*.
1659	January	Marvell elected MP for Hull, Yorkshire, to Richard Cromwell's short-lived parliament.

1660	2 April	Marvell elected MP for Hull in the Convention Parliament.
	1 May	Publication of Charles II's Declaration from Breda promising a 'liberty to tender consciences'.
	29 May	Restoration of Charles II.
	December	Marvell intervened in Parliament on behalf of John Milton.
	29 December	Dissolution of Convention Parliament.
1661	1 April	Marvell re-elected as MP for Hull to Charles II's Long or 'Cavalier' Parliament.
1662	18 March	The House of Commons ordered examination of 'the Difference' between Marvell and Thomas Clifford.
	20 March	The Speaker ordered Marvell to apologize for the quarrel with Clifford; Marvell refused, but was forced to acknowledge that 'he had given the first Provocation'.
	June	Marvell left for Holland in the service of the state and of the Earl of Carlisle.
1663	April	Marvell returned to the House of Commons after absence in Holland.
	July	Marvell went as secretary to the Earl of Carlisle on an embassy to Muscovy, Sweden and Denmark.
1665	5 January	Marvell assaulted a recalcitrant wagoner while en route near Hamburg and was rescued from a mob.
	30 January	Carlisle's embassy returned to London.
	22 February	Second Anglo-Dutch War is declared.
	3 June	Battle of Lowestoft; Edmund Waller subsequently wrote *Instructions to a Painter* in celebration, a work that prompted Marvell and others to participate in an extended controversial exchange.
	13 June	Revised version of *The Character of Holland* was entered for publication in the Stationers' Register.

1666	April	*The Second Advice to a Painter* was likely in manuscript circulation.
	late	Marvell likely wrote *The Third Advice to a Painter*, which was circulating in manuscript by early 1667.
1667	May	Marvell may have married the widow Mary Palmer whose name later appears in litigation over Marvell's estate and whose name testifies to the authenticity of Marvell's poems in the 1681 folio.
	10–13 June	Dutch fleet attacked the Royal Navy at anchor in the River Medway.
	June/July	Marvell wrote *Clarendon's Housewarming*.
	August	Marvell wrote a letter of condolence and epitaphs on the deaths of the two sons of his friend Sir John Trott. Milton's *Paradise Lost* was registered with the Stationers' Company. Marvell was writing *The Last Instructions to a Painter*.
	October–November	In the Parliamentary attacks on the now-disgraced Earl of Clarendon, Marvell spoke against exemplary punishment.
1668		Some scholars seek to date *The Garden* and perhaps other of Marvell's lyrics to this date and beyond.
1670	February	Marvell likely completed the first version of *The Loyal Scot*.
	March	Parliament at work on a new law against religious dissenters that was to become the Second Conventicle Act; Marvell called this 'the Quintessence of arbitrary Malice'.
1671	summer	Marvell wrote the Latin and English versions of the epigram on Colonel Blood's attempt to steal the crown.
1671–2		Marvell wrote Latin verses, *Inscribenda Luparae*, for the Louvre Palace competition.

1672	15 March	Declaration of Indulgence, granting limited religious toleration.
	November	Publication of *The Rehearsal Transpros'd*, which Marvell had been writing through the autumn.
1673–4		Various pamphlet attacks on Marvell in response to *The Rehearsal Transpros'd*.
	May	Samuel Parker's massive counterblast, *A Reproof to the Rehearsal Transprosed*, in the press.
	December	*The Rehearsal Transpros'd: The Second Part* was published.
1674	April–June	Marvell wrote *On Mr Milton's Paradise Lost*.
1676	June	Marvell published *Mr Smirke: Or, the Divine in Mode ... Together with a Short Historical Essay, concerning General Councils, Creeds, and Impositions, in matters of Religion*, a work attacking clericalist claims and excesses.
1677	29 March	Marvell clashed with the Commons Speaker.
	December	Marvell's *An Account of the Growth of Popery and Arbitrary Government* was published.
1678	April	*Remarks upon a Late Disingenuous Discourse Writ by one T. D.* licensed: a defence of clerical moderation and non-doctrinaire Protestantism and Marvell's last publication.
	August	Marvell died of a tertian ague.
1681	January	Publication of *Miscellaneous Poems*.

Like all others who work now on the life and times and writings of Andrew Marvell, we are indebted to Nicholas von Maltzahn's *Chronology of Andrew Marvell*.

ABBREVIATIONS

Chronology   Nicholas von Maltzahn's *An Andrew Marvell Chronology* (Basingstoke, 2005), is throughout referred to as *Chronology*.

Letters   Marvell's letters are quoted from *The Poems and Letters of Andrew Marvell*, ed. H. M. Margoliouth, rev. Pierre Legouis with E. E. Duncan-Jones, 2 vols. (Oxford, 1971); letters are cited parenthetically in the text by page number.

Poems   Marvell's poems, unless otherwise indicated, are quoted from *The Poems of Andrew Marvell*, ed. Nigel Smith, rev. edn (Harlow, 2007); poems are cited parenthetically in the text by line number.

PW   Marvell's prose is quoted from *The Prose Works of Andrew Marvell*, ed. Annabel Patterson, with Martin Dzelzainis, Nicholas von Maltzahn and N. H. Keeble, 2 vols. (New Haven, 2003); the prose is cited parenthetically in the text by volume and page number.

I

DEREK HIRST AND STEVEN N. ZWICKER

Introduction

The making of a *Cambridge Companion to Andrew Marvell* is a more likely enterprise in 2010 than it would have seemed in the late 1980s when Cambridge Companions to individual authors began to appear. Most obviously, the state of Marvell studies has been transformed by new editions of Marvell's poetry and of his polemical writings;[1] we have a more informed appreciation of Restoration politics and religion and of how to track Marvell's presence in those fields;[2] and we have a more finely grained understanding of writing culture, of manuscript and of print.[3] That culture was formed not only of individuals who might have thought of themselves as authors but also of communities that had, in some sense, authorial function – patronage circles, coteries of wit, of partisan affiliation, of spiritual affinity, of gender or perhaps of sexual identity. And in that emerging complication of authorship lies a more fundamental distinction of this moment. The very category of author as subject of study was in the 1980s in some dispute; it had of course been challenged by Foucault's deconstruction of authorship,[4] but now new historicists and cultural materialists were dispersing authorial agency into a broader circulation of social and cultural energy,[5] while discourse analysis of various kinds further complicated the notion of authorship.[6] More broadly too, historians had replaced the old 'history of great men' with a new social history of otherness and dissonance. But from that direction, paradoxically, came an impulse to recover authorship.[7] For what was at stake in the recovery of lost voices was not only identity politics and ideology but as well the conviction that individuals could raise – author – their own voices; ironically, the most progressive of moves in cultural studies depended on a rather regressive model of autonomy. But such tensions can be productive, and it is hard to imagine a more fruitful moment to hazard a volume on that most elusive author Andrew Marvell: isolate, pseudonymous, ventriloquizing, but collaborative and variously bound to networks of patronage and structures of patriarchy. Indeed, all the complexities of authorship now at play and in tension with histories of identity and print culture help us in recovering Andrew Marvell.

Yet the model of authorship still most congenial to modern audiences remains the individual and individuated author as genius. Nor should we be quick to abandon this model for Marvell. A number of essays in the *Cambridge Companion to Andrew Marvell* teach us new ways to appreciate Marvell within those bounds – the lyric grace, the command of cultural registers, the sinuous strength of design, the verbal dexterity and richness of wit. But these essays also teach us to interrogate the model even as they strengthen its claim, for authorship as social practice is newly unfolded by a number of contributors. The sociability of authorship, for example, has been documented as actual collaboration, and elsewhere the late Harold Love has brilliantly illuminated Marvell's verse satires as joint ventures.[8] But there is sociability as well in Marvell's virtual conversations and complicities with ancient and modern voices. The figure emerging from James Loxley's and Paul Davis's chapters, 2 and 3 respectively, in this volume is more deeply implicated in the languages and locutions of other poets than we have, until recently, been able to appreciate. The wonderful paradox that these essays demonstrate is that even as we see how little of Marvell's language belongs exclusively to Marvell, we understand more clearly that the poems could only have been written by him.

Nor is adaptation the practice of Marvell only as a poet. In Chapter 11, Nicholas von Maltzahn demonstrates that Marvell the prose controversialist was a superb mimic, a consummate practitioner of the art of borrowing another man's language and turning it sharply to his own purposes. Imitation allowed mockery and ridicule, but it also enabled Marvell to expropriate, and to redeploy – we might think, for example, and from a very different register, of the way *The Rehearsal Transpros'd* turns the churchmen's figure of a king as nursing father against their own rigour and intolerance. Of course, Marvell was a practised hand in appropriation. He left behind a wonderful trail of exhausted figures and tropes: Petrarchanism exploded by *To His Coy Mistress*, pastoralism drained of rural complacencies, the country house poem dilated almost beyond recognition and to purposes surely beyond Ben Jonson's imagination. But always, in verse and in prose alike, Marvell's programme of competition and possession was as deeply purposive as it was occasional. As Diane Purkiss shows in Chapter 5, Marvell went to school to others to discover how to admire, how to fix in time, the pre-sexual state; she suggests too how extraordinary were his exercises on this theme. The Catullan origins of *The Nymph Complaining for the Death of her Fawn* are not in doubt, but as Matthew C. Augustine demonstrates in Chapter 4, the Nymph is transformed into a figure whose instabilities and erotic indeterminacy cannot be contained by sources and analogues, what Marvell was elsewhere to call

'Roman-cast similitudes'. It has taken a modern age, with its own indeterminacies, fully to open and to be open to the scenes of erotic contemplation, invitation and transgression within Marvell's borrowings and adaptations.

And is there not something particularly of our moment, with its suspicion of the cost of political ideals and ideology, that makes us sensitive as well to the elusive character of Marvell's political identity and practice? For a long time, surely since the eighteenth century, Marvell has been heard as a singular political voice, as high-minded prophet of toleration and liberty; moreover, the figuring of political singularity would have appealed to Marvell's own imagining of himself as political actor – the man who might seize 'the poet's time' to stand against the corruption of his age. But he was as well the politician who reflected on the civil wars as 'a cause too good to have been fought for'. A number of scholars have in recent years excavated Marvell's texts for evidence of political commitments, situating him variously and eloquently within the shifting political consciousness of his times, amidst imponderables and contingencies. But to what degree did these times and contingencies allow Marvell to form a stable political personality – royalist poet? complaisant turncoat? loyalist servant? scourge of popery? emergent Whig? The effort to reduce these categories to logic or to unitary effect, let alone to discover in their midst a stable identity, leads always to exquisite parsing, and at the very least to the suppression of some elements of Marvell's story in favour of others. Consistency is a rare quality, and while John Milton, that paragon of purity and ideological coherence, and mentor and colleague to Marvell, might seem a standard by which to judge the younger man, we should not forget that Milton's own remarkable consistency was an achievement of some self-consciousness, even perhaps of manufacture. Most of Milton's contemporaries were less concerned with self-idealizing, and we may wonder if Marvell himself did not aim to deflate some of that persona in his doubting and ironic tribute *On Mr Milton's Paradise Lost*. And we may wonder too how to put together, how to make coherent, Marvell's later and apparently sterling career as polemicist in what was to become the Whig cause with his submission in 1671–2 of tributary – of abject? – verse on the divinity of Louis XIV's absolute monarchy.

Are there other, newer, ways to understand political identity? In Chapter 7, Phil Withington turns away from that beguiling theme of singularity to focus instead on Marvell's long history as practitioner and rhetorician of and for political community. After all, one of the most significant Marvell archives is the collection of constituency letters he wrote as MP and, Withington stresses, as citizen of Hull. Values of community, and here of commons and closes, are discovered too when we turn from institutions and urban environment to lands and landscape. Marvell's unusual responsiveness to the natural world has often been read as a form of excited spiritualism; in Chapter 8, Andrew McRae gives that responsiveness a striking social dimension that complements but goes beyond Marvell's surprising empathy with those who worked the Yorkshire fields. Indeed, McRae urges, there was something prescient in his capacity to imagine not merely the economies of the land but the violence of human practices.

Violence of feeling, violence of action, these are categories that we do not readily associate with Marvell the meticulous letter-writer, scrupulous parliamentarian, scrupling poet: after all, Michael Schoenfeldt reminds us in Chapter 6, Marvell was a poet absorbed by the very matter of aesthetics, by the epistemologies of representation, by perspectives and prisms, by the music and architecture of verse. And we can think of this poet's anger safely contained by the conventions of art as we look towards the satirist scourging wickedness and vice. But in Marvell's case, we need to note the depth of feeling, the acts and anticipations both of violation and predation embedded and implied not only in his satires but also at a number of junctures in his lyric poetry. In Chapter 5, Purkiss argues for the importance of exemplars and models in comprehending such violence, and indeed Davis goes further, in Chapter 3, by suggesting the presence in Marvell's work of a poetics of violence. In Chapter 12, Smith in turn urges us to consider the violence of the man, the outbursts and fighting in the House of Commons and on the German plains; in this regard, Smith observes as well the irony of a Marvell protesting his own lethargy. Does this irony put an almost confessional spin on the poet's fascination with that increasingly fashionable polarity of *otium* and *negotium*? A history of violence also played its part in Marvell's religion which, as John Spurr argues in Chapter 10, was constituted of contradiction: a delicate spirituality, an unmistakable and growing rationalism, and a violent anger against the bishops and their cruelties. Contradiction is of course not an implausible way of narrating Andrew Marvell, but can we go further? The tensions did not remain wholly in suspension; they drove him, and repeatedly, in two directions. One trajectory ran Marvell towards violence and vituperation, the other dispersed him into that more familiar Marvellian terrain of indeterminacy.

Indeterminacy is the defining condition of Marvell's epistemology. It is surely the defining condition of his poetics, as Augustine emphasizes in Chapter 4 – at the level of language, structures, feeling. And what of the spirit? For a mid-seventeenth-century lyric poet, Marvell is unusually silent on matters of the soul. There are of course the two wonderful dialogues, and his simulacrum of devotional anxiety played out in *The Coronet*; but as Spurr argues in Chapter 10, the pursuit of 'the religious' in Marvell is something of an exercise in infinite regression. Marvell's politics by contrast seem altogether in a different case, altogether determinate, or at least determinable. And yet the very fact of controversy and contradiction among and between those scholars and critics who have so variously construed Marvell's politics is surely its own argument. Here the test case must be Marvell's Cromwell, and in Chapter 9 Joad Raymond amply demonstrates that an interrogatory lies at the centre of all the Cromwell poems. We have long known this of the *Horatian Ode upon Cromwell's Return from Ireland*: it is Marvell's masterpiece of undefinition. As Raymond shows, a similar questioning of the relation of the person to the form drives all three Cromwell pieces – and, we might add, the unsettling representation of monarch and monarchy in *The Last Instructions to a Painter*. And what word more than 'unsettled' might describe the uncertainties of feeling that surround every gesture of erotic attachment in Marvell's poetry? The familiar analytic categories, heterosexual and homoerotic, seem all too fixed for the deep uncertainties of feeling that surround those young girls, those androgynous males, those appetitive and predatory adults who stalk Marvell's writing. But what pushes a pattern of unsettled literary affect towards a deeper indeterminacy are the echoes we may hear of the verse in the traces that remain of the life. Biography aims always to render as whole the necessarily disparate effects of the life, and in Marvell's case that has usually meant the suppression of one part of the lifework in favour of another: exquisite sensibility or patriot hero. But as Smith argues in Chapter 12, the biographer must remain committed to the recovery of the whole, whatever the incompleteness of the life records and however secretive the poet. This is a singular challenge in a case where heterogeneity and indeterminacy are both life and argument, indeed perhaps the life's argument.

Such an Andrew Marvell must seem especially companionable to our own times. 'Shakespeare our contemporary' has been the perennial theme not only of academics but also of a broader cultural appreciation of the ways in which older texts might speak, and might be made to speak, to succeeding generations. And Milton's idealizing of freedom of speech in the activist republic has given him contemporary urgency. But with Andrew Marvell we have had a less certain time hearing his intelligence and sensibility as our own. The twentieth-century Marvell was insistently aestheticized, even etherealized, by the tradition of appreciation that derived from T. S. Eliot. Eliot's denial to the poet of a personality certainly narrowed the grounds for later readers to exercise the faculty of empathy – critical, political, psychological. It is one thing to admire the literary genius, and Eliot did that. But the category of literary genius is always singular, always self-contained. Does it not close off the intimate traffic between circumstance and art and obscure the terrain of uncertainty across which that traffic moved? The various and interlocking perspectives of the *Cambridge Companion to Andrew Marvell* honour Marvell's art and disclose its circumstance; they open as well the indeterminacies which were very much his own, just as surely as they are ours.

NOTES

1. The poems have been edited by Nigel Smith, *The Poems of Andrew Marvell* (Harlow, 2003, rev. edn 2007), for the Longman Annotated English Poets series; the polemical works have been edited by Annabel Patterson with Martin Dzelzainis, Nicholas von Maltzahn, and N. H. Keeble as *The Prose Works of Andrew Marvell* for Yale University Press (New Haven, 2003).
2. On Restoration politics and religion see, for example, John Coffey, *Persecution and Toleration in Protestant England, 1558–1689* (Harlow, 2000); John Spurr, *England in the 1670s: 'This Masquerading Age'* (Oxford, 2000); Tim Harris, *Charles II and His Kingdoms, 1660–1685* (London, 2005); Annabel Patterson, *The Long Parliament of Charles II* (New Haven, 2008).
3. On writing culture see Harold Love, *Scribal Publication in Seventeenth-Century England* (Oxford, 1993); and as well his *English Clandestine Satire, 1660–1702* (Oxford, 2004).
4. Most famously and accessibly in 'What Is an Author?' in Michel Foucault, *Language, Counter-Memory, Practice*, ed. Donald F. Bouchard, trans. Bouchard and Sherry Simon (Cornell, 1977), 113–38.
5. The classic new historicist exploration of authorial agency is Stephen Greenblatt's *Shakespearean Negotiations: The Circulation of Social Energy in Renaissance England* (Berkeley, 1989); see also Jonathan Dollimore and Alan Sinfield, eds., *Political Shakespeare: New Essays in Cultural Materialism* (Cornell, 1985).
6. For a foundational expression of what became known as discourse analysis, see J. G. A. Pocock, *The Machiavellian Moment: Florentine Political Thought and the Atlantic Republican Tradition* (Princeton, 1975).
7. The impulse to recover authorship is evident, for instance, in Paul Seaver's fascinating recovery of an early modern artisan's mentality, *Wallington's World: A Puritan Artisan in Seventeenth-Century London* (Stanford, 1987). See also Germaine Greer, *Kissing the Rod: An Anthology of Seventeenth-Century Women's Verse* (New York, 1988), one of the earliest and most influential anthologies of early modern women's literary voices.
8. Love, *Clandestine Satire*.

Further reading

Editions

The Poems and Letters of Andrew Marvell, ed. H. M. Margoliouth, rev. Pierre Legouis with E. E. Duncan-Jones, 2 vols. (Oxford, 1971). This remains the classic, original spelling edition of Marvell's poems and the only modern edition of his letters. The canon of Marvellian texts has shifted slightly over the years.
The Poems of Andrew Marvell, ed. Nigel Smith (Harlow, 2003; rev. edn 2007), is now the fullest and most fully annotated edition of Marvell's poetry; it is further

distinguished from Margoliouth and Legouis in its modernization of spelling and accidentals.

The Prose Works of Andrew Marvell ed. Annabel Patterson, with Martin Dzelzainis, Nicholas von Maltzahn and N. H. Keeble, 2 vols. (New Haven, 2003); the only complete modern edition of Marvell's prose, fully introduced and annotated.

Criticism

T. S. Eliot, 'Andrew Marvell', first published in the *Times Literary Supplement*, 31 March 1921, repr. in *The Selected Prose Works of T. S. Eliot*, ed. Frank Kermode (New York, 1975).

M. C. Bradbrook and M. G. Lloyd Thomas, *Andrew Marvell* (Cambridge, 1940).

Pierre Legouis, *Andrew Marvell: Poet, Puritan, Patriot* (Oxford, 1965); originally published as *André Marvell: Poète, Puritain, Patriote, 1621–1678* (Paris and London, 1928).

J. B. Leishman, *The Art of Marvell's Poetry* (London, 1968).

John M. Wallace, *Destiny His Choice: The Loyalism of Andrew Marvell* (Cambridge, 1968).

Rosalie Colie, '*My Ecchoing Song*': *Andrew Marvell's Poetry of Criticism* (Princeton, 1970).

Donald Friedman, *Marvell's Pastoral Art* (Berkeley, 1970).

R. I. V. Hodge, *Foreshortened Time: Andrew Marvell and Seventeenth-Century Revolutions* (Cambridge, 1978).

Hilton Kelliher, compiler, *Andrew Marvell, Poet & Politician, 1621–1678: An Exhibition to Commemorate the Tercentenary of His Death* (London, 1978).

Annabel Patterson, *Marvell and the Civic Crown* (Princeton, 1978).

Warren Chernaik, *The Poet's Time: Politics and Religion in the Poetry of Andrew Marvell* (Cambridge, 1983).

and Martin Dzelzainis, eds., *Marvell and Liberty* (New York, 1999).

Derek Hirst and Steven N. Zwicker, 'High Summer at Nun Appleton, 1651: Andrew Marvell and Lord Fairfax's Occasions', *Historical Journal* 36 (1993), 247–69.

'Eros and Abuse: Imagining Andrew Marvell', *English Literary History* 74 (2007), 371–95.

Paul Hammond, 'Marvell's Sexuality', *The Seventeenth Century* 11 (1996), 87–123.

David Norbrook, *Writing the English Republic: Poetry, Rhetoric, and Politics, 1627–1660* (Cambridge, 1999).

Nicholas von Maltzahn, *An Andrew Marvell Chronology* (Basingstoke, 2005).

Blair Worden, *Literature and Politics in Cromwellian England* (Oxford, 2007).

Nicholas McDowell, *Poetry and Allegiance in the English Civil Wars: Marvell and the Cause of Wit* (Oxford, 2008).

2

JAMES LOXLEY

The social modes of Marvell's poetry

Marvell once confessed that he was 'naturally ... inclined to keep my thoughts private' (*Letters*, 166). Many readers over the years have discerned this private figure, reserved though not that austere, moving alone through the self-reflecting worlds of his lyric poetry. *The Garden* finds the Fall in the moment when the original self has to make room for another, rather than in any dalliance with tempting fruit: the human tragedy, it seems, lies in our not being able or permitted to live alone. No wonder, then, that Marvell 'can seem a spokesman for solitariness'. This is the poet as Richard Lovelace's emblematic snail, 'within [his] own self curl'd', and given also to the formal as well as thematic recreation of such tight self-enclosure in his verse.[1] A private, solitary, reflective Marvell has sometimes been separated as cleanly as possible – chronologically – from the Marvell who was a prose controversialist and Member of Parliament during the last two decades of his life.

But *The Garden* may have been written during the earlier of those two decades, and Marvell admitted his inclination to privacy in one of the regular letters concerning public events at Westminster he sent to the civic leadership of Hull: this is a strangely open intimacy, mirroring the intimate publicness of his unprinted and not extensively circulated early political poems. Clearly, solitariness and social engagement, private and public realms and writings, are closely and often perplexingly intertwined in his work. We should perhaps not seek to simplify this by seeing him as a writer for whom 'busy companies of men' (*The Garden*, line 12) figure only as a distraction or departure from the pursuit of a good and literary life. In another letter, this time addressed to an old parliamentary friend, Sir John Trott, after the death of a son, Marvell suggests three prime sources of consolation 'that may strengthen and assist' Trott in his grief. Together with 'the word of God' and 'the books of the Ancients' – deep reservoirs on which to draw, but principally matter for private study or contemplation – he also recommends 'the society of good men', and differentiates this in turn from the lesser help offered by 'diversion, business and activity' (*Letters*, 312–13). Clearly, society to Marvell is not just where fallen humanity unfortunately finds itself, but is instead a site of human flourishing, a place in which we are at home, and a resource to which we can turn in our most troubled moments.

Whatever its thematic claims, even some of Marvell's more solipsistic verse is marked by this sense of a vital sociality. His poetic career does not unfold or develop according to some immanent logic, either formal or subjective, towards an end which was all along its own, even if it can be shown to return repeatedly to particular generic, stylistic and thematic possibilities. It is instead determined, if that is not too strong a word, by the contexts, occasions and relationships with others in which poetry was deemed possible, decorous, or necessary. Proper names, from Richard Flecknoe (*Flecknoe, an English Priest at Rome*) to Archibald Douglas (*Last Instructions to a Painter*) via Robert Witty (*To His Worthy Friend Doctor Witty upon His Translation of the Popular Errors*) and Oliver Cromwell (*An Horatian Ode upon Cromwell's Return from Ireland, The First Anniversary of the Government under His Highness the Lord Protector, A Poem upon the Death of his Late Highness the Lord Protector*), emerge to offer themselves as interlocutors, addressees and focuses of attention; his social relationships, too, shape his engagements with landscape, most notably in the case of the Fairfax family and their estate at Nun Appleton. Marvell's social roles and exchanges surely inflect his poetry; indeed, we might think of his verse as their preserved remainder. The tempting thought that it *might* be such a remainder, and that even those poems that do not sing of their occasion might yet reveal the social context and conventions shaping their composition, drives on much literary-historical work. But although we are not necessarily seeking, as the pioneering historicist critic John Wallace was, a consistent Marvell either behind or within the whole corpus (a historicist version of a formalist ideal, perhaps), its poetic and political discontinuities have not lost their sometimes disorientating awkwardness for historically minded critics.[2] We are still often seeking to answer the question of what Marvell was pragmatically *doing* in writing this or that poem, and to address the issue of why these poems differ so starkly from predecessors or successors. However, since the poems seem to lack a consistent persona or authorial position, the social matrix of their production is essential to any account of that pragmatic endeavour.

Those proper names, and what we know of the poems' publication or circulation before the appearance of the posthumous collection of 1681, give us something to go on. From these details we can concoct the plausible narrative of a journey from the literary circles of 1630s Cambridge, circles which incorporated official occasions for the writing of both vernacular and neo-Latin verse, through the 'poetical academy' of the aristocratic Villiers brothers in Rome after the outbreak of civil war, and back to the sophisticated wits and royalist literary underground of 1640s London. In the following decade Marvell is to be found in attendance on the family of Lord Fairfax, the erstwhile commander of the New Model Army, and then as tutor to William Dutton, a young man entrusted to Cromwell's care. He established a place for himself in the public literary culture of the early Protectorate, and his rhetorical and linguistic skills led to salaried employment in government service. His subsequent career as an MP was accompanied by participation in oppositional coffee house culture and in another literary underground, this time rather more radical. Significantly, this is not just a narrative of a social life to which poetry is incidental, or which it merely records: rather, at all points on the journey verse is an element of the social exchange in which Marvell engages. For this reason, detailing the history of Marvell's poetic career, from this perspective, necessarily involves reference to the practices of literary production and circulation within which he was writing, practices which are not to be isolated from the rest of social and institutional life but are instead continuous with it. As even this brief outline of Marvell's movements suggests, though, no appeal to a general or non-specific sense of literary community, or to a simple model of the literary circle, will prove particularly illuminating. We are clearly looking at different modes or forms of sociality, found in particular configurations and ever-various relations to what lies beyond them. As Judith Scherer Herz has argued, when we talk of the literary circles or communities of this period,

> sometimes we are talking of lived spaces – houses, taverns, universities, Inns of Court, theatres – at other times, of the structure of social relations and gender relations; of brothers, sisters, cousins; of friendship, love, and conversation (in its sexual sense, as well); of patronage and politics; and of intellectual networks and religious affiliations. We are, too, talking of textual spaces: of title pages, of dedicatory poems and epistles, of circles and circulation, and of issues of genre.[3]

Paying attention to such differences will help us to flesh out the narrative of Marvell's poetic movements. However, it will also demonstrate the difficulties inhering in the critical resort to forms of social context as a basis for reading or interpretation, difficulties that Marvell's poetry to some extent acknowledges and exploits. If Marvell's poetry is the object of our critical attention it is also, in Rosalie Colie's enduring phrase, a 'poetry of criticism', a mode of verse writing that both meditates on and works through its own nature and function as poetry.[4] This is a form of self-reflexivity that makes it not so much monadic, sufficient unto and closed upon itself, as awkwardly alive to its readers and methodologically provocative, now, to both critics and historians.

Marvell's earliest surviving works were written for a volume of Greek and Latin poetry produced in 1637 by Cambridge University to celebrate the birth of a Stuart princess. Such celebratory volumes became increasingly common during the reign of Charles I, and testify not only to the place of literary composition in the institutional life of the university but also to the collective cultivation of writing, in classical languages and the vernacular, within its networks. England's only other university, Oxford, had a perhaps more highly developed and vigorously cultivated tradition of this kind of verse writing, and many surviving manuscript collections demonstrate the extent to which verse was composed, transmitted, read and imitated within the social frameworks offered by participation in these institutions. Yet the relationships such verse practice made possible were not all of one kind: they included the bonds between academics, between students, and between tutors and students, all of which could be described variously as ties of fellowship, friendship, familiar rivalries, familial bonds, or erotic attachments. They also included the necessarily inequitable relationships between patrons possessed of institutional authority and their dependants. Such networks also fed off, and opened on to, similar structures in other places. Both Marvell's Cambridge college, Trinity, and Christ Church, the Oxford college most identified with the university's literary circles, had strong links with Westminster School, an establishment that fostered its own verse traditions. Many of those who took part in university literary activities also participated in the life of the Inns of Court, which likewise had longstanding and various forms of literary sociability.[5]

Through the mediation of influential clerics such as Brian Duppa, Dean of Christ Church and a Caroline bishop, university wits could find their writing circulating in court circles, and the official volumes gathered and presented to the monarch to mark important events demonstrate the extent to which university practice could serve courtly occasions. In doing so they played a part in a public practice of verse writing which contributed ceremonially to the business of state, and a younger generation of university poets adapted this Stuart practice to the Protectoral moments that also exercised Marvell's pen in 1654–5 and 1658.[6] A figure such as Duppa was typical, though, in owing his institutional advancement to his dependence on noble patrons who exerted at least influence, and often control, over the mechanisms by which official appointments were made, and in whose households he also served. Such patronage structures, focused most obviously on the aristocracy but also on the more prosperous gentry, confound our modern sense of the distinction between private and public life. Here again literary relationships could be fostered with fellow participants in service and in the more hierarchical exchanges between patron and client.[7] The academy sponsored by the Villiers brothers, whom Duppa had served as tutor, was at least in part just such a structure, though it is of course Marvell's later employment in the

Fairfax household which furnishes us with the most shining evidence of the literary form such relationships could take. His post-Restoration proximity to the elder Villiers, Duke of Buckingham and writer of *The Rehearsal*, his spell in the service of the Earl of Carlisle, and his access to the library of the Earl of Anglesey when writing *The Rehearsal Transpros'd*, show that these kinds of transaction were a longstanding feature of Marvell's public and writerly life.[8]

Equally significant, though, are the interactions between poets in which Marvell participated. Sometimes, as with his elegy on the death of Lord Hastings, he appears to be taking his place among a community of writers all marking the same occasion, and therefore presumably sharing values, a purpose or social bond; elsewhere, as with the poems in praise of Lovelace and Milton that prefaced their published work, he can be seen to be marking or cementing a relationship based on mutual regard and shared commitments, especially to the reading and writing of poetry itself. It is for these kinds of interaction that the language of friendship seems most obviously appropriate: here we detect intimacy, respect or regard, a shared language and shared values. As this kind of relationship may be organized around the public values of politics, for example, or develop within an institutional context, it is not necessarily private, though it is usually imagined as a form of community distinguished from the fulfilment of public or professional roles. Associations of this kind are a notable preoccupation of the literary culture of seventeenth-century England, and are paradigmatically staged in the poetry of Ben Jonson in particular. For Jonson, friendship and its place in social relations are especially urgent topics, and he sought to give more explicit or ritual form to his ideal of literary and learned friendship in the gatherings of his 'Tribe' and the *Leges Conviviales* he proposed for them; he was just as keen to distinguish this amicable mode from the less morally discriminating kinds of club in which other poets of the time engaged.[9] In the England of the 1650s, literary friendship was fostered and codified most clearly in the writings of Katherine Philips and other members of the coterie she explicitly fashioned. Many of her poems to her friends take as their subject the amity they also enact, and she drew treatises on the topic from Francis Finch and Jeremy Taylor, both participants in her circle. Philips's group was not perhaps as closely or exclusively gathered as its use of coterie names might suggest; it certainly overlapped with the perhaps more various group who gathered for concerts at the house of Henry Lawes, the erstwhile court composer.[10] Less well known is the network fostered in the mid to late 1640s by Thomas Stanley, some of whose affiliates were later commemorated in his verse 'Register of Friends'. This names nine contemporaries, including Stanley's kinsmen Edward Sherburne and Richard Lovelace, but there is evidence also to suggest that in the 1640s Stanley constituted and sustained a perhaps wider group of friends as a more formal 'Order of the Black Ribband'.[11] Critics have recently argued that Marvell was to be found in Stanley's orbit at this time, along with contemporaries such as the newsbook writer and pamphleteer Marchamont Nedham, and the younger Cambridge poet and writer John Hall.[12]

Yet this picture of literary circles and friendships, and of Marvell's place within them, is not as simple or clear-cut as it might at first appear. We should certainly not take the declarations and celebrations of friendship to be found in seventeenth-century poetry as merely factual, as if their grammatical mood were always and simply indicative. The ways in which the poetry of friendship speaks of its bonds often suggest a tension between an ideal or promise of amity and the perils that attend its realization. Jonson, for example, manages simultaneously to celebrate the solidity of proper friendship in his poetry while also doubting its capacity to escape the corruption by power or private interest that threatens it: once he has implicated the language of fellowship and the medium of poetry in such corruption, declarations of his own sincerity in this selfsame medium can be affected by his own worried scepticism.[13] The idealizing Platonism of much friendship poetry can also speak not only of a wished-for communion of souls, but also of all the erotic investments and bodily affects that such language renders metaphorical or otherwise sublimates and disavows. Into such writing the sexing of bodies as male or female inevitably enters, to complicate the poetry's apparently secure sense of the bond that it marks; in the same movement, an avowed homosociality finds itself implicated in the homosexuality it is usually at pains to transcend.[14] In a poem entitled 'Friendship' that is obliquely addressed to Stanley, the poet and playwright James Shirley answers verses his friend has written 'in praise of his Mistris' with a poem that steadily displaces the heterosexual utterance that triggers it, declaring instead a love between friends that appropriates the language and vocabulary of desire:

> And yet I have a Mistris all this while,
> But am a convert from that Sex, and can
> Reduc'd to my discretion, love a man,
> With Honour, and Religion; Such a one
> As dares be singly virtuous gainst the Town …
> As handsome as thy Mistris, more divine,
> And hath no fault but that I call him mine:
> My jealousie doth cloud his name, 'tis fit,
> Nor art thou ripe for thy conversion yet.[15]

The poem's epigraph from the third of Virgil's *Eclogues* evokes the pain of a female lover bidding farewell to her male beloved, her sad valediction apparently borrowed by Shirley for his jealous male speaker. It is perhaps also significant that Virgil's poem dramatizes not friendship but a singing contest between rival shepherds who begin the eclogue trading insults, acting out a potentially hostile rather than amicable poetic exchange. Paul Hammond has argued that just these kinds of ironies, disavowals and indirections mark Marvell's lyric poetry, and point not to the communion of souls idealized in the literature of friendship but to more socially fraught ways of being together.[16]

This vision of community was also complicated and compromised in other ways. Stanley, like Philips, was a staunch royalist, and the 'Order of the Black Ribband' of which he and Shirley wrote was apparently a royalist club whose members were enjoined to wear a piece of black ribbon in sympathy with the sufferings of Charles I. John Hall was an intimate of Stanley and Lovelace and addressed poems in friendship to both, at the same time writing vigorously in support of the more radical elements in the parliamentary coalition.[17] Other figures also show how literary amity might reach across the boundaries of political and religious allegiance: the same Thomas May who was to be mercilessly condemned in Marvell's most strongly royalist poem contributed commendatory verses to James Shirley's *Poems* of 1646, despite his involvement in parliamentarian literary activity and Shirley's proclaimed fidelity to the 'Black Ribband'. Marvell himself affirmed his 'esteem' for Samuel Butler's mock-epic poem *Hudibras*, describing it as 'an excellent piece of Wit' despite its satirical attacks on religious nonconformity (*PW*, 1:413). Clearly, literary connections between poets did not always reflect or coincide with shared political commitments. But that does not mean that such literary bonds necessarily reflected instead a shared allegiance to higher values, since the transcendent character of such values was often either hard to establish or compromised by actions and events. An individual's convictions might be complicated enough to elude the crude generalizations of party labels, and party distinctions themselves were not always simple or binary, so some affiliations that look strange from a distance could indeed be based on shared political or religious preoccupations. Furthermore, the shifting imbalance of power throughout the 1640s and 1650s often brought former enemies into new alignments. But Hall, whose position in the later 1640s certainly admitted of some complexity, is recalled by Stanley in his 'Register of Friends' without the fondness shown to his fellows: instead, Stanley revisits the differences between them, almost seeming to continue a polemical quarrel rather than celebrate a friendship. Lovelace, by contrast, contributed an elegy to Hall's posthumously published translation of work by the Greek Neoplatonist Hierocles.[18] And Marvell's public esteem for Samuel Butler did not extend to his witty friend John Cleveland, whose most famous, aggressively royalist poem is satirically diminished in *The Loyal Scot*.

In fact, shared political values might generate forms of collective identity that complicate, rather than simply instantiate, the model of a properly habitable community. The evidence of volumes such as *Lachrymae Musarum*, which brought together a substantial collection of elegies for Lord Hastings, or the great gatherings of commendatory poems prefacing the editions of Jacobean and Caroline writers put out by the royalist publisher Humphrey Moseley, would appear to suggest that royalists sought to reconstitute a destroyed Stuart communal order in choral utterance. This is often described as the literary recreation, in a 'cavalier winter', of the court community that the wars had destroyed, but this underplays the extent to which royalist activity was necessarily both more and less than the continuation of Caroline courtliness.[19] 'Royalism' as a label had no domestic currency prior to the 1640s, and the gatherings of the king's supporters in the war years were inevitably partisan in a manner that court culture could never be (indeed, some of the most prominent courtiers of Charles's pre-war reign were equally prominent in opposing him once sides were taken).[20] The king's rule became the focus for a political desire, and royalism was itself a manifestation of this distance between current circumstances and a longed-for object. Royalist nostalgia for a Stuart unity lost in the outbreak of partisanship is both restorative and reflective: while it seeks to conjure up a faithful recreation of the world it desires, it also recognizes the loss of that world as the condition of its own emergence and even manages to enjoy its own polemically partisan vitality.[21] This is one reason why Charles attracted martyrological language even before his military defeat. Royalism therefore operates in a moment that is self-consciously at odds with itself, necessarily out of joint, and royalist evocations of fellowship or community are marked by a sense of an essential if paradoxical self-estrangement.

This self-estrangement is detectable in the conflicting ways in which royalist writing presents itself. Effort is expended not just on decrying the vulgar, but also on seeing the processes or circles through which loyal utterance writing circulates as the continuation of threatened forms of sociality. In their addresses to each other, royalist writers suggest that they are preserving an otherwise extirpated social order. So it is no surprise to find royalist writers deploring the Babel of disordered voices into which public conversation has descended, or condemning the broadening out of the sphere of political engagement towards a differently imagined public. But at the same time, royalism was a party to this process and eagerly deployed its means, readily embracing the printing press, pamphleteering, newsbooks and popular literary genres. A figure such as John Berkenhead could be a participant in the refined circles of Katherine Philips and Henry Lawes while also serving as one of the most prolific of the royalists' print propagandists in both verse and prose.[22] John Davies, friend to both John Hall and Richard Lovelace, claimed that there were a number of 'secret *Clubs*' into which 'the wits of the ruin'd party' formed themselves in the later 1640s, but he did not think that such communities existed for mutual support or consolation; rather, 'these hatched *Mercuries, Satyres*, and *Pasquinado's* that travelled up and down the streets with so much impunity, that the poor weekly *Hackneyes* durst hardly communicate the ordinary Intelligence'.[23] Humphrey Moseley's editions of courtly writers were aimed at a broader than courtly market, as were the royalist verse miscellanies he also published.[24] The commendatory poems in the many volumes of royalist verse put out by Moseley and others therefore address not just the poets or the inhabitants of the circles in which they move, but also the readers beyond those circles who can now gain access to the work by buying it from a bookseller. To see such writings first as the transactions of an embattled community would be to ignore this primary, if indirect, address to a differently constituted reading public. Such poems in fact often demonstrate an acute awareness of their wider contexts, and in *Tom May's Death* Marvell puts into the mouth of the deceased Ben Jonson a ringing declaration of the royalist poet's public and active role in the contemporary political moment. Yet Jonson's spectrality in this poem, even as he insists on his timeliness, testifies to royalism's complicated sense of its proper moment.

Uncertainties over the nature and extent of literary communities were not peculiar to royalists, despite the fact that their enemies were more optimistic about the opportunities for positive cultural and religious reform presented by the diminution of monarchical and episcopal power, and were more obviously inclined to embrace as beneficial the wider participation in public affairs that accompanied the expansion of parliamentary government and the collapse of the system of book licensing early in the 1640s. Parliamentarian and republican writers articulated normative notions of national, cultural and religious community that they sought to weave into a usually flawed and disappointing reality. Eventually prominent among such principles was a republican ideal of civic and individual liberty that had cultural and literary, as well as political and religious, dimensions.[25] Taking an initially indecisive leave of literary royalism, Marvell's poetry comes to engage with these ideals, though not in any simple fashion. *An Horatian Ode upon Cromwell's Return from Ireland* disavows poetry as a form of idleness or unworthy leisure, the 'numbers languishing' that a 'forward youth' will need to consign to the shade if he is to take his place among the citizenry of the new republic. But these sentiments, of course, are expressed in verse: formally, the poem adapts to its republican context a lyric mode that had been prominently practised in the Caroline past, helping to forge a new idiom of public praise.[26] Yet it has its tonal uncertainties, as if it were not entirely sure of its addressees, or perhaps as if its addressees were not entirely sure of themselves. That the *Horatian Ode* was not committed to the press, unlike so much of the work of his contemporaries at this time, only adds to its complicated sense of its own proper milieu. Later in the 1650s, *The First Anniversary of the Government under His Highness the Lord Protector* explored the meaning and limits of Protectoral rule and its strained relationship both to the republican vision of a public and to radical religious refigurations of the church.[27]

The Restoration satires parody a revived idiom of courtly praise, taking their place in a similarly revived pre-war tradition of scurrilous and fugitive verse attacks, or libels, aimed at court and state. While pre-war satires had often circulated widely in manuscript their Restoration successors could reach print, as Marvell's did, through the efforts of clandestine radical presses.[28] Much of Marvell's verse, therefore, like that of many of his contemporaries, is involved in the active examination and exploration of the social scope and significance of literature, especially as it is opened out into new social contexts and changing forms of publication and circulation. Often, this puts a strain on the relationship between what the poem seems to say and the genre, form or medium of its saying. Such a poetry can hardly be affirming or testifying to its place in given circles or communities, since these circles are themselves not simply given: if Marvell's poetry substantiates a range of social relationships, it also speaks reflexively and critically to the meanings and possibilities with which such poetry, and such relationships, can be invested.

There are some aspects of this picture we still need to consider, though, and doing so brings us up against one of the most characteristic and oft-remarked features of a Marvellian poetics. The evidence furnished by the proper names, specific relationships and particular occasions that shape the poetry notwithstanding, the commitments and the affiliations of much of Marvell's poetry remain perplexingly shadowy, open to being read in wildly differing ways by different critics, and hard to corroborate or pin down through external evidence. While demonstrating that Marvell can plausibly be located in or around the Stanley network at the end of the 1640s, Nicholas McDowell nonetheless has to concede that 'there is no mention of Marvell in Stanley's "Register of Friends" or in any of the writings of the Stanley circle; there is no commendatory poem by Marvell for any of their publications'.[29] Similarly, Nicholas von Maltzahn has remarked on Marvell's only flickering presence in the literary gossip or conversation of post-Restoration London. And assessing the sources that shed light on the printing of Marvell's painter poems in the late 1660s, Martin Dzelzainis comments that 'the one name missing from the file is that of Andrew Marvell himself; but then, like Macavity, he is never there'.[30] There is sometimes surprisingly little to go on, in other words, in determining the extent of Marvell's involvement in specific contexts and social circles. This absence of corroboration is felt all the more keenly because the affiliations and involvements of the poems themselves are often difficult to gauge.

Paul Hammond has persuasively suggested that the poetry generates this difficulty from its somewhat cagey use of 'the grammar of commitment':

> In Marvell's poetry the pronouns 'I', 'you', 'we', and 'they' fashion or inhabit a complex semantic field. They temporarily bring into being an author or speaker, an addressee, an implicit community, but the rather coy way in which they achieve this is a principal component of the elusiveness which many readers find to be characteristic of Marvell's poetry.[31]

Some of those poems that at first sight appear to propose or enact an affiliation can actually be read as holding their addressees at arm's length. Marvell's poem for *Lucasta* – *To his Noble Friend Mr Richard Lovelace, upon his Poems* – implies that Lovelace's work arrives belatedly into a hostile world:

> Our times are much degenerate from those
> Which your sweet Muse with your fair fortune chose,
> And as complexions alter with the climes,
> Our wits have drawn th'infection of our times.   (lines 1–4)

Since 'our civil wars have lost the civic crown' (line 12), Lovelace's book will be assailed by 'Word-peckers, paper-rats, book-scorpions, ... barbèd censurers' (lines 19, 21). The poem then paints a mock-heroic picture of Lovelace defended by an army of female admirers, with Marvell himself comically forced into declaring a commitment:

> And one, the loveliest that was yet e'er seen,
> Thinking that I too of the rout had been,
> Mine eyes invaded with a female spite,
> (She knew what pain 'twould be to lose that sight).
> 'O no, mistake not,' I replied, 'for I
> In your defence, or in his cause would die.'   (lines 41–6)

The specific nature of 'his cause' is a matter of critical disagreement, and Marvell's concluding pledge of allegiance is at odds with a 'studied deployment of pronouns, adjectives and verbs' that 'builds a wall dividing the way things were from the way they are now – and makes it clear that he is on the other side of it from Lovelace'.[32] Such distancing, and its mock-heroic manner, invite critical speculation: principled differences could be postulated, but John Hall – who certainly differed politically from Lovelace – would seem to be more generously encomiastic in his commendatory poem. And this bond isn't the only one that can seem difficult: even Marvell's long-presumed amity and intimacy with Milton, and the poetic tribute to *Paradise Lost* that is its crowning glory, has been read as marked by the ignoble affects of rivalry and jealousy to which Shirley's poem on 'Friendship' confessed.[33]

Yet if Marvell's poetry sometimes undermines its own apparent commitments, its ready way with allusion would appear to indicate a contrasting conviviality. The most recent edition of the poems notes resemblances to works by more than a hundred other poets, many of them the subject of multiple allusions, and many too either his English contemporaries or the ancient and modern Continental poets in whom those contemporaries had a strong interest. It has been suggested that Marvell is not so much a borrower as a sharer, drawing on 'a common and fashionable fund of conceits and topoi', but his allusiveness has also been seen as evidence of his engagement in the kinds of literary circle or conversation for which too little other evidence exists.[34] In alluding to the works of others Marvell establishes a dialogue with them, perhaps demonstrates his proximity and his connection, or even affirms a bond. But allusion is itself an oblique or shadowy way to refer, and requires from those who follow its movements the repeated effort of reading rather than a once-and-for-all decoding. It is 'a very large and wittie figure', a kind of pointing or reference by resemblance which can be both semantically and pragmatically fecund: 'like an echo, it depends on the noise that makes it, but is no less a presence that resounds, reverberates, distorts, mocks, or amplifies'.[35] Its etymological derivation from the Latin for 'play' might suggest, too, that it is not necessarily employed as a reliable means to higher ends; as a form of play, it may be both an end in itself and something set apart from the instrumental uses of language, or even a joco-serious blurring of these categories.

The suggestion that Marvell's poetry 'echoes' the works of others is a familiar one, too, and the fragmentary resemblances between his poems and their possible sources are often described interchangeably both as echoes and as allusions. But Marvell's writing also handles echoing, and therefore allusion, thematically. The main resource for such handling is the myth of Narcissus and Echo as told in Ovid's *Metamorphoses*, an enormously influential text for English Renaissance writers. It was the focus for an innovative retelling by James Shirley, itself echoing Shakespeare's *Venus and Adonis*, which was twice published separately in 1646 and included with his *Poems* the same year. Abraham Cowley's *The Mistress* of 1647 contained a work entitled 'The Echo', the concluding three lines of which resemble phrases from Shirley's poem. Cowley's 'Echo' also resembles verses by the Italian poet Giambattista Marino; Stanley translated them as 'The Eccho' and 'Echo', and published these variants in his collections of 1647 and 1651 respectively.

But other thematic renderings of Echo were possible. She was associated in classical sources with the god Pan as well as with Narcissus: in one such version she redoubles his song, while in another she is the unattained object of his desire. Stanley translated poems by the Greek poet Moschus that give form to both these versions.[36]

In Marvell, echo features at its simplest as an aural realization of agreement or affirmation. The godly settlers of *Bermudas* conclude their song with the wish that their praise of God might 'arrive at Heaven's vault: | Which thence (perhaps) rebounding, may | Echo beyond the Mexique Bay' (lines 34–6), while in *Music's Empire* echoes are 'called ... from their sullen cell' (line 7) to ring out in praise of their 'gentler conqueror' (line 22), possibly Fairfax or Cromwell. Similarly, *Clorinda and Damon* ends with 'flow'ry pastures' (line 27) singing of a Christianized Pan, while 'Caves echo, and the fountains ring' (line 28), repeating to Pan the heavenly music of which he is the source. In all these works we can hear a lyric self-consciousness: echo functions as figure for art, which is itself imagined as a form of re-sounding or affirmation. But the reading of echo as artistic utterance is stated most directly in Marvell's epigrammatic fragment *Upon a Eunuch: a Poet*, which balances the biological incapacity of a poet 'unable to thrust a sickle at the virgin harvest'[37] against a fantastic translation of one Pan myth into the other. He strikes or rapes Echo, and she produces music as his mirroring offspring. Yet this echo could only awkwardly be described as an affirming chorus, complicated as it is by its indications of violence, thwarted masculinity, and compensating hyperbolic fantasy. Invoking the poet as an impotent mower identifies him with the troubled figures of the enigmatic pastoral poems, rather than with the divine Pan or his harmonious tribe. And the consonance between animal gut and human guts in *Flecknoe*, the latter emitting a repining echo of lute strings made of the former, is in fact a bathetic reversal of art's affirmative re-sounding. Another kind of mockery is offered by the linguistic process of repetition itself. The echoing of words can be unsettlingly ironic, confronting speaker and reader alike with a meaning in repetition that undermines what it repeats. An Echo who speaks back necessarily turns the words put to her back on themselves and on to their utterer. As Joseph Loewenstein suggests, this use of echo is also an opening on to satire, and was allegorically recognized as such in classical literature.[38]

Such complications chime with another important aspect of Marvell's poetics, most compellingly articulated in *To His Coy Mistress*. Allusions to Ovid's Latin and to the English translations of the *Metamorphoses* by Arthur Golding and George Sandys have been detected in Marvell's poem; it also features some resemblances to an important section in Shirley's 'Narcissus' in which Echo unexpectedly recovers her capacity to speak her own words and attempts the verbal seduction of the 'coy' focus of her affections. These latter resemblances point to the possibility that the poem as a whole thematically mirrors Shirley's addition to his source. As Nigel Smith has noted, the poem appears to call attention to its debts: when the speaker refers to his 'echoing song', he is pointing out that it is the song of Echo that he echoes.[39] Furthermore, in echoing Shirley's Echo, the poem is returning her to the condition from which she had been so unexpectedly liberated. But the poem's reference to itself as an 'echoing song' is more significant than such brittle wit alone might suggest, and points us towards a more challenging interpretation of the figurative presentation of an echoic art. As Paul Hammond says, 'Marvell thought of his own song as "echoing", not simply in the sense that it reverberates in the vault, but because, like Echo's cries, it can only imitate the fragments of other men's speech'.[40] This is particularly true of *To His Coy Mistress*, which has justly been described as a 'dazzling . . . collage of the best bits of other people's poems'.[41] The Ovidian narrative, though, matters enough to the poetry for it to have been called 'Marvell's private myth', suggesting thematic and formal implications beyond this particular work.[42] Echo's predicament is aligned with Marvell's own allusiveness, posing the more general critical question of how we might comprehend the function of this large and witty figure.

As a mode of copious referentiality, a means of gesturing outwards to the words and work of others, poetic allusion encourages us as readers to trace each of the encounters it stages, to imagine an ongoing conversation, a club or a school or an order, in which Marvell and his poetry are properly at home, and a social bond to which a poem gives form. This is a perfectly reasonable, realistic ambition. But attending only to such a possibility means underplaying or ignoring those qualities of allusion that are most starkly highlighted in its rendering as echo or Echo, and in the identification of poetry and art with this potentially strange kind of re-sounding. The involuntary utterances Echo is able to make are meaningfully, though ironically, expressive, but are at the same time blank, alienated repetitions. In echoic verse words are both owned and disowned, used with their full pragmatic force and held fastidiously between the tongs of quotation. If allusion affirms or identifies, it also distances; if it articulates something as sure as the occasions of a friendship or commitment, it also toys with their vocal manifestation. It complicates the relations it posits.

We might therefore be tempted to see in this an image of Marvell as the 'politic' snail-self of Lovelace's poems, judiciously calibrating his degrees of social involvement and communal affiliation from within the security of a rhetorical shell, tempering his commitments with a range of figurative get-out clauses. But from the perspective of the poetic speaker, echo manifests a relation between words and selves that runs counter not only to an ideal of candid communion, amity or fellowship, but also to any such ideal of careful self-possession. In the Ovidian narrative of Echo we find an allegory of much more psychologically complex relations between desire, consciousness and language, where speaking is not encountered simply as the act of a sovereign, conscious self.[43] Stripped of her capacity to speak her own words, then reduced to this already secondary voice, Echo becomes an image of a selfhood unable properly to speak its own truth. A poetry that invokes such a model is not simply a poetry of personae; it is also one in which the integrity of a speaking persona is retrieved from presupposition, as it is in the compelling peculiarities of *The Nymph Complaining for the Death of her Fawn* and *The Unfortunate Lover*. Marvell's 'echoing song' generates relations between works that might not be completely assimilated to the claims either of the individual or of community; it teases critics, too, in its surprising experimentation with the terms of poetic utterance, disturbing even now the critical principles or assumptions on which our accounts of Marvell's life in writing depend.[44] We can sometimes hear an uncanny music issuing from the Marvellian caves, cells and fountains: not only a familiar kind of voice, a voice at home in itself, its place and its times, but also the impossibly bewitching sound of reverberations never heard before.

NOTES

1. Blair Worden, *Literature and Politics in Cromwellian England* (Oxford, 2007), 54; Richard Lovelace, 'The Snayl', in *The Poems of Richard Lovelace*, ed. C.H. Wilkinson (Oxford, 1930), 136; see also Christopher Ricks, *The Force of Poetry* (Oxford, 1984), 34–59, esp. 58–9, and David Reid, 'The Reflexive Turn in Early Seventeenth-Century Poetry', *English Literary Renaissance* 32 (2002), 408–25.
2. John Wallace, *Destiny His Choice: The Loyalism of Andrew Marvell* (Cambridge, 1968).
3. Judith Scherer Herz, 'Of Circles, Friendship, and the Imperatives of Literary History', in Claude Summers and Ted-Larry Pebworth, eds., *Literary Circles and Cultural Communities in Renaissance England* (Columbia, MO, 2000), 15.
4. Rosalie Colie, *'My Ecchoing Song': Andrew Marvell's Poetry of Criticism* (Princeton, 1970).
5. Arthur Case, *A Bibliography of English Poetical Miscellanies 1521–1750* (Oxford, 1935), 27–63; Harold Love, *Scribal Publication in Seventeenth Century England* (Oxford, 1993), 217–29; Michelle O'Callaghan, *The English Wits: Literature and Sociability in Early Modern England* (Cambridge, 2007), 10–34.
6. James Loxley, *Royalism and Poetry in the English Civil Wars: The Drawn Sword* (Basingstoke, 1997), 18–42; Edward Holberton, *Poetry and the Cromwellian Protectorate: Culture, Politics and Institutions* (Oxford, 2008), 61–118.
7. Ian Green, 'Duppa, Brian (1588–1662)', *Oxford Dictionary of National Biography*, online edn.; Cedric Brown, ed., *Patronage, Politics and Literary Traditions in England, 1558–1658* (Detroit, 1993).

8. Martin Dzelzainis and Annabel Patterson, 'Marvell and the Earl of Anglesey: A Chapter in the History of Reading', *Historical Journal* 44 (2001), 703–26; *Chronology*, 10–11, 71–88, 91–2, 102.

9. Timothy Raylor, *Cavaliers, Clubs and Literary Culture* (Newark, NJ, 1994), 71–110; O'Callaghan, *English Wits*, 35–59; Earl Miner, *The Cavalier Mode from Jonson to Cotton* (Princeton, 1971), 250–82.

10. [Francis Finch], *Friendship* (1654); Jeremy Taylor, *A Discourse of the Nature, Offices and Measures of Friendship* (London, 1657); Carol Barash, *English Women Writers 1649–1714: Politics, Community and Linguistic Authority* (Oxford, 1996), 55–100; Hero Chalmers, *Royalist Women Writers 1650–1689* (Oxford, 2004), 56–72; Ian Spink, *Henry Lawes, Cavalier Songwriter* (Oxford, 2000), 94–9.

11. Thomas Stanley, *Poems and Translations*, ed. Galbraith Miller Crump (Oxford, 1962), xxvi-xxvii, 354–66; Stella Revard, 'Thomas Stanley and "A Register of Friends"', in Summers and Pebworth, eds., *Literary Circles and Cultural Communities*, 148–72; Nicholas McDowell, *Poetry and Allegiance in the English Civil Wars: Marvell and the Cause of Wit* (Oxford, 2008), 13–31. I am very grateful to Dr McDowell for allowing me to read his book in advance of its publication.

12. Hilton Kelliher, compiler, *Andrew Marvell: Poet & Politician 1621–1678* (London, 1978), 33–4; Nigel Smith, '"Courtesie is Fatall": The Civil and Visionary Poetics of Andrew Marvell', *Proceedings of the British Academy* 101 (1999), 181; McDowell, *Poetry and Allegiance*, 13–111; Worden, *Literature and Politics*, 54–81.

13. James Loxley, 'Performatives and Performativity: Ben Jonson Makes His Excuses', *Renaissance Drama* 33 (2004), 63–85.

14. Arlene Stiebel, 'Not Since Sappho: The Erotic in the Poems of Katherine Philips and Aphra Behn', in Claude Summers, ed., *Homosexuality in Renaissance and Enlightenment England* (Binghamton, 1992), 153–71; Harriette Andreadis, *Sappho in Early Modern England* (Chicago, 2001), 76–83, 95–107; Alan Bray, *The Friend* (Chicago, 2003).

15. James Shirley, *Poems* (London, 1646), 68. Sandra Burner, *James Shirley: A Study of Literary Coteries and Patronage in Seventeenth-Century England* (Lanham, MD, 1988), 159, corroborates the identification of Stanley as the poem's addressee.

16. Paul Hammond, *Figuring Sex between Men from Shakespeare to Rochester* (Oxford, 2002), 204–25.

17. Stanley, *Poems and Translations*, xxvi; McDowell, *Poetry and Allegiance*, 53–69.

18. Stanley, 'Hall', in 'A Register of Friends', *Poems and Translations*, 359–60; Lovelace, 'To the Genius of Mr. John Hall. On his exact Translation of Hierocles his Comment upon the golden Verses of Pythagoras', in his *Poems*, 190–92.

19. Miner, *Cavalier Mode*, 282–97; Loxley, *Royalism and Poetry*; Jason McElligott, *Royalism, Print and Censorship in Revolutionary England* (Woodbridge, 2007); Robert Wilcher, *The Writing of Royalism 1628–1660* (Cambridge, 2001).

20. John Adamson, *The Noble Revolt: The Overthrow of Charles I* (London, 2007); Malcolm Smuts, 'The Court and the Emergence of a Royalist Party', in Jason McElligott and David Smith, eds., *Royalists and Royalism during the English Civil Wars* (Cambridge, 2007), 43–65.

21. See Svetlana Boym, *The Future of Nostalgia* (New York, 2001), 41–55.
22. Sharon Achinstein, *Milton and the Revolutionary Reader* (Princeton, 1994), 71–101; McElligott, *Royalism, Print and Censorship*; P. W. Thomas, *Sir John Berkenhead, 1617–1679: A Royalist Career in Politics and Polemics* (Oxford, 1969), 28–196.
23. John Davies, preface to John Hall, trans., *Hierocles upon the Golden Verses of Pythagoras* (London, 1656), sig [b3v].
24. Adam Smyth, *'Profit and Delight': Printed Miscellanies in England, 1640–1682* (Detroit, 2004), 172.
25. David Norbrook, *Writing the English Republic: Poetry, Rhetoric and Politics 1627–1660* (Cambridge, 1998); David Armitage, Armand Himy and Quentin Skinner, eds., *Milton and Republicanism* (Cambridge, 1998); Quentin Skinner, *Liberty Before Liberalism* (Cambridge, 1998).
26. Norbrook, *Writing the English Republic*, 243–71.
27. Derek Hirst, '"That Sober Liberty": Marvell's Cromwell in 1654', in John M. Wallace, ed., *The Golden and the Brazen World* (Berkeley, 1985), 17–53; Worden, *Literature and Politics*, 137–53; Joad Raymond, 'Framing Liberty: Marvell's First Anniversary and the Instrument of Government', *Huntington Library Quarterly* 62 (2001), 313–50; David Loewenstein, *Representing Revolution in Milton and His Contemporaries* (Cambridge, 2001), 143–71.
28. Andrew McRae, *Literature, Satire and the Early Stuart State* (Cambridge, 2004); Harold Love, *English Clandestine Satire 1660–1702* (Oxford, 2004), 21–123.
29. McDowell, *Poetry and Allegiance*, 50.
30. Nicholas von Maltzahn, 'Marvell's Ghost', in Warren Chernaik and Martin Dzelzainis, eds., *Marvell and Liberty* (Basingstoke, 1999), 57; Dzelzainis, 'Andrew Marvell and the Restoration Literary Underground', *The Seventeenth Century* 22 (2007), 405.
31. Paul Hammond, 'Marvell's Pronouns', *Essays in Criticism* 53 (2003), 232, 219.
32. Martin Dzelzainis, 'Literature, War, and Politics, 1642–1668', in David Womersley, ed., *A Companion to Literature from Milton to Blake* (Oxford, 2000), 12.
33. John McWilliams, 'Marvell and Milton's Literary Friendship Reconsidered', *Studies in English Literature* 46 (2006), 155–77.
34. Annabel Patterson, *Marvell and the Civic Crown* (Princeton, 1978), 13, summarizing J. B. Leishman, *The Art of Marvell's Poetry* (London, 1966).
35. John Barton, *The Art of Rhetorick Concisely and Compleatly Handled* (London, 1634), 27; Mary Orr, *Intertextuality: Debates and Contexts* (Cambridge, 2003), 139.
36. Burner, *James Shirley*, 15; *The Collected Works of Abraham Cowley*, ed. Thomas Calhoun, Laurence Heyworth and Robert King, 3 vols. (Newark, NJ, 1989–93), II:270–1; Stanley, *Poems and Translations*, 112 and 120; John Hollander, *The Figure of Echo: A Mode of Allusion in Milton and After* (Berkeley, 1981), 6–22; Joseph Loewenstein, *Responsive Readings: Versions of Echo in Pastoral, Epic, and the Jonsonian Masque* (New Haven, 1984), 10–32.
37. Trans. Smith, *Poems*, 188.
38. Loewenstein, *Responsive Readings*, 18–19.
39. Smith, note in *Poems*, 82–3; Hammond, *Figuring Sex*, 219; Robert Ray, 'Marvell's "To His Coy Mistress" and Sandys's Translation of Ovid's

Metamorphoses', *Review of English Studies* 44 (1993), 386–8; Shirley, 'Narcissus, or The Self-Lover', stanzas 4, 65–80, in *Poems*.
40. Hammond, *Figuring Sex*, 224.
41. McDowell, *Poetry and Allegiance*, 39.
42. Hammond, *Figuring Sex*, 224.
43. Jonathan Goldberg, *Voice Terminal Echo: Postmodernism and English Renaissance Texts* (London, 1986), 14–37; Lynn Enterline, *The Tears of Narcissus: Melancholia and Masculinity in Early Modern Writing* (Stanford, 1995), 167, 174–5.
44. Derek Hirst and Steven N. Zwicker, 'Eros and Abuse: Imagining Andrew Marvell', *English Literary History* 74 (2007), 371–95, especially 390–1.

Further reading

Carol Barash, *English Women Writers 1649–1714: Politics, Community and Linguistic Authority* (Oxford, 1996).
Paul Hammond, 'Marvell's Pronouns', *Essays in Criticism* 53 (2003), 219–34.
Harold Love, *Scribal Publication in Seventeenth Century England* (Oxford, 1993).
Nicholas McDowell, *Poetry and Allegiance in the English Civil Wars: Marvell and the Cause of Wit* (Oxford, 2008).
Earl Miner, *The Cavalier Mode from Jonson to Cotton* (Princeton, 1971).
Michelle O'Callaghan, *The English Wits: Literature and Sociability in Early Modern England* (Cambridge, 2007).
Annabel Patterson, *Marvell: The Writer in Public Life* (Harlow, 2000).
Timothy Raylor, *Cavaliers, Clubs and Literary Culture* (Newark, NJ, 1994).
Claude Summers and Ted-Larry Pebworth, eds., *Literary Circles and Cultural Communities in Renaissance England* (Columbia, MO, 2000).
Blair Worden, *Literature and Politics in Cromwellian England* (Oxford, 2007).

3

PAUL DAVIS

Marvell and the literary past

The literature of the past has a strong presence in the writings of Marvell. In phrase, in genre and in theme, his verse is what he famously calls it in *To His Coy Mistress* – 'echoing song' (line 27) – and his prose works too, for all their polemical topicality, reverberate with memories of earlier authors and texts. Of course, we expect the poets of Marvell's generation to imitate: originality did not become a touchstone of literary value until the middle of the eighteenth century. Many of Dryden's poems cannot properly be understood without a knowledge of Virgil, Horace and Ovid, and even Milton, whose brawny originality exempted him (in the view of Harold Bloom) from the 'anxiety of influence', has in fact been shown carefully to negotiate with a whole host of ancient and modern predecessors. But Marvell is different. The extraordinary extent of his allusiveness has been a central element of his critical reputation ever since T. S. Eliot's famous essay published to commemorate the tercentenary in 1921 of his birth. Eliot heard 'a whole civilization' in four lines of *To His Coy Mistress*:

> But at my back I always hear
> Time's wingèd chariot hurrying near:
> And yonder all before us lie
> Deserts of vast eternity.   (lines 21–4)

But it turns out he didn't know the half of it. Eliot noted a form of poetic surprise invented by Homer, an echo of a line and a half from an ode by Horace or alternatively of a couplet from one of Catullus's love elegies, and some traces of the 'savage austerity' of Lucretius's materialist cosmology in his philosophical epic *De Rerum Natura*. But later commentators have doubled the length of that list, adding a trope from the tragedies of Euripides and Seneca ('Time's wingèd chariot hurrying near'), an epithet stolen from Herrick or Cowley or both ('vast eternity'), and even, in the lines which immediately follow (containing the reference to 'my echoing song'), an 'embedded' translation of a whole epigram from the *Greek Anthology*, written in the third century BCE by one Asclepiades.[1]

The extreme range of Marvell's engagement with the literary past is one of the main reasons he is so challenging to get to grips with as a poet. In the case of other poets, imitativeness is usually a help to the reader; indeed, that was its chief purpose. By situating their work within generally recognizable traditions, early modern poets highlighted the particular areas where they were innovating. Much of Marvell scholarship since Eliot's essay has taken the form of source study conducted on the basis that Marvell conforms to that norm. Reasonably enough: surely we will be in a better position to understand the *Horatian Ode upon Cromwell's Return from Ireland* once we know what exactly Marvell meant by 'Horatian', or *Upon Appleton House, To My Lord Fairfax* once we have determined how far he intended it to be a 'country house poem'. This mode of inquiry has yielded useful discoveries (as we shall see) but its exponential growth over recent years has contributed to what is increasingly being seen as a crisis in Marvell studies. The poetic wood, a number of Marvellians now warn, is in danger of becoming blocked from view behind scholarly trees. And indeed that does not seem unduly alarmist when a critic can claim that everything about *The Nymph Complaining for the Death of her Fawn*, a notoriously elusive lyric even by Marvell's standards, falls into place as soon as we recognize that Marvell was writing in the tradition of 'aulic song known as the *calcya*, composed by the renowned Greek lyricist Stesichorus of Himera'.[2] I do my best in what follows to avoid further narrowing this scholarly impasse, but this essay is written in the belief that it is the peculiar quality of Marvell's relationship with the literary past, as much as the pedantry of scholars, which has put us in it. Accordingly, I seek to bring out that peculiarity by contrasting Marvell's traditionalism with the models of imitation developed by other poets of his era, particularly Ben Jonson and Milton. My other main aim is to suggest links between Marvell's problematic involvements with past literature and his inquiry into a set of intractable problems with which his poems are persistently and brilliantly preoccupied: the problems of time.

The best point of entry into these twin lines of argument is *Tom May's Death*. Considerable uncertainty surrounds the dating of this poem (anything from the late 1640s to the early 1660s is possible), and some scholars doubt that Marvell wrote it at all, chiefly because its apparently royalist sentiments are difficult to reconcile with his support for the Commonwealth. But those dubieties are of a piece with the characteristically Marvellian interest in temporal disruptions and discontinuities developed within the poem. It is in the tradition of Lucianic satire, in which the poet journeys to the underworld and hears the great dead cast judgements on their living descendants – a literary mode which naturally makes emblematic questions about imitation and inheritance. That association is further promoted in this case because the ghost to whom Marvell gives a voice is Ben Jonson. Imitation, as a moral and imaginative process, preoccupied Jonson throughout his works, culminating in his posthumously published collection of critical observations *Timber, or Discoveries* (1640). There, following the lead of classical authorities on imitation such as Quintilian and Seneca, he had emphasized the need for vigilance and discrimination: the past must not be lazily replicated but vigorously reanimated. The Jonson of *Tom May's Death* is the ghostly embodiment of this emphasis. Meeting the newly deceased May at the entrance of the Elysian Fields, he derides him for plotting in his translation of Lucan's *Pharsalia* simplistic parallels between the Roman and English civil wars, failing to see 'How ill the measures of these states agree' (lines 43–4). And he enacts his own contrastively dynamic understanding of history by travestying the opening of May's translation, so that, for instance, 'Warres more then civill on Aemathian plaines | We sing' becomes 'Cups more than civil of Emathian wine, | I sing' (lines 21–2) (May was a heavy drinker).

But Marvell was giving Jonson a taste of his own imitative medicine, rewriting him as he rewrites May. The encounter of the two ghosts is haunted by echoes from the commendatory poem which Jonson provided for the first (not so crudely pro-republican) instalment of May's translation of Lucan. Moreover, the nexus of this link is the keyword 'translated' (i.e. 'travestied') which describes Jonson's upending of May's words but which itself overturns the concluding lines of Jonson's 'To My chosen Friend, The learned Translator of Lucan, Thomas May, Esquire': 'so the worke will say: | The sun translated, or the son of May'. It's not clear who comes off worst in this intertextual crossfire – May for having forfeited the high regard in which Jonson once held him by his increasingly strident republicanism since Jonson's death, or Jonson for having given hostages to fortune by praising May so unguardedly in the first place. Either way, the complex layering of echoes in this early exchange does not sort easily with the famous passage later in the poem heroizing the poet as the guarantor of continuity between past and present:

> When the sword glitters o'er the judge's head,
> And fear has coward churchmen silencèd,
> Then is the poet's time, 'tis then he draws,
> And single fights forsaken Virtue's cause.
> He, when the wheel of empire whirleth back,
> And though the world's disjointed axle crack,
> Sings still of ancient rights and better times,
> Seeks wretched good, arraigns successful crimes. (lines 63–70)

Critics often quote this as representative of Marvell's thinking, but its uplifting certainties derive from Jonson's serenely Elysian point of view. Couched in an emblematic mode widely regarded by this time as old-fashioned in contexts of political debate, the passage develops a one-dimensional image of time that looks nostalgic when set against the multiperspectival vision of history communicated by Marvell's dynamic practice of allusion across the poem as a whole. In fact, in so far as that practice is itself Jonsonian, such a confident invocation of 'ancient rights' (in the civil war period everyone from the fieriest Leveller to the most diehard royalist claimed to be defending these) might be considered a betrayal of Jonson's own critical principles. Perhaps we should have been warned by the little forcing together of present and past, common enough on the face of it but suggestive in the circumstances, which gave Jonson's rhetoric its lift-off: 'Then is'.

Marvell's trumping of Jonson in *Tom May's Death* provides a template for understanding an attitude he often adopts towards the literary past, particularly in the group of shorter love poems and religious lyrics which come first in the running order of the posthumous edition of Marvell's *Miscellaneous Poems* (1681). In these poems, Marvell heeds Jonson's call to revitalize the past but takes it to extremes, developing a reformatory poetics considerably more radical than the essentially conservative Jonson would have been prepared to authorize. At times, in fact, he pushes Jonsonian imitativeness to a point where it almost intersects with the open hostility towards received wisdom characteristic of the other dominant English poet of the generation before Marvell's: John Donne.[3] 'Who makes the Past, a patterne for next yeare', Donne declares in his great New Year's Day verse letter to his friend Sir Henry Goodyer, 'Turnes no new leafe, but still the same thing reads.' Marvell's early lyrics are made out of past books, but he sometimes seems Donne-ishly intent on tearing those books to pieces rather than, as Jonson might, merely taking leaves out of them. Thus, in *Bermudas*, he systematically rewrites phrases from Edmund Waller's *The Battle of the Summer Islands* (1645), cancelling its courtly and classicizing vision of paradisal eroticism in favour of a godly presentation of the islands as a rediscovered Eden.[4] And in *A Dialogue between the Soul and Body*, much of the first stanza (spoken by the Soul) is translated from the Jesuit Hermann Hugo's Latin emblem book *Pia Desideria* (1624), before the Body, in the second, capsizes Hugo's otherworldly mysticism, starting with the Pauline epigraph which epitomizes his hatred of the flesh, 'Who will deliver me from the body of this death', which now appears as 'O who shall deliver me whole, | From bonds of this tyrannic soul' (lines 11–12).

The scholar who discovered those echoes in *A Dialogue between the Soul and Body* concluded that Marvell was playing 'humorous havoc' with Hugo.[5] But in the two poems generally regarded as the most characteristic and achieved of Marvell's early lyrics – *The Coronet* and *To His Coy*

Mistress – allusiveness is bound up with real violence. These poems are not often aligned, but they make a natural pair: both are unusually rich in echoes even by Marvell's standards, closely dependent on specific 'metaphysical' sources, and both are unusually tightly structured (elsewhere, when writing in the metaphysical mode – in *The Gallery*, for instance, or *Mourning* – Marvell abandons the syllogistic cohesion which Donne and his followers so prized). Their structures are underpinned by an almost identical rhythm: in each, a frame of logical argument, painstakingly assembled over the course of the first two thirds of the poem (32 out of 46 lines in *To His Coy Mistress*; 18 out of 26 in *The Coronet*), is destroyed in a violent spasm of emotion in the final third. And in both cases, most strikingly of all, what is being lashed out against includes Marvell's own fastidious historical sensibility, the intricate responsiveness to the past characteristic of his 'echoing song'.

In *To His Coy Mistress*, the turn comes after the lines so admired by Eliot for their attentiveness to tradition, and it may have been because Eliot recognized the next paragraph in which the speaker openly propositions the mistress as an implicit attack on that traditionary temper that he noted the change of tone but did not go on to discuss it. Harried by lust, the lover now harasses the mistress with formulations of temporal immediacy ('Now, therefore, while . . .', 'instant fires', 'Now . . . while we may', 'And now', 'at once') and as he does so the allusive range of his language contracts accordingly. Previously he expressed himself in canonically established phrases like 'Time's wingèd chariot' and 'vast eternity'; now he tastelessly improvises hyper-Donnean mixed metaphors about rolling 'strength' and 'sweetness' into 'one ball' (scholars are still arguing about whether it's a cannonball, a medicinal bolus, or the philosopher's stone) and tearing pleasures through 'the gates of life' (in some manuscripts it is 'grates' instead, and editors often give as their reason for choosing one or the other that it is the most bizarrely novel).[6] Slow-grown literary eloquence is a nicety he no longer has time for. His desire is carnal, and such bookishness is for 'vegetable' lovers.

The effect is even more marked in *The Coronet*. Here no one disputes that Marvell is reflexively concerned with aspects of his own technique. The poem has been called a 'palinode' (a formal response to a previous poem),[7] such is its dependence on George Herbert's 'A Wreath', and 'A Wreath' belongs to the subset of poems in *The Temple* which explicitly address the problems of writing devotional verse. Marvell shares Herbert's general misgivings about poetic artifice, but he inflects them in the particular direction of allusiveness. 'A Wreath' made no mention of time but *The Coronet* is thoroughly chronological: its speaker, realizing he has 'long, too long' crowned his saviour's head with thorns (line 1), takes apart the garlands of flowers that 'once' adorned his shepherdess's head (line 8) 'And now' sets about re-weaving them to make a coronet such as Christ has 'never yet' worn (lines 11–12); he soon discovers, however, that his handiwork has been infiltrated by 'the serpent old', and so calls on Christ 'at once' to 'disentangle all his winding snare' (lines 20–21) and 'shatter too with him my curious frame' (line 22). The 'frame' in question, of course, is *The Coronet* as well as the coronet; Marvell's poem is 'curious' (artful) not merely in the broad sense of being elegantly composed but more specifically because of its refined literary-historical sensibility. It most resembles the coronet in having been re-woven out of a pre-existing 'Wreath' – Herbert's – plaited together with other posies culled from far and wide in *The Temple* ('Through every garden, every mead | I gather flow'rs' [lines 5–6]). Its most artful echo coincides with the moment when the speaker turns vengefully against his own creation: reworking 'winding stair' (from Herbert's 'Jordan (I)', an attack on the sensuous complication of secular verse) into 'winding snare' is exceptionally nimble-fingered even for Marvell. So if Christ answers the speaker's prayer and tramples the flawed gift of the coronet underfoot, He will particularly be grinding into the dust Marvell's gift for 'echoing song'.

The endings of the two poems have proved highly controversial; does Marvell endorse or deplore their aggressive impulsiveness? In the case of *To His Coy Mistress*, the latter view currently prevails: the lover is being exposed as a sexual predator. But in that of *The Coronet* the balance of opinion is on the other side: the shepherd/poet manifests exemplary Puritan anxiety about human works. Taken together, though, they make it clear that violent spontaneity fascinated Marvell. The fact that he brought that fascination so hard up against his imitative poetics is susceptible of a range of interpretations. In the purely secular terms of *To His Coy Mistress*, it perhaps suggests that Marvell sometimes resented the way his nervy historical self-consciousness made passionately direct modes of utterance all but inaccessible to him (a number of his commentators certainly do suggest this). But add in the religious dimension of *The Coronet*, and the possibilities ramify. Most obviously, we might conclude that Marvell's Protestantism dictated an iconoclastic attitude to literary traditions. Witness his reworkings of Roman Catholic devotional modes. When he reworks the Jesuit Henry Hawkins's essay on 'The Deaw' in *On a Drop of Dew*, he displaces the figure of Mary, and in *Eyes and Tears* he turns a Counter-Reformation genre into a philosophical one.[8] The nunnery episode of *Upon Appleton House* provides the perfect image for this imitative aesthetic: the moment when William Fairfax, smashing the convent wall to liberate his bride-to-be, Isabel Thwaites, lets fresh Protestant air into 'th'unfrequented vault' and 'The relics false were set to view' (lines 259–61). But there is another more radical possibility: namely, that Marvell was drawn to the idea not just of rewriting the Roman Catholic past but of destroying the (literary) past altogether. Such apocalypticist contempt for human history as a winding snare, a Gordian knot that Christ would soon cut and the sooner the better, was very much in the air at this time. To explore further its bearing on Marvell's 'echoing song' we must move on to the poem around which controversy over his uses of past literature has at present come to revolve: *An Horatian Ode upon Cromwell's Return from Ireland*.

The problems start with the title. What did Marvell mean by 'Horatian'? Horace is a singularly various poet. This applies not only across his output as a whole (the Horace of the *Satires* is not the Horace of the *Epistles*) but also within individual works, and particularly within the *Odes*. The multifacetedness of these four books of lyrics is nowhere more evident than in their treatment of the questions about poetry and power which lie at the heart of the *Horatian Ode*. Horace can be said to advocate withdrawal or engagement, and a whole gamut of intermediate postures, depending on which particular ode is at issue. But in the case of the *Horatian Ode* this is left crucially unclear: it is not an imitation of a single Horace ode but a composite of more or less distant and more or less fleeting echoes of several (Marvell's latest editor lists I. ii, xxxv and xxxvii, IV. iv, v, xiv, and xv).[9] What is more, the composite is highly unstable. Draw out the links with *Odes* IV.iv which hails the return of Drusus Nero after defeating Hannibal, and Marvell begins to sound like a cheerleader for Cromwell; focus on the relation to *Odes* I.xxxvii which applauds Cleopatra for the dignified manner of her suicide after the battle of Actium, and Marvell's heart seems most to be in his famously pathetic description of Charles I's execution. Anyway, the poem the *Horatian Ode* most closely echoes is not a Horatian ode at all, but Thomas May's translation of Lucan's *Pharsalia*.[10] In combining elements from two of his classical predecessors, Marvell was practising the highest form of imitation by Jonson's lights: past writers were to be imitated in groups as a guard against overdependence on a single authority. Again, though, Marvell takes Jonsonian orthodoxy to extremes. In addition to multiple Horaces and Lucan, Pindar, originator of the sublime ode, has a significant presence in the poem; turning from particular authors to traditions more largely, its generic identity proves equally multifarious, encompassing not only various subcategories of ode, but also pastoral, elegy, and the masque.[11] This historical overdetermination makes the poem supremely difficult to interpret. Rosalie Colie once called Marvell 'the poet with too many personae';[12] in the *Horatian Ode* he is the poet with too many pasts.

It was Cromwell himself who drove Marvell to these extremes. For he was revolutionizing not merely the form of the English polity but the laws of space and time themselves:

> 'Tis he the force of scattered Time contracts,
> And in one year the work of ages acts:
> While heavy monarchs make a wide return,
> Longer, and more malignant than Saturn:
> And though they all Platonic years should reign,
> In the same posture would be found again.

This makes Cromwell sound like an ideally plural and dynamic imitator (monarchs, by contrast, impotently replicate the past). Marvell may even have been remembering George Chapman's praise poem on *Sejanus* where Jonson is figured as a 'wealth-contracting Jeweller' gathering 'Pearles and deare Stones' from the 'richest shores & streames' of the ancient literary world.[13] But the passage quoted above is from Marvell's *The First Anniversary of the Government under His Highness the Lord Protector* (lines 13–18); the Cromwell it celebrates is the Protector who has agreed to confine his power within the 'frame' provided by the (reassuringly familiar, quasi-monarchical) Instrument of Government. The earlier Cromwell of the *Horatian Ode* is a less Jonsonian animal. Fresh from his triumphs in Ireland and riding a surge of millenial fervour at home, he may be preparing a more violent rewrite of history. He

> Could by industrious valour climb
> To ruin the great work of time,
>   And cast the kingdoms old
>   Into another mould.   (lines 33–6)

Is the fabric of time warped or torn there? Or, to put it in the literary terms broached by Marvell's phrasing ('the great work of time' is in part a book, and 'cast' together with 'mould' may suggest printing), can Cromwell's revisionary energies be contained within the norms of imitation? If he tears up the history books he will make 'echoing song' obsolete, and in fact he may already have done this (it is impossible to tell whether 'Could' describes a future possibility or a past action). But would that be the end of civilization or the dawning of the apocalypse? This question informs the extreme allusiveness of the *Horatian Ode*. Crammed with pasts, the poem's slight tetrameters and trimeters strain to comprehend Cromwell within the traditional purlieus of historical judgement, as 'the swelling hall' of Fairfax's Appleton House 'does sweat, | And scarce endures the Master great' (*Upon Appleton House*, lines 49–51). But this barely sustainable imitativeness fosters a yearning for release into a simpler God-given narrative. Forcing the historicity of early modern poetics to a crisis (as a star collapses into a black hole under the pressure of its own density), the *Horatian Ode* allows the hope that 'Foreshortened Time its useless course would stay, | And soon precipitate the latest day' (*First Anniversary*, lines 139–40).

So far we have seen how Marvell analyses Jonsonian norms of imitation from within, conforming to them but extrapolating them to drastic lengths. But there are places in his work where he stands outside those norms altogether, refuses to accept their premises. This drift in Marvell's thinking about the past has been largely overlooked by commentators fixated on the more eye-catching models of metapoetic 'parody' or Protestant 'conversion'. It is felt most strongly in one of the lesser poems from the Nun Appleton grouping which marks the next phase of Marvell's career following the *Horatian Ode*: *To His Worthy Friend Doctor Witty upon His Translation of the Popular Errors*. Witty was a Hull physician acquainted with the Fairfax family; the 'popular errors' repudiated in the treatise he had translated were medical. But Marvell praises him for combating the spread among English poets of a noxious attitude towards the literary past:

> Some in this task
> Take off the cypress veil, but leave a mask,
> Changing the Latin, but do more obscure
> That sense in English which was bright and pure.
> So of translators they are authors grown,
> For ill translators make the book their own.   (lines 3–8)

'Some' decorously mentions no names, but the theory of free translation these lines attack had strong royalist associations. Marvell's discrimination between authors and translators reverses the tendency to collapse that distinction instigated by Sir John Denham's influential praise poem 'To Sir Richard Fanshawe upon His Translation of *Pastor Fido*' (1647). Alleging that free translators 'obscure' the 'bright and pure' sense of their originals with 'a mask', Marvell aligns them with the defining excesses of Caroline court culture: Laudianism, which caked on to the gospel a greasy rouge of ceremonial and liturgical innovations, and the masque itself, that homonym for the Stuart aesthetic of prodigality and deception. Here what his Protestantism entails in respect of the literary past is not reformatory zeal but mistrust of innovation. Nor should it be supposed that Marvell's approval of Witty's non-interventionist approach was tailored exclusively to the special circumstances of the translatorial mode. On the contrary, his epigrammatic gibe at 'ill translators' who 'make the book their own' is deliberately phrased as a challenge to one of the central tenets of the classical orthodoxy of transformative imitation. 'Nostra faciamus' ('let us make [the past] our own'), Seneca had urged in his 84th Epistle, a founding statement of that orthodoxy; and, in their practice of imitation, Jonson and 'sons of Ben' such as Denham and Fanshawe had answered that call.

Two of Marvell's essential characteristics as a poet suggest that the aversion to emulativeness he expressed in *To His Worthy Friend Doctor Witty* was native to him. The first is his disinclination to publish. Not only did he stop printing his poems after the early handful of occasional pieces he contributed to royalist anthologies; with the sole exception of *The Last Instructions to a Painter* at the other end of his career, he also appears to have taken steps to restrict, if not entirely prevent, their manuscript circulation. The 'stigma of print' was a bit out of date in Marvell's day, particularly where political poems were concerned, a throwback to the coterie sensibility of Donne and Herbert at a time when Milton was demanding that poets help make 'cloistered virtue' a thing of the past. But more important, it is fundamentally at odds with the purpose of imitation, as Jonson had understood it and even more so as Milton did. To imitate was to stake a claim to authority. In Jonson's case, the authority sought was largely personal, in Milton's more broadly national, but both recognized classical prestige could only be gained on the public stage. The lack of such a public context where Marvell's imitative conduct is concerned makes statements about the revisionary impact of his interactions with the literary past potentially disproportionate. Take the *Horatian Ode*. One widely influential recent reading aligns it with the 'drastic revision of Caroline *prosphonetika*' (that is, 'return' poems) and royalist Horatianism more generally being undertaken by republican writers at the turn of the 1650s.[14] However, those writers were noisy denizens of the public sphere, poet-journalists such as John Hall and Henry Marten, whereas Marvell's ode had only a private circulation. If Marvell was enlisting in the cultural campaign to republicanize Horace, it was as an armchair warrior.

The second thing about Marvell that qualifies the prevailing view of him as a boldly transformative imitator is that he wrote mostly in lyric modes, which cannot easily sustain the set-piece effects of reconceptualization possible in more discursive or narrative contexts. Lightness and grace were prized in early modern lyric, and while Marvell's lyrics certainly test the limits of these categories, they do not (in notable contrast to Donne's) jettison them entirely. In a Marvell lyric, beauty remains an end in and of itself – and imitation is an indispensable means to that end. For Marvell the literary past was as often a storehouse of treasures as it was a mausoleum of relics. Here we might invoke the paradigm of 'setting', discussed earlier in relation to the nunnery episode of *Upon Appleton House*, in a less aggressive connection: that of a jeweller setting a precious stone as a means of bringing out its native lustre. Consider again the passage Eliot singled out from *To His Coy Mistress*. Marvell's reuse of the epithet 'vast eternity' from Herrick and Cowley has little or nothing to do with differences between his (putatively) Puritan and their Anglo-Catholic eschatology and plenty to do with the sensual qualities of the phrase. Its seductive capaciousness permits the lover, even as he threatens the coy mistress with a sexless perpetuity if she persists in rejecting his advances, to give further earnest of the immense erotic delights that await if she yields. Certainly Marvell has plumped up the epithet's charms by accessorizing it with 'deserts' (thereby showing off its 'st' cluster to best advantage), as against the more dowdily familiar oceanic terms ('Sea', 'course') in Herrick and Cowley. But it would be misleading to call that a transformation, let alone to claim that Marvell has thereby made the epithet his own.

In those two general respects, then, resistance to the interventionist model of imitation was native to Marvell: in his poetic genes, so to speak. But it has a particular relation to his work in the mode which prompted him to think most broadly and deeply about the past – pastoral. That it was in an Appletonian context that he spoke out most strongly against those who made past books their own is no accident, for such a stance readily equates to tendencies in Marvellian pastoral. Its green consciousness, for instance: the 'Fond lovers' attacked in the third stanza of *The Garden* as 'cruel as their flame' because they 'Cut in these trees their mistress' name' (lines 19–20, 23–4) are gougingly self-assertive *re*writers (the speaker's sentiment is gently underscored by its being so deeply traditionalist, a pastoral cliché). Or its hedonism; in this connection, the relevant stanza of *The Garden* is the fifth:

> What wondrous life is this I lead!
> Ripe apples drop about my head;
> The luscious clusters of the vine
> Upon my mouth do crush their wine;
> The nectarene, and curious peach,
> Into my hands themselves do reach.   (lines 33–8)

It comes as no surprise to discover that this produce has dropped into Marvell's lap from a previous poetic garden, an ode by the Polish poet Casimire Sarbiewski which was itself a rewriting of the Song of Solomon.[15] The inactive imitativeness of the lines is of a piece with their speaker's indolent sensuality. It is the peach that is 'curious' (the adjective, remember, had connoted inventive allusiveness in *The Coronet*), not he or Marvell. Tellingly too, he doesn't eat the grapes: metaphors of ingestion and digestion underpin classical accounts of imitation, and are endemic in Jonson whose ideal imitator above all 'feedes with an appetite, and hath a Stomacke to concoct, divide, and turne all to nourishment'.[16]

At this point, a scheme for mapping Marvell's various imitative behaviours over the course of his career suggests itself, according to which an activist posture operative particularly in the explicitly Protestant lyrics and the Cromwellian poems is counterbalanced by a less interventionist tendency especially prominent within the pastoral poems. As a general guide, that has some merit. Marvell's single most untransformative encounter with a piece of past literature, his virtually line-for-line translation *The Second Chorus from Seneca's Tragedy Thyestes* (which implicitly takes issue with a previous looser rendering by Cowley, double the length of the original) provides the setting for his simplest profession of ruralist disengagement. There he longs to be 'Settled in some secret nest' and 'far off the public stage | Pass away my silent age' (lines 4–7), and makes a start on that new quiet life in the act of close translation, silencing and secreting himself behind the voice of his Stoic predecessor. But we have already seen that some of Marvell's most audacious remouldings of past literature feature elements of calm continuativeness; and it is most unlikely that his many versions of pastoral would manifest a uniformly static traditionalism. For the desire to take refuge in the past is a desire it has always been in the nature of pastoral to inspect. Critics sometimes forget this, presenting any advance on golden-age nostalgia in Marvell's pastorals as a sophisticated debunking of classical naïveties. But pain and loss inescapably attend efforts to escape to a better place and time in ancient pastoral. Death has always been in Arcadia. Nothing could be less original than the awareness of the complications besetting the wish for a return to original purity which Marvell (unbeknownst to the speaker of the poem) registers in the eighth stanza of *The Garden*:

> Such was that happy garden-state,
> While man there walked without a mate:
> After a place so pure, and sweet,
> What other help could yet be meet?
> But 'twas beyond a mortal's share
> To wander solitary there:
> Two Paradises 'twere in one
> To live in Paradise alone.   (lines 57–64)

The flaw in this sort of reasoning (the speaker is wishing himself unborn) had been pointed out again and again to young women reluctant to move on from their virginal past in the 'persuasions to love' poems which proliferated in the 1630s and 1640s. Compacting it into a grammatical *trompe l'oeil*, a brief blurring together of the subjunctive mood and the past tense (''twas' | ''twere'), is the distinctively Marvellian touch.

Similar confusions and deceptions involving the past tense underpin the quartet of poems featuring Marvell's most enduring pastoral creation – Damon the Mower. *The Mower against Gardens* is 'focussed around a shift' at its mid point 'from the past tense to the subjunctive mood';[17] *Damon the Mower* hinges on dramatically ironized 'use of the historic present tense';[18] *The Mower to the Glow-worms* is a single sentence made up of three quatrains of subordinate clauses in the present tense which turn out in the fourth to depend on a main verb in the past; and *The Mower's Song* revolves around a refrain which is set in the past in the first three stanzas ('When Juliana came ...') but breaks through into the present in the fourth and fifth ('For Juliana comes ...'). These effects are the natural punctuation for Damon's story, a tragi-comedy of unrequited love not so much for Juliana as for an ideal past. It is an inherently literary story (without ever approaching arid meta-poeticality). Here Damon's occupation is fundamental. It used once to be claimed that by making him a mower instead of a shepherd Marvell was breaking with the past of pastoral, perhaps in tacit endorsement of the revolutionary agrarianism of the Levellers and the Diggers. Actually, though, mowers do crop up here and there in classical pastoral (notably in Theocritus's 10th *Idyll*) and even in the (supposedly ultra-nostalgic) pastorals of 'Cavalier' lyricists such as Thomas Randolph (a key source for the Mower poems). Still, mowers were rather less central to pastoral tradition than shepherds, and this is at the root of Damon's problems. From the outset, in *The Mower against Gardens*, even before Juliana has shaken up his pastoral world, he is using the past to shore up his tottering sense of self, attacking the (very far from novel) practice of grafting as a corruption of the original purity of nature in terms so ultra-traditionalist as to suggest insecurity. This insecurity may stem from Damon's conditions of employment: mowers were hired for only two months of the year. But he is also overcompensating for a pastoral inferiority complex (like someone dubiously related to a historic family who trumpets its pedigree). Marvell was fond of such frame-breaking turns of wit; the most striking case in his poems even suggests he particularly associated the device with mowers – the moment in *Upon Appleton House* when Thestylis, bringing lunch to 'the mowing camp', 'cries, "He [the narrator] called us Israelites; | But now, to make his saying true, | Rails rain for quails, for manna, dew" ' (lines 402, 406–8).

Marvell's practice of allusion in the Mower poems deftly consolidates the reflexive dimension of Damon's story; echoes bounce off Damon's words, one moment harmonizing sympathetically with his time consciousness, the next teasingly counterpointed against it. Or both at once, as happens in the central instance, one of the most unmistakable recalls of the literary past in all of Marvell: 'Nor am I so deformed to sight, | If in my scythe I lookèd right' (*Damon the Mower*, lines 57–8). That first phrase is a direct translation of the half-line 'nec sum adeo informis' from Virgil's 2nd eclogue, in which the shepherd Corydon unavailingly woos 'his master's pet' Alexis. So clear is this allusion that it is as if Damon himself (rather than Marvell) were quoting Virgil, a feeling strengthened by the witty appositeness of the Virgilian phrase to Damon's circumstances: he proves he is not 'informis' (unshapely) by the literary shapeliness of his speech. However, behind that primary echo more distant reverberations are audible, and these create interference with Damon's purposes. Virgil's 2nd eclogue was itself a rewrite of Theocritus's 6th *Idyll* where the unsuccessful wooer is indeed 'informis' – a Cyclops. This queers the purist pitch of Damon's pastoralism, partly to comic effect, but more darkly too, for it is at just this point that his increasing sense of estrangement from his pastoral environment begins to issue in fantasies of Cyclopean retaliation, centring on his scythe:

> What, though the piping shepherd stock
> The plains with an unnumbered flock,
> This scythe of mine discovers wide
> More ground than all his sheep do hide.   (lines 49–52)

This is a powerfully emblematic image – a blanket of whiteness yanked aside to reveal the bare earth beneath – and one of the things it emblematizes is emulative imitation. Damon is now a 'discoverer', restlessly cutting through the woolly-mindedness of pastoral: sheep no longer mean innocence to him but inexperience. With his scythe, he exposes what they 'hide' (with their hides – a grim pun), undermines the shepherd's dispensation and so supplants him ('mine' next to 'discovers' blends subversion with possessiveness).

But Marvell himself does not indulge in such retaliatory undercutting. He does not exert his superior self-awareness over Damon. He does not 'discover' the mower's naïveté, shear off the fleecy delusions of grandeur he has wrapped around himself, leaving him to shiver in blasts of readerly contempt. Such ironies as he ventures at Damon's expense are carefully restrained, never escalating to the pitch of sarcastic exposure. Inevitably estranged like Damon from originary (literary) innocence, Marvell does not take his disillusionment out on Damon as Damon takes his out on nature. Incapable of tolerating the irrecoverability of the past, Damon ends up in *The Mower's Song* vowing to eradicate it altogether, to devastate his environment (and himself) so thoroughly that nothing will remain to remind him of the world he has lost (the change in the tense of the refrain articulates this desire for a totalizing present-ness unadulterated by memory). But Marvell was more tolerant: he could let the past that could not be his be. This imaginative tolerance is the key to the 'odd literary achievement' of the Mower poems, as David Kalstone has finely described it: 'odd' in that Marvell's 'restlessness or wariness' about the pastoral past 'does not seem to destroy the pleasure [he] takes in reviving or giving life to certain conventions like the one behind Damon the Mower's lament'.[19]

A decade or so after Marvell wrote the Mower poems, something like the destruction of the past envisaged by Damon took place within English culture. The Restoration restored the monarchical past by sweeping away the more recent republican and Cromwellian pasts. The accession of Charles II was officially backdated to the moment his father was executed, and the programme of legislation enacted under the Commonwealth and the Protectorate was cut down at a stroke. The 1650s were no more. In the past there was general agreement among critics that this catastrophic rewriting of history made a decisive impact on the shape of Marvell's career. The Marvell of the Interregnum died out and was replaced by one better adapted to the new cultural environment of the Restoration: lyric gave way to satire, pastoral to party politics, ambivalence to partisanship. But that view is rather outdated now; recent studies have tended to emphasize areas of continuity between Marvell's pre- and post-Restoration writings. To judge from the title of his most controversial Restoration work – *The Rehearsal Transpros'd* (1672) – his relations with the past are one such area. It reads like a description of the transformative mode of rewriting exemplified in his early devotional and love lyrics. Sure enough, Marvell did not just rehearse *The Rehearsal*, the previous year's smash-hit dramatic burlesque of the Poet Laureate John Dryden, but brilliantly transposed it into new satiric circumstances. The central character 'Bayes' is no longer Dryden but the Tory churchman Samuel Parker who had taken a leading role in the campaign against the policy of toleration for the Nonconformist sects; and the original's parody of the gross unrealistic excesses of Dryden's dramaturgy has bifurcated into mockery both of Parker's ludicrously exaggerated representations of the Dissenters as proponents of religious anarchy and his own self-aggrandizingly heroic pretensions to be the last bastion of 'the church in danger'. This reconfiguration is extended by the presence of other literary pasts, notably that of chivalric romance: Marvell repeatedly casts Parker as a latter-day Don Quixote. The transposition is, then, both dynamic and plural. But most of all, there is implicit within it a rethinking of the cultural and historical past that is as multidimensional as anything to be found in the corpus of Marvell's Interregnum imitations. The association of religious nonconformity with solipsistic emotionalism ('enthusiasm', in the argot of the day) had been a mainstay of Anglican polemic for decades, and was particularly exploited by Tory propagandists in the Restoration to cast religious dissent (however moderate) as a throwback to the radical Puritanism of the 1640s. By contrast, writers like Dryden and Parker prided themselves on their urbane rationality which they presented as distinctively modern. The romance mode had lately been used to reinforce this contrast in Samuel Butler's bestselling *Hudibras* (1665) whose Puritan anti-hero is straight out of Cervantes. Marvell's rotations of the literary past in *The Rehearsal Transpros'd* were intended to turn those various ideological tables.

But in the Restoration an entire new dimension was added to Marvell's complex responsiveness to literary history: now among the pasts he particularly had to respond to was his own. Annabel Patterson has shown that in the best of his Restoration satires, *The Last Instructions to a Painter* (1667), Marvell occasionally 'parodies, by echoing, his own heroic poetry of the Commonwealth era' in order to enforce a sense of the disjunction between the noble Cromwellian past and the ignominious Stuart present.[20] The course of the relationship between Marvell's Restoration and Interregnum poetic selves, however, did not always run so smooth – particularly not where his personal history intersected with that of the poet whose career the loss of the republican past had most publicly deformed: Milton. *On Mr Milton's Paradise Lost*, written to commend the second edition of the epic in 1674, is usually taken as an acknowledgement on Marvell's part that he has accommodated himself to the new cultural dispensation whereas Milton has remained heroically true to the radical past. But this is not the whole story. The argument of the poem in fact takes place against a backdrop of multiple literary pasts, and leads to the conclusion that Milton is revolutionary in his deep traditionalism and Marvell backward-looking in his shallow modernity. Here Marvell was taking his cue from Milton's own writing about *Paradise Lost*. In his famous prefatory note Milton had defended his choice of blank verse as 'an example set, the first in English, of ancient liberty recovered to heroic poem' – a claim at once to unprecedentedness ('the first in English') and traditionality ('ancient liberty'). Rhyme, too, he had called both 'modern' and 'barbarous'. Marvell may have meant to imply a similarly double historical movement when he confessed to being 'transported by the mode' of rhyme, since the verb 'transport' particularly describes Satan's progressive regression in *Paradise Lost*.[21] But what most reveals Marvell's retrograde modernity is the presence in his poem, beneath its stratum of Miltonic allusion, of a deep-lying seam of Jonsonian echo:

> When I beheld the poet blind, yet bold,
> In slender book his vast design unfold,
> Messiah crowned, God's reconciled decree,
> Rebelling angels, the forbidden tree.
> Heaven, hell, earth, chaos, all; the argument
> Held me a while misdoubting his intent,
> That he would ruin (for I saw him strong)
> The sacred truths to fable and old song
> (So Sampson groped the Temple's post in spite)
> The world o'erwhelming to revenge his sight.   (lines 1–10)

It was discovered a few years ago that this critical scenario of initial misgivings subsequently rescinded is closely modelled on Jonson's 'To my chosen Friend, The learned Translator of Lucan, Thomas May, Esquire',[22] which itself depends upon Horace's self-comparison with Pindar in *Odes* IV. ii. The effect of the allusion is to honour Milton as the latest in a line of sublime poetic innovators, while consigning Marvell himself to the lower rank of traditionalists who take fright at such daring inventiveness. Indeed, consigning him to the very back of that cautious company: for Marvell was also alluding to his own previous allusion to Jonson's poem in *Tom May's Death*, and whereas there he had trumped Jonson in imitative adventurousness, now he exposes himself as more Jonsonian than Jonson in the extent of his rule-bound conservatism. Jonson has one period of 'doubt' lasting six lines before being 'ravish'd with just wonder' at May's genius; Marvell goes through three distinct phases of 'misdoubting', 'fear' and 'Jealous' anxiety, taking twenty-four lines to be 'convinced' of Milton's achievement (lines 6, 12, 18, 25).

Of course, that was all wittily done. Marvell's self-presentation as poetic quailer is filtered through a layer of Horatian irony. Such irony was all the rage in Restoration culture: even as *On Mr Milton's Paradise Lost* was published, Dryden was slugging it out with the Whig dramatist Thomas Shadwell for the disputed title of heir to this Horatian/Jonsonian ethos of metropolitan suavity. So by aligning himself with this tradition, Marvell was giving himself one foot in the Stuart past and another in the Stuart present. But he was also removing himself from the middle distance in between the two, that of the English republic (no time for such Horatian elegance). This hallowed space Marvell now left clear for Milton. Once again comparison with Jonson marks him out as ultra-retiring as he does so: when Jonson overcame his doubts about May, he was 'ravish'd' up into sympathy with him; what Marvell is eventually 'convinced' of about Milton is that 'none will dare | Within thy labours to pretend a share' (lines 25–6). The lone survivor of the apocalyptic 1650s, Milton has escaped history. He is inimitable, has no future in 'echoing song': 'no room is here for writers left, | But to detect their ignorance or theft' (lines 29–30). In the past, in the *Horatian Ode*, Marvell had said the same of Cromwell, urging Nature to 'make room | Where greater spirits come' (lines 43–4), but back then an understructure of Lucanian resonance had implied he himself might become the poet of this new Cromwellian order, ecstatically tearing his verse through the grates of history into the eternal present of the millennium. Now that prophecy is revised: it is Milton who inflicts Lucanic 'ruin' on 'old song' (lines 7–8). The destiny left to Marvell emerges from what is perhaps the most far-reaching instance of self-quotation in his Restoration verse. It has been known for some time that the passage describing how Milton soars 'above human flight ... aloft | With plume so strong' recalls some lines from stanza VII of *The Garden*:

> My soul into the boughs does glide:
> There like a bird it sits, and sings,

Then whets, and combs its silver wings;
And, till prepared for longer flight,
Waves in its plumes the various light.   (lines 52–6)[23]

But the recent claim that Marvell wrote *The Garden* not during his Nun Appleton period but after the Restoration dramatically extends the echo's range of suggestion.[24] Verbal overlaps with pastoral verse contained in Katherine Philips's *Poems* (1667) and Abraham Cowley's *Several Discourses by Way of Essays, in Verse and Prose* (1668) suggest that the poem may have been written or at least revised in the late 1660s. The former possibility is fascinating enough – that Marvell was pastiching his Appletonian past (convincingly enough to dupe generations of readers) – but the latter possibility may be the more distinctively Marvellian. The Restoration poems that Marvell was echoing are extremely well known; the reason it took so long to spot the echoes is that they are also extremely nostalgic, deliberate throwbacks to a Cavalier idiom of halcyon retirement. 'Echoing song' in this case simultaneously updates and backdates. As Milton broke through into a timeless present in *Paradise Lost*, Marvell in *The Garden* went back to the Restoration future.

NOTES

1. See Smith's notes on the passage in *Poems*, 82; and for more on the Asclepiades case, in the context of Marvell's debt to the *Greek Anthology* more generally, Stella Revard, 'Intertwining the Garland of Marvell's Lyrics: The Greek Anthology and Its Renaissance Heritage', in Claude J. Summers and Ted-Larry Pebworth, eds., *On the Celebrated and Neglected Poems of Andrew Marvell* (Columbia, MO, 1992), 29–46.
2. Paul R. Sellin, ' "The Nymph Complaining" as a Stesichorean *Calcya*', in Summers and Pebworth, eds., *Celebrated and Neglected Poems*, 86–100 (at 92).
3. Jeremy Maule brilliantly and capaciously surveys 'Donne's vigorous attacks on, and arguments with, the concept of the past as well as its local inhabitants' in his essay 'Donne and the Past', in Helen Wilcox, Richard Todd and Alasdair MacDonald, eds., *Sacred and Profane: Secular and Devotional Interplay in Early Modern British Literature* (Amsterdam, 1996), 203–21.
4. Annabel Patterson, *Marvell: The Writer in Public Life* (Harlow, 2000), 66–9.
5. Kitty Scoular Datta, 'New Light on Marvell's "A Dialogue between the Soul and the Body" ', *Renaissance Quarterly* 22 (1969), 242–55 (at 246).
6. Smith's note on the phrase is symptomatic: 'Randall . . . argues in favour of "grates" on the grounds of its frequency as an image of a fortified door . . . But Wilcher's sense that the unexpectedness of "gates of life" (reversing "gates of death" and the commonness of "iron grates") "has the ring of Marvellian wit" is more convincing' (*Poems*, 84).
7. By Donald Friedman, in *Marvell's Pastoral Art* (Berkeley, 1970), 80.
8. Patterson, *Marvell*, 63; Smith, in *Poems*, 50.
9. Smith, in *Poems*, 268.
10. R. H. Syfret, 'Marvell's *Horatian Ode*', *Review of English Studies* 12 (1961), 160–72.

11. See David Norbrook, *Writing the English Republic* (Cambridge, 1999), 269–70; for pastoral, see Judith Haber, *Pastoral and the Poetics of Self-Contradiction: Theocritus to Marvell* (Cambridge, 1994); for 'Cavalier' lyric, see Norbrook, *Writing the English Republic*, 266–7; for the masque, see Muriel C. Bradbrook, 'Marvell and the Masque', in Kenneth Friedenreich, ed., *Tercentenary Essays in Honor of Andrew Marvell* (Hamden, CT, 1977), 204–23 (at 213–14).

12. Rosalie Colie, *'My Ecchoing Song': Andrew Marvell's Poetry of Criticism* (Princeton, 1970), p. 3 n. 2.

13. Chapman, quoted in Peterson, *Imitation and Praise in the Poems of Ben Jonson* (New Haven; 1981), 14; Marvell's immediately preceding line describes Cromwell as 'the jewel of the yearly ring' (line 12).

14. David Norbrook, 'Marvell's "Horatian Ode" and the Politics of Genre', in Thomas Healy and Jonathan Sawday, eds., *Literature and the English Civil War* (Cambridge, 1990), 147–69 (I quote from 163).

15. Marvell is echoing the translation of *The Odes of Casimire* by one 'G.H.' published in 1646; on Sarbiewski's general reputation in England at this period, and Marvell's particular relation to him, see Maren-Sofie Rostvig, 'Benlowes, Marvell, and the Divine Casimire', *Huntington Library Quarterly* 18 (1954), 13–35 (these echoes are discussed at 27).

16. Burrow, 'Combative Classicism: Jonson, Milton, and Classical Literary Criticism in England', in Glyn P. Norton, ed., *The Cambridge History of Literary Criticism*, Vol. III, *The Renaissance* (Cambridge, 2000), 491–2 (the quotation is on 492).

17. Note by Smith, in *Poems*, 133.

18. Christine Rees, *The Judgement of Marvell* (London, 1989), 155.

19. David Kalstone, 'Marvell and the Fictions of Pastoral', *English Literary Renaissance* 4 (1974), 174–88 (at 187).

20. Patterson, *Marvell*, 104–5.

21. Marvell perhaps had in mind God's notoriously punning remarks at the beginning of his conversation with the Son in Book III of *Paradise Lost*: 'seest thou what rage | Transports our Adversary . . . | so bent he seems | On desperate revenge, that shall redound | Upon his own rebellious head' (lines 80–1, 84–6).

22. By Andrew Shifflett: see his essay '"By Lucan Driv'n About": A Jonsonian Marvell's Lucanic Milton', *Renaissance Quarterly* 49 (1996), 803–23.

23. The echo is discussed, for instance, in Joseph Anthony Wittreich, Jr, 'Perplexing the Explanation: Marvell's "On Mr Milton's *Paradise Lost*"', in C. A. Patrides, ed., *Approaches to Marvell: The York Tercentenary Lectures* (London, 1978), 280–305 (at 299–300).

24. This claim was originally advanced by Allan Pritchard in his essay 'Marvell's "The Garden": A Restoration Poem?', *Studies in English Literature* 23 (1983), 371–88; it has been widely (though not universally) accepted, notably by Smith who dates the poem '1668' (*Poems*, 152).

Further reading

Colin Burrow, 'Combative Classicism: Jonson, Milton, and Classical Literary Criticism in England', in Glyn P. Norton, ed., *The Cambridge History of Literary Criticism, Vol. III, The Renaissance* (Cambridge, 2000), 487–99.

Rosalie Colie, '*My Ecchoing Song': Andrew Marvell's Poetry of Criticism* (Princeton, 1970).

John Creaser, 'Marvell's Effortless Superiority', *Essays in Criticism* 20 (1970), 403–23

Kitty Scoular Datta, 'New Light on Marvell's "A Dialogue between the Soul and the Body"', *Renaissance Quarterly* 2 (1969), 242–55

T. S. Eliot, 'Andrew Marvell', in his *Selected Essays* (1932), reprinted in Elizabeth Story Donno, ed., *Andrew Marvell: The Critical Heritage* (London, 1978), 362–74.

Judith Haber, *Pastoral and the Poetics of Self-Contradiction: Theocritus to Marvell* (Cambridge, 1994).

David Kalstone, 'Marvell and the Fictions of Pastoral', *English Literary Renaissance* 4 (1974), 174–88.

J. B. Leishman, *The Art of Marvell's Poetry* (London, 1966).

Jeremy Maule, 'Donne and the Past', in Helen Wilcox, Richard Todd and Alasdair MacDonald, eds., *Sacred and Profane: Secular and Devotional Interplay in Early Modern British Literature* (Amsterdam, 1996), 203–21.

Annabel Patterson, *Marvell: The Writer in Public Life* (Harlow, 2000).

Richard S. Peterson, *Imitation and Praise in the Poems of Ben Jonson* (New Haven, 1981)

Allan Pritchard, 'Marvell's "The Garden": A Restoration Poem?', *Studies in English Literature* 23 (1983), 371–88.

Maren-Sofie Rostvig, 'Benlowes, Marvell, and the Divine Casimire', *Huntington Library Quarterly* 18 (1954), 13–35.

Andrew Shifflett, '"By Lucan Driv'n About": A Jonsonian Marvell's Lucanic Milton', *Renaissance Quarterly* 49 (1996), 803–23.

4

MATTHEW C. AUGUSTINE

Borders and transitions in Marvell's poetry

Andrew Marvell is a writer deeply identified with particular locales and enclosures. Despite recent interest in his occasional and polemical writings, he is still first and foremost the poet of gardens, those lush, mysterious haunts we know so well from *The Garden*, from *Upon Appleton House, To My Lord Fairfax*, or from *The Nymph Complaining for the Death of her Fawn*. More generally we think of Marvell as a pastoral poet, ever attendant to the green business of the world, familiar of Daphnis and Chloe, Ametas and Thestylis, and not least Damon the Mower. His most famous poem, *To His Coy Mistress*, has as its backdrop the Yorkshire countryside and was likely written, as we believe the great part of his lyrics were, while Marvell was in residence at Nun Appleton.[1] Later in the 1650s, we might think of Marvell in his employ at the Latin Secretary's Office, perhaps writing there *A Poem upon the Death of O. C.*; and in the 1660s we might think of him in lobbies and committee rooms of Parliament, writing letters to the Hull Corporation or collecting gossip and slander for the 'advice to a painter' poems.

But to situate Marvell and his writing life within such determinate boundaries belies the often migratory character of his professional and writerly occupations. Left parentless by the death of his father in January 1641, Marvell shuttled back and forth between Cambridge and London before disappearing to the Continent probably in autumn 1642, just as civil war broke out in England. We know almost nothing of this period in his life beyond what Milton says in a 1652 letter recommending Marvell to John Bradshaw, that 'he hath spent foure yeares abroad in Holland, France, Italy, & Spaine, to very good purpose, as I beleeve, & the gaineing of those 4 languages'.[2] It has been conjectured that he was at this time tutor to some young lord on his Grand Tour, and at least one poem dates from this sojourn abroad: the barbed lampoon *Flecknoe, an English Priest at Rome*. By November 1647 Marvell was back in England, though his movements and activities remain sketchy through the end of the decade; 'some poems that he wrote over the next three years imply close contact with literary circles in

46

London'.[3] In 1650 he entered the service of Sir Thomas Fairfax as tutor to the retiring lord-general's daughter; he would take up similar employment with Oliver Cromwell, serving for several years in the mid 1650s as governor to the Lord Protector's ward and prospective son-in-law William Dutton, with whom Marvell again travelled the Continent. There followed the appointment as assistant Latin Secretary, and then, of course, Marvell's long and improbable parliamentary career, punctuated by his farthest travel – an embassy to Russia – and the hectic and often furtive business of his last decade and a half: backbench wheeling and dealing, controversy and polemic, opposition satire, much of it anonymous, much of it dangerous, all of it brilliant and brutal.

This essay will suggest how mobility and professional itinerancy inflect Marvell's body of writing: his range of reference, his themes and subjects, his generic choices, perhaps most of all his very habits of thought and argument. More than this, however, borders and transitions both organize and impel Marvell's art: he does not long stand in one place or inhabit a single perspective; rather Marvell's is a poetry and a psychology of looking in two directions, of standing at the margins, of occupying a position neither outside nor genuinely inside prevailing structures of political identity, of spiritual economy, of erotic desire. There is, of course, a technical side to Marvell's exploration and exposition of the liminal; indeed questions of presence, identity, and difference are inscribed at an almost elemental level in Marvell's art, in punning wordplay that foregrounds the indeterminacy of language, exploiting the porous boundaries between words and other words, other meanings, other contexts. Such concerns are also manifested in Marvell's affinity for dialectics, those slippery contests of binaries and oppositions staged in pastoral dialogues and in philosophical lyrics, and marshalled as political calculus in the *Horatian Ode upon Cromwell's Return from Ireland*. And everywhere there is traffic between and among genres and modes, their particular ways of seeing and saying.

Beyond (though always in conjunction with) these issues of poetic form, borders and their transgressions are ineluctably thematized across Marvell's works: border crossing that structures narrative, as in the poet's amble over the Nun Appleton estate, and that sets in motion the story of *The Nymph Complaining* and subtends that poem's remarkable series of transformations and metamorphoses. The Unfortunate Lover, that singularly Marvellian creature – by traumatic birth and cruel care fashioned 'Th'amphibium of Life and Death' (line 40), fated to be caught 'betwixt the flames and waves' (line 47) – epitomizes both the plight and the imaginative potency of in-betweenness. And there is in this poet's lyric voice always the trace of other texts and other voices, ancient and modern. But Marvell's liminal sensibility does not end at the edge of his lyric verse. The *Poem upon the Death* is self-consciously situated on a tremulous political threshold; and in *The Last Instructions to a Painter*, Marvell writes himself and in turn the reader into an inescapable problematic of within and without, of resistance to and complicity with the passionate distempers of the Stuart polity.

The drift of language

Puns seem so much a part of the fabric of Marvell's verse that we hardly notice them, unless it is to appreciate Marvell's Latinity, or to unfold some crucial double meaning out of a line or stanza in which a pun figures. But to wander about the pun-scape of the poetry is also a way of walking into Marvell's broader poetic and thematic concerns with identity and difference and with borders and transgressions. As Jonathan Culler notes, 'Puns present the disquieting spectacle of a functioning of language where boundaries – between sounds, between sound and letter, between meanings – count for less than one might imagine and where supposedly discrete meanings threaten to sink into fluid subterranean signifieds too undefinable to call concepts.'[4] Most obviously, puns are the device of bathetic humour or sexual innuendo, where their effect is to blur the boundaries between proper and inappropriate discourse, between high and low, the poetic and the demotic. But Marvell's investment in puns is not usually bathos, or at least never simply bathos; rather the pun functions as a kind of hinge for Marvell's unstable perspectivism. Even in poems such as *A Dialogue, Between the Resolved Soul, and Created Pleasure*, wordplay is not the less disquieting for being tactful or even elegant. Indeed, such puns are all the more disquieting for their apparent innocence.

We might begin in familiar territory, with a memorable pun from a well-known poem, *To His Coy Mistress*. The pun occurs in the second stanza, where the speaker turns from the witty dilations of 'world enough, and time' to conjure 'Deserts of vast eternity':

> Thy beauty shall no more be found;
> Nor, in thy marble vault, shall sound
> My echoing song: then worms shall try
> That long preserved virginity:
> And your quaint honour turn to dust;
> And into ashes all my lust. (lines 25–30)

The theme of *To His Coy Mistress*, as T. S. Eliot noted long ago, 'is one of the great traditional commonplaces of European literature':[5] pleasure must be seized in the heat of youth, before the body and its capacity for enjoyment decay. But Marvell's rendering of this argument rewrites the stock trope of human transience in brutally literal terms, as the abject desolation of the body: 'then worms shall try | That long preserved virginity'. The indelicate pun on 'quaint' in the following line – the adjective means 'prim' or 'fastidious', but the context clearly puts the noun of Chaucerian bawdy (Middle English 'queynte'='cunt') into play – punctuates this obscene parody of sex. Yet in so doing, surely the pun tampers with the persuasive force of the central lines of the poem: not, as some critics have felt, because it makes the poet seem to leer where he should be serious, but because the pun allows a further intrusion of the grossly physical, and perhaps then suggests an aversion to, a repugnance for the female anatomy, a repugnance that the metaphysic of the final stanza cannot wholly diffuse or dispel.

To remain for the moment in the family of bawdy puns, let us consider a passage near the end of *Upon Appleton House*:

> But now away my hooks, my quills,
> And angles, idle utensils.
> The young Maria walks tonight:
> Hide trifling youth thy pleasures slight.
> 'Twere shame that such judicious eyes
> Should with such toys a man surprise   (lines 649–54)

In previous stanzas, the poet has laid himself down on the riverbank to fish; Maria thus finds him in an embarrassing state of discomposure, and in a posture that seems to signify moral laxity. Marvell counterpoints the poet's recumbency with Maria's uprightness, his 'trifling youth' with her 'judicious' maturity. The figurative work of the scene is extended and complicated through puns that tangle together angling, autoeroticism, and the writing of poetry. For 'toy' in early modern usage primarily means 'an act or piece of amorous sport', but also marks out a piece of wit, 'a jest, joke, pun', or, more broadly, 'A fantastic or trifling speech or piece of writing'.[6] Quills can likewise be taken as instruments of writing as well as fishing, and even casual readers of Shakespeare will know that to take one's pen in hand is always to cruise the pun. Here wordplay inscribes a double movement within the moral economy of the poem, transgressing most radically where it corrects most steeply. That there is a generic dimension to that economy is certain – Maria's entrance calls the poet back to his original project, the poetry of praise, a task from which he has strayed in moving outward from Appleton House to the estate's formal gardens, its water meadows, its woods and riverbanks, a schema that sees the poet dissolve from philosophic purposiveness into pastoral distraction. Punning in this stanza is thus a way of indulging not just sexual but also generic waywardness and in the very space that sexual and generic waywardness are ostensibly arrested and reversed.

But we are only getting part of the story of puns in Marvell's poetry if we limit ourselves to plays on words that court the forbidden or taboo, for Marvell's puns have been admired by no less exacting a critic than William Empson precisely for their tact and justness. 'The most obvious way to justify [puns] is by derivation,' Empson writes, though he goes on to allow that 'a pun may not need to be justified by derivation because the word itself suggests the connection by which it is justified'.[7] Here Empson quotes the Soul responding to the temptation of Music in Marvell's *A Dialogue, Between the Resolved Soul, and Created Pleasure*:

> Had I but any time to lose,
> On this I would it all dispose.
> Cease tempter. None can chain a mind
> Whom this sweet chordage cannot bind.   (lines 41–4)

'It is exquisitely pointed', Empson insists, 'especially in that most cords are weaker than *chains*, so that the statement is paradox, and these *chords* are implacable, so that it is hyperbole.'[8] There is, however, an interpretive blindness in Empson's question, 'How is the poet's making of puns justifiable?' when he fails to ask, 'How is the Resolved Soul's making of puns justifiable?' The Resolved Soul is of course a device through which the poet speaks, but so are all poetic figures. And if we take the fiction of the poem seriously, which means that we should not conflate poet and persona, we find that even as it rejects the temptations of the material world, the Resolved Soul cannot raise itself out of the materiality of language, that the soul 'stumbles', in its spiritual trial, on the pleasures of the word.

The dialogue is framed by a narrator who hails in mock-epic fashion the arming of the Resolved Soul for battle with 'Nature', or 'Created Pleasure'. With each successful test of its resolution, the soul seems to ascend closer to heaven. No quarter is here granted to 'pleasures less', that is, to material pleasure. Unlike, say, *The Garden*, this dialogue argues the soul's happiness exclusively in terms of its division from and denial of sense satisfactions. Where such strict discursive boundaries are drawn, the pun is bound to be problematic; and can puns be innocent of pleasure? Let us listen to the temptation and hear once more the Resolved Soul's response:

> Pleasure
> Hark how music then prepares
> For thy stay these charming airs;
> Which the posting winds recall,
> And suspend the river's fall.
> Soul
> Had I but any time to lose,
> On this I would it all dispose.

> Cease tempter. None can chain a mind
> Whom this sweet chordage cannot bind.   (lines 37–44)

'Airs' is of course a pun, playing upon the senses of 'winds' and 'melodies'; 'chordage' is an even better pun, condensing a metaphysical conceit into a single word. Yet for all its economy, the pun nevertheless discloses, indeed calls attention to and exploits for effect, the gap in time between signifier and signified: the pun takes a moment to land. This seems pointedly ironic if the reader is supposed to identify with the soul's spiritual urgency – it 'cannot stay | To bait so long upon the way' (lines 17–18), has not 'any time to lose' (line 41) – for the pun retards our progress as readers, sends us circling back to sound it out. Perhaps by this we are made aware – made wary – of tending to the progress of our own soul; we catch ourselves 'falling away' from spiritual purpose. But of course the Resolved Soul's pun is itself carefully indeed perfectly made, and does not its artfulness belong within the precincts of Created Pleasure? Put more sharply, is not the pun born out of the erotics of language, a responsiveness to what Culler identifies as 'the call of the phoneme'? The soul is here offered and supposedly turns aside the temptation of 'charming airs' – and yet the soul's riposte is full of music. The poem celebrates the soul's self-enclosure, 'its pure and circling thoughts', to quote Marvell's *On a Drop of Dew* (line 25), and at the same time reveals something of the soul's naïveté, its imbrication in the material world, and more specifically in language: the pure thought is always mediated, bent by the material word. This superb lyric – the first poem in the 1681 folio – puts us on notice that language is a double-edged instrument, and it cuts in several directions.

Otium and *negotium*

The pressure of contradictory forces is apparent at the level of language, but also at the level of form, in the dialectical movement of thought that drives so many of Marvell's best poems. This structure is most obvious in Marvell's handful of debate poems, *A Dialogue, Between The Resolved Soul, and Created Pleasure* and *A Dialogue between the Soul and Body*, along with *Clorinda and Damon, Daphnis and Chloe*, and *Ametas and Thestylis Making Hay-Ropes*. As Robert Polito observes, however, 'There is something misleading about the application of a metaphor of debate to these poems . . . Both generically and in common parlance, "debate" implies a conclusion and a victor, but neither of these exists in Marvell's poetry.'[9] We have already seen how compromised is the soul's 'victory' over pleasure in their debate; of the dialogue between soul and body Rosalie Colie comments that Marvell 'presents them [soul and body] so that their traditional independence and opposition are seen to be illusory'.[10] However, Marvell's most rigorously dialectical poems take more subtle forms and attend to more subtle occasions than these genre exercises. These can feel a bit like warm-ups for Marvell's signal performances in poems such as *The Garden*, which stands as a kind of *locus classicus* for thinking about his address to the world as man and poet – about how he inhabits a set of positions and perspectives without ever coming to rest in one or the other, hovering always betwixt and between.

In their very different ways both *The Garden* and the *Horatian Ode* treat a common problem, that of *otium* and *negotium*, leisure and engagement, retirement and activity. *The Garden* opens by briskly proposing a set of arguments on behalf of either term:

> How vainly men themselves amaze
> To win the palm, the oak, or bays;
> And their uncessant labours see
> Crowned from some single herb or tree,
> Whose short and narrow vergèd shade
> Does prudently their toils upbraid;
> While all flow'rs and all trees do close
> To weave the garlands of repose.   (lines 1–8)

Palm, oak, and bays, as any good edition will note, are emblems of military, civic, and literary accomplishment. In a characteristic piece of wit, Marvell pretends that these tokens are pursued not as symbols but as plants, and they are made comically trivial next to the ample comfort and repose of the garden's flowers and trees. Wordplay impels and deepens this contest between the hurry of civilization and the equipoise of seclusion and withdrawal: on the side of *negotium* we have 'uncessant labours' and 'toils', on the side of *otium* 'repose'; on the side of *negotium* the 'single herb or tree' and its 'narrow vergèd shade', on the other the abundance and plenitude of 'all' and 'all'; confusion and self-deception versus (implicitly) quiet and self-knowledge. But here Marvell also deposits a central irony: art and poetry (the 'bays') clearly belong to the side of *negotium*, to the world of ambition and striving counterpointed with the garden world of retirement and ease. Yet poetry is of course the very instrument of that comparison, and so belongs at once to self-deception and to self-knowledge, to blindness and to insight – a resonant Marvellian paradox.

We might be inclined to think that the seclusion of the garden would be ascetic, as compared to the license and licentiousness of the busy world, but while Marvell does insert pleasure into the lockstep of his dialectic, the equation is by no means one of presence and absence. 'No white nor red was ever seen | So am'rous as this lovely green' (lines 17–18). Red and white are emblematic of human passion, though for Marvell, here and elsewhere, green is the true shade of eros. In the poem's accounting, human lovers are '[f]ond' and 'cruel', 'fond' gathering 'foolish' together with 'affectionate', 'cruel' reminding us of love's destructive flames and consuming fevers. The narrow compass of human love and its restrictions, its singularity, are also brought into contradistinction with a love for nature, a love that preserves rather than destroys, enjoys boundless variety rather than the tyranny of two: in the famous central stanza ripe apples drop about the speaker's head, grapes 'crush their wine' upon his mouth, nectarines reach into his hands, and 'Stumbling on melons, as I pass, | Insnared with flow'rs, I fall on grass' (lines 39–40). We can thus further extrapolate the dialectic: on the side of *otium*, voluptuous nature, polymorphous pleasure, and the fall into innocence; on the side of *negotium*, women, sex, and the fall into sin.

With the body thus absorbed into the garden's matrix of pleasures, the mind 'Withdraws into its happiness' (line 42), turning inward to survey the world of mental forms. 'Know thyself' is a Delphic prescription, but it also has a Christian analogue: 'The kingdom of God cometh not with observation; neither shall they say, Lo here! or, Lo there! For behold, the kingdom of God is within you' (Luke 17: 20–21). And sure enough, the reflexive mind here prepares and prefigures the soul's self-perfection:

> Casting the body's vest aside,
> My soul into the boughs does glide:
> There like a bird it sits, and sings,
> Then whets, and combs its silver wings;
> And, till prepared for longer flight,
> Waves in its plumes the various light.　　　　　(lines 51–6)

The rewards of civilization are material, the rewards of the garden spiritual; in the world of *negotium* man seeks fame and fortune, in that of *otium* he seeks self-knowledge and salvation. *And yet*: in stanzas six and seven the turn inward also clearly entails the risk of falling into ecstatic solipsism. The mind exults in its power not just to represent to itself that which exists but to create 'Far other worlds, and other seas, | Annihilating all that's made | To a green thought in a green shade' (lines 46–8). The soul, freed from the body, flies up into the tree where it 'whets, and combs its silver wings', an act of purification, of making itself ready for the next world, but as well an act of vainglory. 'How vainly men themselves amaze' – can we help but think that the poem's relentless dialectical strategies have in these passages somehow gotten confounded? That the opposition of *otium* and *negotium* has dissolved into interpenetration? Two concluding stanzas do little to ease us beyond this impasse, seeming rather to deepen the problematic. For in stanza eight, Marvell wistfully imagines what it would have been like to inhabit the delicious solitude of that *other* garden, before Eve, the apple, and the Fall, again conjuring an ideal solipsism only to walk away: ''twas beyond a mortal's share' (line 61). And in the final verse, the poet actually walks out of the garden and – we may feel – out of the poem, leaving us to sift the pieces of a puzzle.

It is this programme of statement, qualification and retreat, this subtle motion by which a set of values is inverted and reversed, something is transformed into its opposite, that identifies Marvell's liminal cast of mind. Though *The Garden* may be an intellectual exercise, it is not merely an intellectual exercise: its point and counterpoint are almost certainly tuned to the real-world circumstances of Marvell's patron Thomas Lord Fairfax and of so many others. Marvell entered Fairfax's service in the summer of 1650, shortly after Fairfax had laid down his post as supreme commander of the Parliamentary army rather than lead the invasion of Scotland. There was fear of a Scottish assault on England under the banner of Charles King of Scots, but Fairfax made a principled decision not to make pre-emptive war 'upon a neighbour nation, especially our brethren of Scotland, to whom we are engaged in a solemn league and covenant'.[11] Though we cannot be sure, we can well imagine that Marvell wrote *The Garden* – and its formidably longer companion piece *Upon Appleton House* – with a view to entertaining his patron and perhaps also to soothing his conscience. Clearly *The Garden* devises a way of thinking about retirement from the world and its cares and responsibilities that discovers dignity and even higher purpose in pastoral retreat; but there is, in the ultimate irresolution of the poem's dialectic, also something discomfiting, some unquiet and uncertainty, and this too belongs to Marvell.

The poetics of liminality

Marvell's 'liminal sensibility' is inscribed in his poetry at the level of form and theme, but there are also imaginative dimensions to Marvell's concern with borders and liminalities. In this there is no better place to start than with Marvell's arrestingly strange paean to love and loss, *The Nymph Complaining for the Death of her Fawn*. Almost everywhere this poem presents an occasion to remark various forms of border traffic; indeed, the poem's narrative turns comprise an important element of its labile, indeterminate character. The poem begins in the traumatic present with the senseless shooting of the fawn by marauding troopers, an event generic expectation tells us ought to be the narrative and affective centre of the poem. However, the central seventy or so lines of *The Nymph Complaining* circle back in time to recount the nymph's aborted affair with 'Unconstant Sylvio', a huntsman who 'grew wild, | And quite regardless of my smart, | Left me his fawn, but took his heart' (lines 34–6). As the nymph's punning couplet suggests, the fawn becomes a surrogate for the departed Sylvio. So, embedded in the nymph's complaint we find a startling erotic pastoralism. But past pleasure is everywhere shadowed by present grief; an idyllic future for the fawn can only be imagined counterfactually: 'Had it lived long . . .' At the same time, the fawn's death and transfiguration reprise in different form the nymph's pastoral fantasy of the fawn metamorphosed into a creature of lilies and roses. Erotic pastoral and funerary ode are competing discourses in *The Nymph Complaining*, yet each is shot through with linguistic and affective traces of the other, just as the narrative present permeates the narrative past, and just as the artefactual future projected at the end of the poem is marked by a sentient future that was never anything but impossible.

Of the many questions raised by this précis of the poem's narrative, poetic and thematic structures, we might first ask, what are troopers doing at the border of the nymph's garden? It is as if, one critic has wryly commented, 'the characters from another poem have for a moment burst into this one and left behind something to interpret'.[12] The intrusion, moreover, consists not only in the appearance of carbine-toting soldiers on the fringe of the nymph's pastoral domain but also in the appearance of 'troopers' in the nymph's lyric vocabulary. In English, 'troop' had long referred to a military body, but 'troopers', as a designation specifically for mounted soldiers (these troopers are 'riding by'), only came into the language around 1640. It is a word of new and specialized coinage, but pastoral complaint is a conventional and 'timeless' genre. In the very first couplet of the poem we are plunged into a drama of transit and transgression across borders: the troopers' violation of the nymph's garden represents the collision of a private and literary realm with a public and historical one. Once opened to historical consciousness, the nymph's elegiac recording of the fawn's death takes on complex and surprising significance:

> Ungentle men! They cannot thrive
> To kill thee. Thou ne'er didst alive
> Them any harm: alas nor could
> Thy death yet do them any good.   (lines 3–6)

> Though they should wash their guilty hands
> In this warm life-blood, which doth part
> From thine, and wound me to the heart,
> Yet could they not be clean: their stain
> Is dyed in such a purple grain.
> There is not such another in
> The world, to offer for their sin.   (lines 18–24)

It is hard not to hear sacred overtones in this account: the innocent fawn, as M. C. Bradbrook and M. G. Lloyd Thomas pointed out long ago, is reminiscent of the beloved roe or hart of the Song of Solomon;[13] the stain on the hands of the troopers recalls Pontius Pilate; purple is traditionally used in churches to mark the season of Advent and the coming kingdom of Christ.

This much is undeniable – but to read the death of the fawn as allegory does not make sense of the historical specificity of 'troopers' and its association with the New Model Army, as Edward Le Comte notes in asking (albeit sardonically): 'If allegory is our game, why may we not say that the faun stands for Merry England, mortally wounded in the civil war?'[14] Even better, why may we not say that the fawn stands for the Anglican Church, which had been dissolved after the civil war by the victorious Puritan faction, its bishops abolished, its prayerbooks banned. After all, though Marvell celebrates Cromwell in the *Horatian Ode* of 1650 as the great 'climacteric' of reformed freedoms, his capacity in the same poem to admire Charles's deportment on the 'tragic scaffold', and ruefully to acknowledge the king's possession of 'ancient rights', surely argues Marvell's capacity in *The Nymph Complaining* to mourn the stricken church. Or perhaps, then, the fawn represents Charles I, whose 'martyrdom' was widely connected with Christ's, and whose titular role as 'Supreme Governor' also makes him an obvious synecdoche for the Anglican Church? So has the case been argued, with various echoes and allusions – from Scripture to Virgil to Ovid to *Britannia's Pastorals* – adduced as corroboration of its religious or political significance.

Allegory, however, proves a rather slippery slope on which to build an argument that encompasses this protean poem. Indeed, if the central panels of the poem have any 'ulterior' meaning, it is erotic rather than political or religious. The nymph, we observe, nourishes her pet in such a way as to conflate the eroticism of nursing with that of amorous foreplay, suckling the fawn at her fingertips:

> With sweetest milk, and sugar, first
> I it at mine own fingers nursed.
> And as it grew, so every day
> It waxed more white and sweet than they.
> It had so sweet a breath! And oft
> I blushed to see its foot more soft,
> And white (shall I say than my hand?
> Nay any lady's of the land). (lines 55–62)

Here is a scene, certainly, of erotic displacement, but the libidinous energy does not constitute psychic overflow from the nymph's relationship with Sylvio; rather the nymph seems to be incorporating the fawn into an essentially narcissistic drive. The nymph's own body is the erotic baseline of the passage ('shall I say than my hand?'), and it is the elemental whiteness and sweetness of her fingers that the fawn absorbs through the medium of milk and sugar. We might note the fantastically transformative properties of that absorption: while it is the fawn's breath that sweetens, it is its foot (so the nymph imagines) that softens and whitens. This erotic congress is one of virtual transpeciation: the boundaries between 'nymph' and 'fawn' are here dissolved, their identity as discrete bodies and discrete subjectivities ecstatically surrendered. The progress of the nymph's 'dream', moreover, presents us with successive images wherein leakage similarly occurs between subject and object, self and other: the white fawn lies down in a bank of lilies only to disappear into the 'flaxen lilies' shade' (line 81); it hungrily devours roses 'Until its lips ev'n seemed to bleed' (line 84); the fawn then 'print[s] those roses on my lip' (line 86), 'bleeds', to pick up the word used two lines previously, on to and into the nymph, leaves its indelible 'mark'. We might think back to the end of *Eyes and Tears*: 'Thus let your streams o'erflow your springs, | Till eyes and tears be the same things: | *And each the other's diff'rence bears*' (lines 53–5; my emphasis), a figure echoed wonderfully in the nymph's apotheosis on the fawn, 'Had it lived long, it would have been | Lilies without, roses within' (lines 91–2). Even the space of the garden has the quality of being betwixt and between: 'I have a garden of my own,' the nymph says, 'But so with roses overgrown, | And lilies, that you would it guess | To be a little wilderness' (lines 71–4).[15]

What are we to make of these intractably strange erotic tableaux and indeed of all the other scenes of lingering fascination with the liminal body in *Young Love*, in *The Picture of Little T. C. in a Prospect of Flowers*, or in *Upon Appleton House*, to name but a few? We can no longer think that Sylvio represents the 'true' site and form of desire in this poem or the fawn a pathetic simulacrum of that desire; to the contrary, it seems that Sylvio's evacuation, along with the removal of the imperatives and teleologies of heterosexuality, actually opens the possibility of pleasure. Men in this poem are symbols of violence and violation, not sexual allure. The creatures of Marvell's erotic landscape are liminal, indeterminate figures: the nymph is part 'mythic being' part 'country girl', and on the cusp of childlike innocence and 'adult' sexuality; the fawn is resolutely designated 'it', never 'he' (or 'she'), and so deeply anthropomorphized that the language of the poem easily lets us forget that the fawn is not a human being but equally not an animal. 'Fawn' itself is an ambiguous term, indicating a yearling deer of either sex. Moreover, what the structure of desire – and of pleasure – manifested in *The Nymph Complaining* reminds one most of is certainly not heterosexuality, nor those grey eminences 'homoeroticism' or 'bestiality', but Freud's polymorphous perverse, a mode of pleasure not focused but roaming, as it were, all over the body. The pleasure of the text, the structure of the reader's 'erotic' relation to Marvell's poem is or ought to be 'polymorphously perverse' as well. Denied the consistency and coherence – denied the comfort – of allegory, the reader must be content to 'roam all over' the poem, allowing its fragmentary bits of story, its various 'overtones' and 'undertones', to shimmer in and out of view.

The Unfortunate Lover is a poem no less strange or challenging than The Nymph Complaining; taken together, these poems mark out a territory – and a poetics – of thought and feeling that belong alone to Marvell. For all their apparent tonal and dramatic differences, both texts are extraordinary in the resourcefulness with which they mobilize generic conventions and codes to support and also to baffle and obscure a welter of meanings that reach from the broadly topical and political to the intensely private and personal. The Nymph Complaining is a pastoral complaint capacious enough to shelter allegories of the Crucifixion, of the martyrdom of Charles I and of the collapse of the Anglican Church, while also disclosing, however obliquely, the poet's deepest fantasies and longings. In The Unfortunate Lover, Marvell inscribes within the Petrarchan narrative of frustrated desire, that most conventionally interior of forms, not just as has been argued a singular history of the self but as well the recent history of the state.

After a nostalgic first stanza spent admiring those lovers 'Sorted by pairs' (line 3) who still play amid 'Fountains cool, and Shadows green' (line 4), the poem careers into Petrarchan love's characteristically heavy weather:

> 'Twas in a shipwrack, when the seas
> Ruled, and the winds did what they please,
> That my poor lover floating lay,
> And, ere brought forth, was cast away: (lines 9–12)

> The sea him lent these bitter tears
> Which at his eyes he always wears:
> And from the winds the sighs he bore,
> Which through his surging breast do roar.   (lines 17–20)

The sea voyage as metaphor for the perils of amorous attachment is the organizing trope of Petrarch's celebrated Sonnet 189 ('My ship is sailing, full of mindless woe'), where the mainsail on the ship of love 'by wet eternal winds distraught, | With hopes, desires and sighs is made to rend' (lines 7–8), while 'A rain of tears, a fog of scornful lines, | Washes and tugs at the too sluggish cords' (lines 9–10).[16] One cannot help but think this lyric stands somewhere behind Marvell's. More generally, we recognize in Marvell's poem, especially in stanzas six and seven, the familiar elemental oppositions of Petrarch's Songbook (Il Canzoniere), the burning and freezing, the flames and waves, as well as the flaunting of wounds. But more even than a setting of his life – and Marvell's taste for marine metaphors is clear – the emotional 'weather' of Petrarchanism is also the substance of the Unfortunate Lover's being: he literally 'cries seas' and 'sighs winds', he is a kind of Aeolus, carrying the storm within him wherever he goes.

Yet for all its inventiveness, beyond a certain technical respect for the poem critics have found little to like about *The Unfortunate Lover* – Marvell's witty and sophisticated dilation of Petrarchan poetics has met most often with puzzlement, and occasionally with scorn. The cause for both of these reactions lies in the feel of narrative texture and detail in *The Unfortunate Lover*, a feeling that is at once specific and maddeningly elusive. Who is the Unfortunate Lover? He was born into a tempest, and as the final stanza tells us, 'by malignant stars, | Forced to live in storms and wars' (lines 59–60), language that instantly conjures the turbulence of the recent civil conflict. Moreover, he is an 'unfortunate', a figure whose defining circumstance is suffering, but who is also defined – and even exalted – in his own imagination by suffering. Should we remember the martyred king pictured emblematically amid storms on the frontispiece of his spiritual autobiography, the *Eikon Basilike*? – the king who affected to write of his solitude at Holmby, 'I come farre short of Davids piety; yet since I may equall Davids afflictions, give Mee also the comforts, and the sure mercies of David'; 'Let my sufferings satiate the malice of mine, & thy Churches Enemies. But let their cruelty never exceed the measure of my charity.'[17]

Has Marvell then folded into Petrarchan lineaments a royalist polemic, a story about the tragic love of Charles I for his people, his affliction at their hands, his destiny to suffer and to redeem and to be redeemed by suffering? If 'polemic' is too strong a word, might we say that Marvell projects an eschatological vision that in some way demands the sacrifice of the king? It does not seem altogether unreasonable; but what then are the historical coordinates of that curious and sensational scene in which the Unfortunate Lover falls into the 'cruel care' of 'corm'rants black' (lines 29, 27)? Here, Margarita Stocker conjectures, 'The clerical cormorants are "black" because of their clerical garb,' and she further intimates that the scene somehow describes the Anglican episcopacy nurturing Charles's ambitions for personal rule while subtly undermining his political authority.[18] Robert Wilcher, perhaps more plausibly, sees the cormorants as the Scottish Presbyterian clergy who were the king's gaolers after his capture by the Scots at Newark.[19]

Yet historical allegory does not take into account the personal significance these rapacious figures may have held for Andrew Marvell. Though himself a clergyman's son, the poet nourished a lifelong anger at clerical tyranny and abuse, and it may be tempting to see in the Unfortunate Lover's ordeal with the cormorants – an ordeal that ruinously fashioned the lover to his erotic destiny – an element of lived trauma.[20] But however biographically we might wish to read these figures, it is important to insist on the poetics of radical interpolation in *The Unfortunate Lover* no less than in *The Nymph Complaining*: of private and public, of personal and political, of real and imaginary. Such interpolation depends of course upon an ability to trade in a number of voices. This can take the form of punning wordplay and destabilizing ironies, but beyond such local effects these poems manage several stories simultaneously, stories that both complement and complicate one another. And we might note as well the striking intertextuality of Marvell's work, that extraordinary pattern of echoes, allusions, imitations and parodies in his poetry, the conjuring up of ancient and modern texts to work on behalf of poet and poem, to supply texture and depth, but also to be revised and re-evaluated. Out of this verbal, and surely psychic, economy of the liminal – the painful yet pleasurable singularity of the life lived 'betwixt and between the positions assigned and arrayed by law, custom, convention, and ceremonial'[21] – Marvell's art emerges: how else are we to understand the Unfortunate Lover transformed into 'the only banneret | That ever Love created yet' (lines 57–8),[22] or the Nymph Complaining become self-creating artefact, a statue engraved by its own tears?

Here we might end, though to do so would be to recapitulate conventional divisions between Marvell's lyric achievements and his political verse. But Marvell's political verse reveals a writer still deeply engaged by and with dialectics, always looking in two directions – a poet still writing within and at the same time writing against convention, and still very much an inhabitant of margins and borders. Above all, we find Marvell still incising private meaning within the political, as in the lyrics he incised political meaning within the personal and the private – and from a vantage point that seems systematically located within and without. To make this case, I will focus on the two poems that might appear to have least of the liminal, that appear the most partisan.

Many critics have thought the *Poem upon the Death of O. C.* the least accomplished, least interesting, indeed least 'Marvellian' of the Cromwell poems. In this text Marvell's famous indeterminacies supposedly fall away, his disinterested intelligence giving over to pathos and turgid conventionality. Yet at least one serious attempt has been made in recent years to align the *Poem upon the Death* with the great ode and *The First Anniversary* in terms of how it 'contemplates the complexity of historical means and the contingency of power',[23] and it is worth taking seriously this poem and what it says of Marvell's sensitivity to the problematics of borders and margins.

It is true, as Robert Wilcher writes, that the poem 'contains much that is predictable – the storm that raged as he [Cromwell] lay dying was a sign of "what pangs that death did Nature cost" (line 112); "Valour, religion, friendship, prudence died | At once with him" (lines 227–8); his "honour, praise, and name" will live "As long as future time succeeds the past" (lines 285–6)'.[24] Nevertheless, Marvell's initial and most sustained vehicle for comprehending Cromwell's death, and for venerating his life, is not the conventional stuff of martial courage and spiritual rectitude (though Marvell does deploy those materials in the poem) but rather the highly unconventional topos of domestic affection. Love and grief, according to Marvell, were the agents of Cromwell's mortal fate, his death rendered a kind of empathic suicide in response to the loss of his favourite daughter Elizabeth to long illness:

> Who now shall tell us more of mournful swans,
> Of halcyons kind, or bleeding pelicans?
> No downy breast did ere so gently beat,
> Or fan with airy plumes so soft an heat.
> For he no duty by his height excused,
> Nor though a prince, to be a man refused:
> But rather than in his Eliza's pain
> Not love, not grieve, would neither live nor reign:
> And in himself so oft immortal tried,
> Yet in compassion of another died. (lines 79–88)

What better measure of a man than as a father? the poem asks, and here is a father who, though exalted, never neglected his duties of affection, who placed paternal affection above duties of state, indeed above his own mortal life. In a Christic act of self-abnegation, Cromwell relinquishes mundane glories to join Eliza in the eternal life beyond. To be sure, Marvell is trading on pathos here but always to strategic effect: placing Cromwell in these domestic scenes softens not only the anticlimax of Cromwell's death (he 'Deservèd yet an end whose ev'ry part | Should speak the wondrous softness of his heart') but the fears and resentments of those who saw in Cromwell radical, even tyrannical ambition. Here, as in the *Horatian Ode*, Marvell argues privacy and retirement, the domestic sphere, as Cromwell's native element, thus framing his remarkable career as the selfless pursuit of a providential calling. The lustre of Cromwell's martial and political success is heightened by the foil of his sympathetic nature while at the same time his motives are subsumed into the work of fate.

Writing against the tradition that has seen the elegy 'as a series of abstract gestures', Ashley Marshall insists that the elegy 'departs … notably from elegiac custom in its unremitting emphasis on the personality of Oliver himself rather than on an archetype'.[25] For Marshall, the passage that most stands out is thus Marvell's description of viewing the Lord Protector's corpse – 'I saw him dead' (line 247) – which strikingly personalizes both the subject of the elegy and its author: since the public saw only an effigy of Cromwell at his official funeral, the lines place Marvell in intimate proximity to the body and claim a very human and privileged relation between poet and Protector. Yet more striking is Marvell's fantasy of Cromwell's domestic life, and indeed his imaginative projection of himself into those deeply intimate and familiar scenes. Here is Marvell chronicling Elizabeth Cromwell's sickness, and the history of affection between father and daughter:

> Straight does a slow and languishing disease
> Eliza, Nature's and his darling, seize.
> Her when an Infant, taken with her charms,
> He oft would flourish in his mighty arms;
> And, lest their force the tender burden wrong,
> Slacken the vigour of his muscles strong.　　　(lines 29–34)

The passage makes a strong impression of Marvell's bearing witness to these fond interactions; yet Elizabeth Cromwell was hardly a child when she died. She was, in fact, born in 1629, when Marvell was eight years old, and by the time he came into Cromwell's service Elizabeth was already in her twenties.

These vividly rendered vignettes are fashioned not from memory but from fantasy, motivated by and overlain with Marvell's own psychic longings and perhaps also his own psychic wounds. What those wounds may be is hard to say, but it is equally hard to deny the longing for paternal protection and affection. Marvell explicitly admits into the scene the possibility of the child's being hurt or 'wrong[ed]' in the arms of patriarchy; however, Cromwell 'Slacken[s] the vigour of his muscles strong', at once deflating the threat to the child – the martial arm becomes protective cradle – and augmenting Marvell's brilliantly counterintuitive portrait of Cromwell as man of feeling. In creating the fiction of his own presence at this moment of familial comfort and ease, Marvell also writes himself, literally and figuratively, into the space of Cromwell's domestic affections. He thereby manages to accomplish what seems like an astonishing bit of private wish fulfilment even as he pursues a rhetorical strategy that is calibrated precisely to the exigencies and realities of the political moment.

Yet there was a further dilemma to be resolved besides that of framing the public and private aspects of Cromwell's person in ways both satisfying to his friends and ameliorating to his enemies – and that was of course the problem of the Protectoral succession. Oliver twice refused the title and office of 'king', and despite being charged in the 'Humble Petition and Advice' of 1657 to denominate a successor, he never did so publicly. In any case, though, Oliver's eldest son Richard was proclaimed Lord Protector the day after his father's death. There is every sign that Richard's emergence initially met with wide public support. From very early on, however, Richard's experience and force of character were at issue, and by November 1658 rifts were already forming between the new Lord Protector and the military. There were 'some secret murmurings in the army as if his highnes were not generall of the army as his father was',[26] and soon enough there was a general unrest and uncertainty as to the future of the republican experiment.

It is into this pitch of uncertainty that Marvell wrote the Cromwell elegy, taking up the succession explicitly in the poem's final stanzas. That the lines endorse Richard's protectorship is clear, and yet there is a certain cognitive dissonance to the passage, as where Marvell writes, 'How he becomes that seat, how strongly strains, | How gently winds at once the ruling reins?' (lines 313–14). 'Strongly strains' and 'gently winds' consort rather oddly together and suggest a rather different push–pull from what is ostensibly being described: when the reins pass to milder hands, horses threaten to gallop out of control. There are other such crosscurrents here, most noticeably Marvell's insistent counterpointing of Richard's mildness to Oliver's potency at the same time as he proclaims that 'A Cromwell in an hour a prince will grow' (line 312). In his support of Richard it seems fair to say that Marvell is 'neither assured nor assuring',[27] but it is not a fault in the poem; rather the disequilibrium of the envoy reflects and enacts yet again the condition of occupying a borderland. Marvell could not perhaps have seen that he was standing on the fault line between Commonwealth and Restoration: behind him were eight years of republican government under Cromwell's extraordinary star, but with Cromwell's setting, the design of providence was suddenly dimmed, inchoate, seeming to wait upon another son of destiny. Richard may have been the leading candidate for that role, and we do not have to doubt the sincerity of Marvell's endorsement, but in the shadows of the envoy there lurks that other 'prince', Charles II, and it is not without irony that the cracks and divisions in the polity that emerged after Oliver Cromwell's death would be healed not by Richard's but by Charles's 'milder beams'.

If critics have thought that Marvell nodded in writing the *Poem upon the Death*, some have wondered how *The Last Instructions*, in its rhetorical violence and abundant cruelty, can belong to the same poet who wrote *The Garden* or the *Horatian Ode*. That this view underestimates Marvell's ability to inhabit and ventriloquize different positions and rhetorics should be apparent. But it also fails to apprehend the central dilemma of the *The Last Instructions*, which is nothing if not Marvellian: it is the problem of within and without, of where writer and reader stand in relation to the poem's programme of complicity and resistance, and it is written into the very heart of this text. The strategy of Marvell's argument is to connect private vice with public ruin and disorder, to identify the diseased appetites of royal bodies with the disease of the body politic. As in much clandestine satire of this period, the poem engages the reader in a series of voyeuristic acts, demystifying and degrading the court by revealing the physical grossness of courtiers, and by making the reader witness to their most secret and humiliating acts and arts. The individual portraits are devastating enough, but we need also remember that in Restoration satire the geometry of sexual subjection is almost always inscribed as political allegory.[28] The real scandal of Castlemaine's affair with her lackey, for example, is not sexual degradation but inversion of hierarchy. Voyeuristic looking, moreover, here penetrates the privacy not just of the closet but of the psyche as well: Castlemaine 'Her wonted joys thenceforth, and court, she shuns, | And still *within her mind* the footman runs' (lines 83–4, emphasis mine).

Yet not only to imagine and represent those acts that might, if only hypothetically, be glimpsed by the well-placed observer, but also to fashion to view the secret thoughts and desires of Lady Castlemaine (or as happens later in the poem, the predatory fantasies of the king) is perforce to indulge – perhaps even to outgo – the very distempers the poem ostensibly aims to lash and correct. Of course, there has always been an uneasy complicity between the methods of the satirist and the vice and excess that so exercise him: as Alvin Kernan sardonically notes, 'Inevitably when [the satirist] dips into the devil's broth in order, he says, to show us how filthy it really is, he gets splattered.'[29] The danger of contamination and complicity is powerfully heightened in a poem like *The Last Instructions*, which achieves its most dazzling effects through the device of voyeurism.

This problem is writ large in the poem's most dramatic sequence, the fiery apotheosis of young Archibald Douglas, who in the Dutch invasion of the Thames in the summer of 1667 burned alive in his ship rather than surrender. The scene of Douglas's immolation has long perplexed critics. Its manner and tone are distant from the scabrous satire that surrounds it, an intrusion of Ovidian pastoral into the midst of folly and vice. Recent scholarship has at least made clear certain of the thematic and argumentative functions of Marvell's treatment of the 'loyal Scot'. Though Douglas was in fact a married man in his thirties, Marvell provocatively figures his hero as both virgin and androgyne. Frozen on the cusp of adult sexuality, Douglas 'is a denial of sexual desire: he is innocence in a world of corruption, beauty among the deformed'.[30] His passion is spent in civic sacrifice and public defence, not in the throes of idle lust. Such arguments undeniably hold explanatory power; but I want to end by framing a puzzle that they do not entirely solve. Here is some of the language from this remarkable scene:

> Much him the honours of his ancient race
> Inspire, nor would he his own deeds deface;
> And secret joy in his calm soul does rise,
> That Monck looks on to see how Douglas dies.
> Like a glad lover, the fierce flames he meets,
> And tries his first embraces in their sheets.
> His shape exact, which the bright flames enfold,
> Like the sun's statue stands of burnished gold.
> Round the transparent fire about him glows,
> As the clear amber on the bee does close[.]   (lines 673–82)

Archibald Douglas – with 'secret joy in his calm soul' – looks at General Monk looking at him die. In an extraordinary inversion of the Renaissance trope of orgasm as a 'little death', Douglas's actual death in the flames of the *Royal Oak* is here figured in the most explicit terms as the height of erotic ecstasy; yet more provocatively, the ecstasy of Douglas's destruction is compounded by its being observed. But it is not just Monk who watches Douglas die: through the eyes of the poet, we, too, look on, and it is here that our aesthetic appreciation for Marvell's incandescent verse becomes inextricable from what seems for this poet to be the frisson of imagining the holocaust of this unsullied creature of innocence and virtue. In this Marvellian moment, then, we are standing at the centre of the poem's positive argument, its greatest example and counter to the forces of vice and darkness, and at the same time we are drawn irresistibly into a shocking web of voyeurism and self-display.

Here we are positioned, as so often in Marvell's work, both within and without: even as we inhabit the perspectives and affects of the 'lookers' and the 'looked-at' inside the poem, we are aware of the poem's status as text and of voyeurism as textual strategy. Unlike Monk or Douglas – actors within but not consumers of the poem – we can read the scene against the raw images and energies of satire that surround it and in relation to the pastoral materials and conventions that lie behind it. To identify in *The Last Instructions* the partial and fluid conjunctions of poet, character and reader, and to locate identification and difference within the convergence of disparate meanings and modes, is also to be reminded of the play that structures so much of Marvell's poetry. That play begins at the level of language, Marvell's puns providing a means of blurring the very arguments and distinctions he would appear to refine and uphold. But Marvell goes beyond the fields of language to exploit – sometimes indeed to explode – the conventions and codes of Renaissance poetics, to assert and then to dissolve the boundaries between and among literary kinds, to fuse the languages and meanings of public and private, to intermingle the history of nation and self. It is surely no coincidence that liminality should also have constituted for Marvell a psychic economy of pain and discomfiture as well as of supreme and supremely creative pleasure.

NOTES

1. Though see Allan Pritchard, 'Marvell's "The Garden": A Restoration Poem?' *Studies in English Literature* 23 (1983), 371–88, and Paul Hammond, 'The Date of Marvell's "The Mower against Gardens"', *Notes and Queries* 53 (2006), 178–81, for arguments re-dating lyrics once thought to belong to the Nun Appleton period to the Restoration.
2. Milton to John Bradshaw, 21 February 1652, in Frank Allen Patterson *et al.*, eds., *The Works of John Milton*, 18 vols. (New York, 1931–8), XII:330.
3. W. H. Kelliher, 'Andrew Marvell', *Oxford Dictionary of National Biography*, online edn.
4. Jonathan Culler, 'The Call of the Phoneme', in Culler, ed., *On Puns: The Foundation of Letters* (Oxford, 1988), 3.
5. T. S. Eliot, 'Andrew Marvell', first published in the *Times Literary Supplement*, 31 March 1921, repr. in Frank Kermode, ed., *The Selected Prose of T. S. Eliot* (New York, 1975), 163.
6. See the *Oxford English Dictionary* entry for 'toy', n^1, n^{3a}.
7. William Empson, *Seven Types of Ambiguity*, 3rd edn (New York, 1966), 104, 105.
8. *Ibid.*, 105.
9. Robert Polito, 'A Pair of Andys: Looking at Andy Warhol through Andrew Marvell's Eyes, and Vice Versa', *The Poetry Foundation* (online journal, 2008), no pp.
10. Rosalie Colie, '*My Ecchoing Song*': *Andrew Marvell's Poetry of Criticism* (Princeton, 1970), 57.
11. Bulstrode Whitelocke, *Memorials of English Affairs*, new edn, 4 vols. (London, 1853), III:209.
12. Stanley Fish, 'Marvell and the Art of Disappearance', in Michael P. Clarke, ed., *Revenge of the Aesthetic* (Berkeley, 2000), 30.
13. See M. C. Bradbrook and M. G. Lloyd Thomas, *Andrew Marvell* (Cambridge, 1940), 46–50.
14. Edward Le Comte, 'Marvell's "The Nymph Complaining for the Death of her Fawn"', *Modern Philology* 50 (1952), 100.
15. For a fuller unfolding of the erotics of the nymph's garden see Matthew C. Augustine, '"Lillies without, Roses within": Marvell's Poetics of Indeterminacy and "The Nymph Complaining"', *Criticism* 50 (2008), 255–78.
16. Francesco Petrarca, *Sonnets and Songs*, trans. Anna Maria Armi (New York, 1946).
17. *Eikon Basilike – The Pourtraicture of His Sacred Majestie in His Solitudes and Sufferings* (London, 1649), 210, 211.
18. Margarita Stocker, *Apocalyptic Marvell: The Second Coming in Seventeenth Century Poetry* (Brighton, 1986), 285.
19. See *ibid.*, 286, and Robert Wilcher, *The Writing of Royalism, 1628–1660* (Cambridge, 2001), 306–7.

20. This story is told in Derek Hirst and Steven N. Zwicker, 'Eros and Abuse: Imagining Andrew Marvell', *English Literary History* 74 (2007), 371–95.
21. Victor Turner, *The Ritual Process: Structure and Anti-Structure* (Chicago, 1969), 95. Turner is a cultural anthropologist whose work on ritual and rites of passage – the latter constituting for Turner the paradigmatic liminal phenomenon – has been widely influential.
22. On the relation between poesis and suffering in Marvell, and especially in *The Unfortunate Lover*, see Lynn Enterline's brilliant study 'The Mirror and the Snake: The Case of Marvell's "Unfortunate Lover"', in her *Tears of Narcissus: Melancholia and Masculinity in Early Modern Writing* (Stanford, 1995), 146–88.
23. Ashley Marshall, '"I saw him dead": Marvell's Elegy for Cromwell', *Studies in Philology* 103 (2006), 500.
24. Robert Wilcher, *Andrew Marvell* (Cambridge, 1985), 172.
25. Marshall, 'Marvell's Elegy for Cromwell', 501.
26. John Thurloe, *State Papers*, ed. Thomas Birch, 7 vols. (London, 1742), VII:374.
27. Marshall, 'Marvell's Elegy for Cromwell', 499.
28. On the 'pornopolitics' of Restoration satire see Harold Love, *English Clandestine Satire, 1660–1702* (Oxford, 2004), esp. 21–65.
29. Alvin Kernan, *The Cankered Muse: Satire of the English Renaissance* (New Haven, 1959), 24.
30. Steven N. Zwicker, *Lines of Authority: Politics and English Literary Culture, 1649–1689* (Ithaca, 1993), 114.

Further reading

Harry Berger, Jr, 'Andrew Marvell: The Poem as Green World', in *Second World and Green World: Studies in Renaissance Fiction-Making* (Berkeley, 1988), 251–323.
Warren Chernaik, *The Poet's Time: Politics and Religion in the Work of Andrew Marvell* (Cambridge, 1983).
William Empson, 'Marvell's Garden', in *Some Versions of Pastoral* (London, 1935; repr. New York, 1974), 119–48.
Joan Faust, 'Blurring the Boundaries: *Ut pictora poesis* and Marvell's Liminal Mower', *Studies in Philology* 104 (2007), 526–55.
Donald Friedman, *Marvell's Pastoral Art* (Berkeley, 1970).
Jonathan Goldberg, 'Marvell's Nymph and the Echo of Voice', in *Voice Terminal Echo: Postmodernism and English Renaissance Texts* (New York, 1986), 14–37.
Paul Hammond, 'Marvell's Ambiguities', in *Figuring Sex between Men from Shakespeare to Rochester* (Oxford, 2002), 186–225.
Derek Hirst and Steven N. Zwicker, 'Andrew Marvell and the Toils of Patriarchy: Fatherhood, Longing, and the Body Politic', *English Literary History* 66 (1999), 629–54.
Michael Long, *Marvell, Nabokov: Childhood and Arcadia* (Oxford, 1986).
Annabel Patterson, *Marvell and the Civic Crown* (Princeton, 1978).
Balachandra Rajan, 'Andrew Marvell: The Aesthetics of Inconclusiveness', in C. A. Patrides, ed., *Approaches to Marvell: The York Tercentenary Lectures* (London, 1978), 155–73.
Harold Toliver, *Marvell's Ironic Vision* (New Haven, 1965).

5

DIANE PURKISS

Thinking of gender

The twin issues of Marvell's representation of gender and Marvellian sexuality are at their most visible in the bodies of the nuns of Appleton and their desires. Exceptionally, *Upon Appleton House, To My Lord Fairfax* inaugurates its bid to establish the supremacy of the contemplative paterfamilias across the defeated bodies of nuns, whose portrayal includes a subtle but unmistakable representation of lesbian desire:

> Each night among us to your side
> Appoint a fresh and virgin bride;
> Whom if Our Lord at midnight find,
> Yet neither should be left behind.
> Where you may lie as chaste in bed,
> As pearls together billeted.
> All night embracing arm in arm,
> Like crystal pure with cotton warm.   (lines 185–92)

The question is whether the text will really allow itself to consider those desires as legitimate, or whether it rather inoculates itself against those longings by rendering them seductive. In this, it is Milton who is Marvell's stylistic master, risking moral confusion by allotting the best tunes to the devil, and, as with Milton, this has led to some misreadings.[1] The Fairfax family's acquisition of former monastic lands was typical of families of their class; they were occupying lands formerly used by a convent, now 'ruin[ed]', and their conversion of them to a right use, the uses of family and heterosexuality, is about resisting the sensuous allures of overtly feminized missteps and building a new and properly reproductive nation. Lesbian desire is presented as a response to and also as a cause of isolation from the family. Here, the perversions (for that is what they are to Marvell) are tempting precisely because they do not know themselves as desire. If they did, they could be resisted. So the poem is trying to make the nuns' allurements visible enough to allow them to be labelled and resisted.

Crucial to the legitimation of both the Protestant church and the Fairfaxes are the lines 'Thenceforth (as when th'enchantment ends, | The castle vanishes

68

or rends) | The wasting cloister with the rest | Was in one instant dispossessed' (lines 269–72). Generic laws – evil enchantments defeated by forces of good – make the overthrow of conventual rule in England seem inexorable. Spenser is the narrative ancestor of this idea – the triumph in arms of the Protestant cause is the subject of Book I of *The Faerie Queene* – but there are other, less comfortable antecedents in play. Has Marvell Giambattista Basile's *Pentamerone* in mind, and, if he has, what light does this cast on the nuns? While enchanted, Basile's Sleeping Beauty is ravished and impregnated, casting the nuns in an ever more perverse light. Equating the history of Catholic England not merely with the past, as James Holstun suggests, but with violent folktale, a national 'old wife's tale' full of ignorance, Marvell urges us all to grow up.[2]

The nuns' seductive exploration of erotic possibilities outside the heterosexual family is not, however, the poem's only alternative to that norm. Rather, the author's own solitary reveries provide a genuine alternative to and also a metaphor for the stoically retired paterfamilias. Marvell is concerned to sustain a sharp contrast between these solitudes and the nuns' illicit togetherness; his reveries are pastoral, natural, while theirs are the result of and metaphorized through craft and artisanal labour. Marvell asks the brambles to chain him and the briars to nail him, while woodbines bind and vines lace him closely. The nuns, conversely, offer commodities such as lilies, crystal, cotton. Marvell's eremitic and Edenic singleness is the alternative obverse of the nuns' unnatural longings; the latter exist to sanction and make space for the former. What makes Marvell unique is not his crass commitment to the heterosexual nor his dismissal of lesbian desire, but the way his poem seeks, questions, probes, interrogates, and invents. Some experiments succeed and others fail.

Why might 1651 seem an appropriate moment for this particular exploration? Why did nuns' sexuality seem especially relevant as a way of defining paterfamilial retirement and title to land? While Philip Schwyzer has recently argued that ruined monasteries do not form a large part of the English imagination, his work neglects the role they play in the Catholic polemic which was of particular and apparently pressing concern during the civil war years.[3] Alison Shell shows that monastic lands came to appear 'cursed', their decay or infertility an explicit rebuke from God. In particular, they could be cursed by lack of productivity. Fairfax, with only one child, could be construed as cursed, and further cursed to continue the unacceptably unalleviated femininity of the nuns.[4] In Marvell's tale, it is the nuns and not the Fairfaxes who are a palimpsest, or, rather, the nuns and their desires constitute an erasure which has the paradoxical effect of highlighting what appears in their place. The cult of the Virgin Mary became newly problematic as a result of

Queen Henrietta Maria's devotional practices.[5] Fairfax represents the masculinity which defeated the allegedly papist army of William Cavendish, the future Duke of Newcastle; he also signifies the reconquest of Northern femininity by Protestant masculine virtue, and his estate is represented as feminized 'territory' that is rightfully his precisely because it was previously in improper use. The satirical context in which lesbianism is used to portray the intrigues in Henrietta Maria's circle of courtly female intimates further contextualizes Marvell's seductive, even erotic satire. The erotic and the satirical overlap so strongly in seventeenth-century polemic that the presence of the sensual is not enough to imply that it is truly the central topic. Rather, political opponents can be vilified alongside erotic and even pornographic stimulus.

Sexuality and gender in *Upon Appleton House* are presented as a series of explorations of the arts of the possible and the desirable. For Marvell, lyric is a place in which one can explore heterosexuality – desire and its destinations – from the point of view of an outsider, even an alien. Defamiliarizing the heterosexual and exploring what else might be preferable can be exploratory and even loving. Marvell's metaphysical lyrics are not straightforward, but rather act as interrogations of the heterosexual, attempts to imagine or reimagine what heterosexuality might mean. The fact that the so-called 'metaphysical poets' engaged with sex at all seems to have obscured the oddity of the engagement, a point appreciated by John Dryden, who wrote that '[Donne] affects the metaphysics, not only in his satires, but in his amorous verses, where nature only should reign; and perplexes the minds of the fair sex with nice speculations of philosophy, when he should engage their hearts, and entertain them with the softnesses of love'.[6] Writing about sex is always at odds with the expression of desire, because writing (and reading) are antithetical to passionate immersion in the moment. Descriptions of desire and its outcomes always stand back from what they seek to describe, calculatingly, or even comically, and thus it is no surprise to find metaphysicals the masters of satire that deploys sex and sexuality. Hence lyric (which at its inception often sought to naturalize the homoerotic) evolves into a denaturalization of the heterosexual. The problem with gender and sexuality studies and the critical discourses they produce is that they often assume that heterosexuality can never be reimagined or re-envisaged in any truly radical way; the only way to re-envisage the heterosexual is often assumed to be to replace it with the homoerotic. However, the more extreme the vertical elaboration of gender, the more unnatural and even menacing a heterosexual desire is seen to become to masculinity. In the very business of seduction, heterosexuality risks exposing itself as perverse, a possibility Marvell ceaselessly probes. What if there is nothing odder than heterosexual reciprocity and reproductivity?

What if the norms of heterosexual climax and fulfilment are actually tanta-mount to the violence of predators, the unbearable wildness of desert sands, or the amorousness of vegetal unruliness? What if the goal of lyric poetry itself is the estrangement of heterosexuality, while seduction poems, aimed across a gulf of understanding, treat all their hearers as virgins to whom sexuality will be eerie and other? To whom desire itself is alien? Marvell turns his Martian gaze on the heterosexual and either reinvents or turns away. Where does he turn? We shall see that the poems in praise of the unreachable virginity of little girls and the political satires that use femininity to represent corruption and greed are of a piece with the valorizations of Cromwellian phallicity and the seduction poems. All these are discourses which take unto themselves as an object a body which cannot itself experience desire, or even the desire to desire. This mythical prelapsarian body is fully isomorphic with the phallus in a way no homo- or any other kind of eroticism can include or account for.

The sheer weirdness, the magical realism of Marvellian sexual metaphor, is therefore not simply a series of codes for a series of drearily familiar scenarios, but the very point of the poetry. Take *On a Drop of Dew*; perfectly readable as an allegory of desire and consummation, it also estranges us from those overfamiliar sensations. The sexualization of the dew's semen-like fertilization of the blowing roses can be read as a puzzled investigation of reproductivity by other means; the polymathic pleasure of the clear dew and the blowing roses does not endorse but calls into question its apparent cognate in human heterosexuality. Not so much provoking a knowing grin as a puzzled frown, the poem takes the all-too-common cavalier lyric and uses its metaphors to prise open the ostensible naturalness of breeding by human sex – which is less enticingly sensual, it turns out, than we might expect, and subject also to a kind of impotence: 'Could it [the fountain] within the human flower be seen | Rememb'ring still its former height' (lines 21–2); however, such priapic delights turn out to be unavailable. The apparent symmetry Nigel Smith observes in both halves of the poem could also be understood in terms of the sexed body, and in terms especially of the Galenic body,[7] but the mirroring of body and soul poses a problem for such an understanding because the union of soul to crude matter is made to seem at best unfortunate, especially given Marvell's source for this lyric in the third-century Greek hymn of Synesius of Cyrene, who bluntly describes the body as fated to decay.[8] Rather, sexuality is ultimately rejected in favour of the mystical subsumption of body and soul together into the larger liquid glory of God, an arena of pleasure unknowable from the sexually supine postures imagined at the outset. *Ros*, Marvell's Latin version of *On a Drop of Dew*, is even more overt because here the dew is a drop of Aurora's sweat. The drop is a little girl, in fact a shy virgin, one who naturally repudiates the sexual.

To His Coy Mistress

In Marvell's most famous lyric, seduction becomes a way not of endorsing but of interrogating pleasure. *To His Coy Mistress* slyly undermines cavalier lyric. The poem exposes and destroys what we might call the thrusting rhythms of heterosexuality. The whole point of the first section is to explore an utter alterity of pleasure, an antipodes of desire. As in the drop of dew, this exposes the mirror image of straight seduction as anything but straight. If 'vegetable love' is envisaged, then animal love becomes bestial, too rash, too unadvised, too sudden. The priapic joke about a vegetable love growing vast but slow is also a wry comment on the male body and its deficiencies. Petrarchan devotion, too, is satirized in the schedule of praise allotted to each body part; the quasi-religious excess of going around the body bit by bit is portrayed as both comically inadequate and hopelessly abject. This devotion becomes merely a lie, a promise broken even as it is made. The empire metaphors which characterize other poetries of desire are here re-imagined as a blissful and eremitic infertility. What in Herrick was 'the sea | Of vast eternity' is simply a place where there is no one – Marvell and his beloved can see it, but it lies before them, distant and unreachable.

The chariot hurrying behind the poem is desire. What the poem longs for is a desire without urgency, without time, but it wryly concludes that the only place for such utter alterity is the grave; Marvell's song will not echo in the conventional pastoral landscape but in the tomb. Or rather, it won't. There is an overturning of the cult of relics analogous to Appleton House here because for the Catholic Church 'long-preserved virginity' is immune to the attacks of worms. The worm, a treble signifier (phallic joke/Edenic serpent/agent of decay) is able almost literally to deflower the woman and remove her, no restore her, to a grisly naturalness she can hardly help but shun. Since her virginity cannot last forever, then … But this also advertises the deadly qualities of consummation, an apprehension reinforced when the poem tries to find words in which to imagine it.[9] The lovers become birds of prey, devouring time in a manner which recalls the myth of Kronos swallowing his children, and this is opposed to being eaten by the agonizingly slow jaws of time.[10] Similarly violent, the image of the lovers who 'tear our pleasures with rough strife' (line 43) presents the erotic not as a refuge from the *agon* of mortality but as its ultimate expression. The slowness of being deflowered by worms is to be pushed aside by the violence of lived heterosexuality. The juxtaposition of 'tear' and 'rough strife' with the image of the iron gates pertains to time, but beneath there is a deeper and more unsettling suggestion of violation, even of rape. The gates of life implicitly oppose the gates of death, too, and are thus suggestive of birth, and of the opening of the female body. But these denotations seem too precise. What the poem does is generally posit consummation in the mortal body as violent and also as intrinsically inscrutable. The natural imagery of (say) cavalier Thomas Carew's 'The Rapture' is swept aside in favour of the twinned impossibilities of wormy defloration and ravishment.

The text with which we are familiar is that printed in the 1681 folio, but the poem also exists in a manuscript version dated to 1672;[11] in his study of the manuscript and print versions of the poem, Paul Hammond concludes that the manuscript copy brought the poem into line with 1670s eroticism, a performance in a bolder heterosexual idiom; but in fact the 1670s manuscript can be seen as both bowdlerizing and making more explicit. The 1672 version substitutes 'thighs' for 'the rest', but to maintain rhyme it deletes 'breast' and replaces it with the sentimental and far less explicit 'eyes'.[12] Perhaps this was because 'the rest' had become unreadable. Superficially, 'the rest' implies that the speaker will not bother to specify the parts to be described over 30,000 years, inviting the lady to imagine an itemized catalogue. But *she* has to fill in this blank; often misread as a blazon in the era when historians of gender felt confident about how to read such a thing, this is actually the refusal of one, even the *haughty* refusal, a tease in itself. The lady is free to imagine an itemization of every eyelash, while the male seducer grins knowingly over her head at the astute reader, who is invited to understand 'the rest' not as a list of discrete parts, but as the *telos* of the entire journey, the vulva or vagina. The 1681 printing alterations do not make it sexier; they are explicatory. But they do – and this is important – delete the possibility of slow enumeration of every part as a fantasy. Patient, curious exploration of what desire might be like without time is deleted from what was a powerfully unseductive seduction poem. Perhaps this points to the Restoration anxieties about virility which dominate Marvell's own satires.

By violence

The sheer violence of Marvell's erotic lyrics has rarely been noted; Johnson wrote of metaphysical lyric as where 'The most heterogeneous ideas are yoked by violence together; nature and art are ransacked for illustrations, comparisons, and allusions; their learning instructs, and their subtilty surprises; but the reader commonly thinks his improvement dearly bought, and, though he sometimes admires, is seldom pleased.'[13] The quotation has become such a cliché that its implications of surprise and violation are not noticed. For instance, in Marvell's *The Unfortunate Lover*, the Caesarian birth which so upset critics of an earlier generation invites a vehemently satirical reading of the Quixote-like protagonist. Unnatural birth is coupled – in every sense – with the unnaturalness of bodily union achieved through eating and being eaten by cormorants, while the heroic Promethean lover, clad only in his own blood, is a disturbed and disturbing image of the price of 'normal' love. The Petrarchan images here turned to hyperbolae are an interrogation of the heterosexual unions conventionally described in them. In *Daphnis and Chloe*, love is likened to cannibalism; 'Rather I away will pine | In a manly stubbornness | Than be fatted up express | For the cannibal to dine' (lines 69–72). Similarly violent imagery surfaces in *The Gallery*, with Clora wavering between murderous sadism and pastoral innocence. The displaced violence of naval and military images problematizes love: in *The Fair Singer*, 'all my forces needs must be outdone | She having gainèd both the wind and sun' (lines 17–18). *The Match* brings the unlikeliness of mummified age-prevention and artillery powderkeg explosions to bear on passion, both themselves forms of unnatural violation – a farfetched series of events implies that love is impossible, or nearly so, and this is supported by a final hyperbolic claim: 'we alone the happy rest, | Whilst all the world is poor, | And have within ourselves possessed | All Love's and Nature's store' (lines 37–40). As in other poems, a kind of violence is done to the value of amorous metaphor. Exaggeration becomes a kind of hyperinflationary currency.

In the Mower poems, the themes of violence are coupled with the opening of the question of where innocence can be located. Spoken by the touchingly naïve rustic Damon, the poems break with pastoral in that the desiring voice is not the nurturing shepherd but the destructive mower, who is nevertheless the defender of a natural order he himself violates with his own (often overtly phallic) weapon. The persona is based on the crassly masculine Polyphemus of Theocritus's Idyll XI, whose failure to seduce the nymph Galatea is inevitable given their extreme difference, a difference that denaturalizes the heterosexual. In the Mower poems too, reproductivity sometimes seems suspect and heterosexuality dangerous. To 'graft upon the wild the tame' (*The Mower against Gardens*, line 24) calls reproductivity into question. To speak of an unnatural garden as a 'green *seraglio*' and to add that it 'has its eunuchs too' (lines 27) makes of the gardener an effeminate Eastern tyrant, bent on vexing nature to 'procreate without a sex' (line 30). Stoneless cherries imply emasculated, even eunuched cherries, since 'stone' is also a term for testicles. Nigel Smith sees this as a riposte to Cowley's enthusiastic endorsement of natural destruction of virginity: 'even Daphne's coyness he does mock | And weds the cherry to her stock [...] | Even she, that chast and virgin tree, | Now wonders at herself, to see | That she's a mother made | And blushes in her fruit' (lines 23–8).[14] In Cowley, grafting affirms heterosexual norms, but in Marvell a graft suggests that reproductivity always threatens an unnatural effeminization. This is reaffirmed in *Damon the Mower*, where Juliana is compared to the Dog Star, which was supposed to threaten disease by heat and dryness, and therefore to be analogous to the effects of male sexuality upon male health. Images of erotic heat reinforce the menace. The image of 'the sun himself' who 'licks off my sweat' (line 46) suggests that an unspecific sensual bodily realm of pleasure may be restorative as opposed to the menace of desire and consummation. The anxious vaginal imagery of 'About me they contract their ring' (line 64) and the strange, Achilles-like wounding of the mower's own ankle testify to anxiety. The blow is like a loss of virginity, an eroticism that doesn't fit any known template or narrative. Damon compares the wound to love, but this overt heterosexual conclusion is erased by Damon's final figuration of death as the ultimate paramour, a mower like himself who will wound him further. It is this pairing or desert-like end of all pairings which finalizes the poem's searchings. But this is not straightforward lyric homoeroticism in the pastoral world, of the kind we might associate with Virgil or Richard Barnfield or even Marlowe or Shakespeare. Indeed, here the pastoral homoerotic is as bent out of shape as heterosexual Petrarchanism is elsewhere in Marvell, since what is desired is a narcissistic self-reflection, a guarantee of existence, a regression that can only be confirmed in pain. There is more violence and loss of innocence in *The Mower's Song*, where Juliana becomes the mower, creating another analogy of alterity between Damon and the grass, which grows luxuriant, while the mower is 'trodden under feet' (line 16). This further denaturalizes and un-pleasures heterosexuality. *Ametas and Thestylis Making Hay-Ropes* is similar: apparently simple, it offers an understanding of the heterosexual as dependent for its stability on opposition, resistance and naysayings – perverseness, in fact. Ultimately, the lovers abandon the pastoral craft of hayrope-making in order to confer the looser bond of kisses on each other. The lines of the poem themselves, woven together, seem unfinished, like the abandoned hay-rope. Paradoxically, something strong, secure and finished is not constructed but *abandoned* by the enactment of heterosexual desires. Is there, the poems ask, another way?

Marvell and girls

Marvell locates an alternative narrative of sexual consummation in the movement through which a 'green girl' becomes capable of 'bearing', floriferous or fructifying. The repeated references to young girls raise an obvious question for a twenty-first-century reader. Should we worry about the plethora of young girls here? Should we leap to the conclusion that there is sexuality here, as some critics have done? Patient exploration will show that they are indeed the destinations of desire, but in a complex rather than in a simple way. What is desired is not the conquest of a young girl, not her induction into sexuality, but a particular and culturally marked moment *before* the genesis of masculinity can begin, for in Marvell it is masculinity on which cultural pressure is felt. Earlier critics identified this preoccupation with girls as a return to what they termed the 'green world', but they overlooked the gendered and sexualized connotations of the word 'green' that required the signifier of a prepubescent girl to exemplify them.[15]

In order to understand the young girl, it is helpful to begin with Mary Fairfax and *Upon Appleton House* because not even the most anxious or suspicious critic is likely to believe that she is an erotic figure. Indeed, Maria is an *anerotic* figure, displacing the anxiously depicted lesbian eroticism of the nuns whose place has been taken by the Fairfaxes.[16] Mary Fairfax appears in the poem just as the estate or country house celebration of retirement almost threatens to stop the poem completely:

> But now away my hooks, my quills,
> And angles, idle utensils.
> The young Maria walks tonight:
> Hide trifling youth thy pleasures slight.
> 'Twere shame that such judicious eyes
> Should with such toys a man surprise.
> She that already is the law
> Of all her sex, her age's awe.   (lines 649–56)

In the word 'surprise' there is glancing allusion to virgin goddesses – Artemis, Athene – whose leisure is surprised by an unlucky mortal, but in those legends it is men who surprise the goddess and not vice versa. In *Upon Appleton House* virgin sternness becomes a surprise to men, whose contamination by 'pleasures' unspecified is condemned by the nuns. Marvell is thinking among other things of the moral allegorization of the myth of Diana and Actaeon, where Actaeon's dogs represent his own passions, which tear him to pieces. The poet's fishing becomes a brutal disruption of Edenic stasis. Maria's stasis in singular girlhood also halts the garden, halts nature itself, turning it to a vast hush. She is also the maker of the garden since ''Tis she that to these gardens gave | That wondrous beauty which they have' (lines 689–90). This is because the gardens not only reflect but also express her qualities. Maria, as her name suggests, is both connected to and contrasted with the nuns who precede her, who represent her protective virginity and its creation of a *hortus conclusus* space, but who cannot make it fecund and productive.[17]

Maria's virgin seclusion also makes her an apt image of her father's retirement, in opposition to celebrations of his public role. Here Marvell is thinking not only of Evander in the *Aeneid*, but also of the various stoical *contemptus mundi* poems of Elizabethan and Jacobean retirement, and even of Shakespeare's late romances, in which the father finds rest from politics or labour only in a natural space with a daughter. While Fairfax himself in his own poems celebrates ruins as metaphors for an absolute retirement, Marvell sees Appleton House as something that has to be snatched *from* ruin(s). This idea is given corporeal form in the poem when Isabella Thwaites is snatched by William Fairfax in the poem's dramatic staging of the capture of virginity by the active male. That trope of setting the girl in motion in order to rescue her also has a cognate in Thomas Fairfax's own experience during the civil wars, where his own child was threatened by the conflict which she now symbolically closes out. He writes:

> [M]y daughter, not above five years old, being carried before her Maid, endured all this retreat a Horseback, but Nature not being able to hold out any longer, she fell into frequent swoonings, and in appearance was ready to expire her last.[18]

This is Mary, now the goddess-like bringer of stasis and repose. When Marvell writes that 'The gard'ner had the soldier's place' (line 337) and of the nursery as a magazine, the stoves as winter quarters, and so forth, he is contrasting the arts of the garden with the arts of war by drawing attention to the oddity of the comparison, and so emphasizing the arts of peace by the inclusion of a girl nearly destroyed by war. The metaphorical Maria's future fecundity is represented by the plethora of meanings she generates. So fecund an image is Maria that she also represents the Fairfaxes' legitimate occupation of the land by all-but-literally tying them in with its history in the image of Maria as the mistletoe growing on the Fairfax oak and the druid image that accompanies it. Maria is precisely the longed-for garden space of a femininity conflated with the garden itself.

But why is the green girl such an apt metaphor for the green world? This same trope – the conflation of the girl with nature itself – animates *Young Love*, based as it is on the Anacreontic Greek lyric that solicits the love of a very young girl. But Marvell adapts that pretext to make the girl even younger than she is in the original. While the Anacreontic poem registers the girl as unripe grain and grapes, Marvell describes her as blossoms that are 'too green'. Green signifies blossoms that are not yet ripe *even as blossoms*, blossoms that have not yet begun to become fruit, let alone to ripen. In *Young Love*:

> Common beauties stay fifteen;
>   Such as yours should swifter move;
> Whose fair blossoms are too green
>   Yet for Lust, but not for Love.   (lines 9–12)

Here it is clear that Marvell is out to disclose not the eroticization of the child but the pleasure of a child who is enjoyed precisely because she is not eroticized, or even because she has a magical power not to be eroticized however much she is urged or chided forwards. '[O]ur sportings are as free | As the nurse's with the child' (lines 7–8), writes Marvell, now constructing a female–female pre-sexual state of sensuous play to contrast with the worrying animal masculinity of the bulls and rams. The kid is wanton not because it is sexual, but because its lack of sexuality leaves it freer to explore its own senses. Such young bodies have the power associated with Maria Fairfax, the power to draw the old back into their own 'green world' of unregulated pleasure.

The idea of the 'green girl' is foundational in Marvell's work. Central to it is the idea of a sensual pleasure that precedes and therefore holds at bay troubling eroticism, an idea even more evident in relation to another poem, *The Picture of Little T. C. in a Prospect of Flowers*. T. C. is a green girl too: 'In the green grass she loves to lie | And there with her fair aspect tames | The wilder flowers, and gives them names: | But only with the roses plays; | And them does tell | What colour best becomes them, and what smell' (lines 3–8). Again the girl, lost in her own 'golden age' of childhood – yes, that idea *is* present here, early though it might seem – and the flowers, especially the brief-flowering roses, are engaged in seductive play. At the beginning of her own life, the girl can act like Milton's Eve, and name the flowers; indeed, infant play has become a kind of Eden here. The girl is the principal metaphor for an Edenic moment which extends to embrace a goddess-like purity, since 'wanton Love shall one day fear, | And, under her command severe, | See his bow broke and ensigns torn' (lines 12–14). She is linked with the artificial prolongation of that moment by the underlying Persephone myth, which is evoked in the violets that are one of Persephone's chief symbols. She is asked to use her almost supernatural power to command nature in order to 'procure | That violets may a longer age endure' (lines 31–2). Violets are especially linked with the deaths of girls and with transience, which is why Laertes wishes that from Ophelia's fair and unpolluted flesh violets might spring. This will be an alteration in state for Ophelia, who was called a 'green girl' by her father earlier in the play when she interpreted Hamlet's overtures roman-tically rather than seeing their sexual menace. Persephone represents the violation of a young girl, herself a flower.

As well as Persephone, the goddess Flora is vital here. In Ovid's *Fasti*, his poetic portrayal of Roman festival practices, and in Renaissance iconography she is an ambiguous figure.[19] In the myth the nymph Chloris, whose name means 'green', is ravished by Zephyrus, the West Wind, and is reborn as Flora, goddess of flowers. Hence Flora represents not so much fertility but in particular the moment in spring when the greenness of new growth (Chloris) breaks into multicoloured flowers. The Romans themselves understood this not only as April breeding lilacs out of the dead land, but also as the greensick young girl becoming the displayed object of desire. Plain green becomes gaudy or bedizened. This is why the Floralia, the Roman festival of the goddess Flora, was also a festival associated with prostitutes, a tradition reflected in Venetian art. To go from Chloris to Flora is for Marvell to fall.

In classical mythology, the conflation of young girls with flowers always implied a sexual threat; Persephone, for instance, called 'a fairer flower by gloomy Dis' by Milton, is one of many young girls who are picking flowers when they themselves plucked. Catullus writes in his formal epithalamion, or wedding song, 'Just as a flower that grows in a garden close, apart | Unbeknown to sheep ... | Many boys have longed for it and many girls: | But when its bloom is gone, nipped off by a fingernail, | Never boy has longed for it and never girl | A maid too while untouched is dear to her family | But when she loses her flower | Then no-one wants her.'[20] So while cavalier poets urged girls to gather their rosebuds, Marvell reverses the image, insisting that girls should try to prolong deferral and delay. Be green for as long as possible, he urges. Avoid flowers.

Marvell's green girls include Maria, T. C., the Nymph Complaining, and Marvell's forever-green Daphne and Syrinx: in *The Garden* that 'Apollo hunted Daphne so | Only that she might Laurel grow; | And Pan did after Syrinx speed, | Not as a nymph, but as a reed' (lines 29–32). These women represent the ultimate conflation of girl and garden. Laurels and reeds remain green and never break into colour – they remain Chloris and are never Flora. Of course, all seduction poetry depends on a lady's no to set it in motion. And the laurel and the reed are symbols of poetry itself. Marvell is linking poetry and poetic fame to the 'no' of a woman who will forever be a girl. And the same thing, or something similar, happens in *The Nymph Complaining for the Death of her Fawn*, in which the fawn's death allows it to be arrested at a pre-sexual moment before it can become 'Lilies without, roses within' (line 92). The very moment of arrest is captured in a work of art: 'First my unhappy statue shall | Be cut in marble; and withal, | Let it be weeping too: but there [...] | There at my feet shalt thou be laid, | Of purest alabaster made: | For I would have thine image be | White as I can, though not as thee' (lines 111–22).[21] The last line confesses, however, to the inadequacy of art as a means for preserving the moment of cessation of movement; the statue cannot stop the moment of decline from perfect whiteness, just as the poem cannot preserve either nymph or fawn at the moment of pastoral bliss when both are at one with a cleansed world.

Why lilies and why roses? The fawn is conflated with both. In John Gerard's *Herball*, the white lily is the madonna lily, which – significantly – flowers *before* the red rose.[22] So the lily is about an *earlier* period of life. Lilies famously last only a day or two in flower, so they signify a moment that can easily be lost, subject to the ruinous hand of time. Gerard also says that it is called Juno's rose, because it 'as it is reported came up of her milke that fell upon the ground. But the Poets feign, that Hercules, who Jupiter had by Alcimena, was put to Juno's breasts whilest she was asleepe; and after the sucking there fell away an abundance of milk and that one part was spilt in the heavens, and the other upon the earth; and that of this sprang the Lily.' In Gerard, then, the lily signifies the infancy and nourishment of a hypermasculine hero. But the milk also signifies *not* nourishing the hero since it spills because Juno snatches her breast away as soon as she wakes and realizes what is happening. The lily is about infancy, but also loss of the mother.

This is the symbolic key to the situation. Roses, on the other hand, are associated with a particular form of pastoral, Anacreontic pastoral, which for the Renaissance means a poetry about the naughty boyish games of a baby Cupid who 'doth wrap his head round with garlands of rose'.[23] The rose here is a symbol of the sensuous child, cleansed of anything actually erotic. Here is a psychic pattern, a repeating figure in Marvell's symbolic universe, the figure of a young girl or feminized young boy who stands at the brink of an adult world understood as perilous and who is celebrated for not having yet crossed the line into that world.

It is an error to see these figures as tainted by paedophilia; they signify a phase of masculinity which is associatively linked with childhood.[24] Renaissance writers understood masculinity as born from a childhood located in the feminine world, even as sculpted painfully from a girlish self accustomed to feminine pleasures. The reason for this was that male childhood experience was split in two by an event marked by breeching, the putting on of doublet and hose. This could sometimes be merely a symbolic moment, but it was also the name for a far more radical change; better-off boys were handed over to the care of tutors or to school, while other boys were given over to a master to be trained as apprentices. Before breeching, boys inhabited a female world, signified by the long gowns they wore, a world ruled by the mother and by female servants. After breeching, these servants were often dismissed completely, and male attendants were installed. This was the beginning of masculinity, which had to be born painfully from a cosy feminine world, and maintained by learning and beatings. It meant parting with the mother and entering a world in which for people of Marvell's and Fairfax's class, a different language – Latin – was spoken.

School was an all-male world in which behaviour was enforced by severe beatings. Renaissance boys were at school all day and many were at all-male boarding schools. What they learned was seen as incomprehensible to their mothers and sisters; Latin language study, it has been suggested, was a kind of puberty rite from which masculinity was made.[25] But since it was hard and alien, early childhood may have been seen as a kind of lost Eden, and it would be aptly represented as a little *girl*, or as a markedly feminized little boy – Cupid, for example – because it was associated with femininity, because sisters didn't have to leave it behind.

Marvell makes a further association, a symbolic retelling of this childhood trauma, between leaving home to go to war and leaving femininity to go to school, and further between leaving the old royal regime behind for the republic and this traumatic breach in childhood. But he is also worried by the notion that retirement is somehow feminine – precisely because it is so desired, it becomes troubling to him. In the recurring figure of a little girl in a garden, as a sign of all that is private, enclosed, retired, *safe* from the public world of war and politics and the state, we have nothing less than a retreat from masculine pain into a child's world of feminine pleasure, a retreat that is also and sometimes explicitly a retreat from adult sexuality. There is a longing for safety, for maternity, which masculinity must disavow. And it is coupled with an anxiety about the fragility of psychic defences, because these feminine worlds of childhood are always being menaced or even broached by masculinity in the form of education, or in the form of the poet and poems themselves, signs of education. If we hear the tone of the poem correctly, there is an effect of enormous and tragic distance; grief and horror can only appear in the heavily mediated and disguised form of an overtly simple pastoral, voiced by a little girl whose own simplicity prevents her from understanding the complex emotions to which her own speech alludes. It is a figuration not just of innocence but also of inexperience. And the poem at once longs for the nymph to be a refuge and presents her as ultimately vulnerable. Longings for femininity in a masculine world – longings to inhabit a feminine space – can only be ignoble and embarrassing.

If the political poems/prose and the politics of the lyrics equate that greenness with a lost political Eden in keeping with republican claims for an originary constitution, the added impetus is the acute anxieties about masculinity induced by Charles/the regicide/Cromwell. Cromwell is constantly and enviously signified being born again as a force of masculinity from within that feminized world. In a very dark allusion to Homer's portrayal of Hector's doomed son Astyanax, Marvell depicts Cromwell holding his baby daughter Elizabeth, and makes an explicit contrast, as Homer does, among the warlike male body, the softness of the baby, and the softness of the maternal breast:

> Her when an infant, taken with her charms,
> He oft would flourish in his mighty arms;
> And, lest their force the tender burthen wrong,

> Slacken the vigour of his muscles strong;
> Then to the mother's breast her softly move,
> Which, while she drained of milk, she filled with love.
>
> (*A Poem upon the Death of his Highness
> the Lord Protector*, lines 31–6)[26]

Cromwell's restraint in deliberately weakening his muscles, deliberately softening his body, figures him not merely as protector of the vulnerable, but also as in control of his body and its acts. Rather than possessing, penetrating and exploiting femininity, Cromwell protects it in its greenness. Cromwell's hard muscles, available though still relaxed, are counterpointed by a source of feminine nurturance of which he is the guarantor. Here is the godly paterfamilias innately – and literally – the Protector.[27] Like Maria Fairfax in *Upon Appleton House*, Elizabeth offers a way *out* from the burden of masculinity, a burden of violence borne by sexuality. The green girl can contain masculinity without diluting it. One of the attractions of Cromwell for the nation was that he offered an apparently secure masculinity, one unlikely to collapse miserably into femininity, one able to resist the longing to be a little girl at mother's knee. That pre-civilized childhood state was the only one in which man could walk 'without a mate' and escape the burdens of violence and eroticism. Yet precisely because it was so ideal, it also represented a stasis which the active male was obliged to resist. It was only after many years of civil war had made the violence of masculinity seem repugnant that a stoical withdrawal into the feminine golden age of the garden of childhood could be imagined without disgrace.

The Last Instructions to a Painter

Without Cromwell, however, the risk of the softening of the nation became unbearable. Marvell's *The Last Instructions to a Painter* envisages the process already under way. The metaphoric architecture links sexual disorder with political chaos, and both with effeminate softness:

> Witness, ye stars of night, and thou the pale
> Moon, that o'ercome with the sick steam didst fail;
> Ye neighbouring elms, that your green leaves did shed,
> And fawns that from the womb abortive fled   (lines 69–72)

The correspondence between these lines and the enigma of *The Nymph Complaining* has not previously been noted, but here images of defloration are metonymically and metaphorically aligned with images of miscarriage. Anne Hyde's poisons menace the chastity and reproductivity of a green girl whose pure body becomes alien to her. Hyde thus becomes the witch whose sexualized body defines and limns the clean body of the girl.[28] Here, as so often in Milton, virginity and the clean, contained womb are not opposed but linked. Read retrospectively in relation to the earlier poem and its puzzles, the fawn itself becomes readable precisely as an abortion, the standard metaphor for the failure of the female body to do as it ought. Hyde's black magic attacks the female regularization of the moon, and brings about defoliation, always a metaphor in Marvell for lapse from the natural order. Other failed reproductivities dominate *The Last Instructions*. The general excise tax proposed by the Court party in 1666 is a demon baby who 'Frighted the midwife and the mother tore' (line 132). This baby, reminiscent of the satires representing the Rump parliament and the radical sects, figures the tax as a kind of semiotic disorder.[29]

The eunuch

In this context, we can look back at Marvell's response to those who satirized him. The principal Marvellian arena and gendered and desiring alterity is solitude. This may have been why an accumulation of references to Marvell as eunuch led him to respond, but we should not assume that response to be biographical.[30] John Cleveland's poem 'The Antiplatonick' helps us to understand what it meant to be called a eunuch:

> Give me a lover bold and free,
> Not Eunucht with formality
> Like an Embassador that beds a queen
> With the nice caution of a sword between.[31]

To be 'eunucht with formality' is not to be incapable of a sexual act, but to be incapable of spontaneity. We could well read Marvell's status as eunuch as a response to his careful octosyllabic lines, and their formality; their neatness seems to forbid emotional or even sexual outbursts.[32] We could also read the epithet as a response to Marvell's relations with the Cromwellian government. Eunuchs were the sign of a tyrant, and a foreign tyrant at that. So when Marvell responds to the slights in his Latin epigram *Upon a Eunuch: a Poet*, he does so in defence not of his person but of his poetry:

> And do not believe that you are sterile, albeit, as an exile from women, you are unable to thrust a sickle at the virgin harvest or to sin in our manner. By you will Fame be forever pregnant, and you will lay hold of the nine sisters from the mountain, while Echo, repeatedly struck, will give birth to music as your offspring.
> (trans. Smith, in *Poems*, 188)

The key words in interpreting these Janus-faced lines are *rapies*, where the Penguin translator has 'snatch' and Smith has 'lay hold of'; and *repetita*, where the former has 'often struck' and Smith has 'repeatedly struck'.[33] There are reasons why the lines invite a sexual interpretation, but even if we assign one to them we lose the doubleness of the Latin. *Rapio* carries the classical meaning: seize, snatch, plunder, *not* rape. Here, however, the poet's violent potency is invoked as the source of poetry; both the muses and Echo will be ravished in order to make them (re)productive, and the poet portrays himself as active, violent, refuting his critics by laying claim to hypermasculinity on Parnassus, whatever his defects elsewhere. But placing heterosexual and in this case violent and overweening masculine desire in the context of the despoliation of pastoral nymphs estranges the very potency Marvell's critics appear to praise. The doubleness of the vision contained in *Upon a Eunuch* is symptomatic of a Marvell for whom the heterosexual can never be anything other than a fascinatingly alien conundrum.

NOTES

1. Morgan Holmes, 'A Garden of Her Own: Marvell's Nymph and the Order of Nature', in Goran V. Stanivukovic, ed., *Ovid and the Renaissance Body* (Toronto, 2001); see also the essays in Richard Burt and John Michael Archer, eds., *Enclosure Acts: Sexuality, Property, and Culture in Early Modern England* (Ithaca, NY, 1994), as well as Derek Hirst and Steven N. Zwicker, 'Andrew Marvell and the Toils of Patriarchy: Fatherhood, Longing, and the Body Politic', *English Literary History* 66 (1999), 629–54.
2. James Holstun, ' "Will You Rent Our Ancient Love Asunder?": Lesbian Elegy in Donne, Marvell, and Milton', *English Literary History* 54 (1987), 835–67.
3. Philip Schwyzer, *Archaeologies of English Renaissance Literature* (Oxford, 2007).
4. Alison Shell, *Oral Culture and Catholicism in Early Modern England* (Cambridge, 2008), 31–2.
5. Erica Veevers, *Images of Love and Religion: Queen Henrietta Maria and Court Entertainments* (Cambridge, 1989).
6. John Dryden, *Discourse Concerning the Original and Progress of Satire*, in *The Essays of John Dryden*, ed. W. P. Ker, 2 vols. (Oxford, 1900), II:19.
7. See Thomas Laqueur, *Making Sex: Body and Gender from the Greeks to Freud* (Cambridge, MA, 1990).
8. The connection of *On a Drop of Dew* with the epigrams of Synesius is noted by Smith (*Poems*, 39), following Stella Revard.
9. Catherine Belsey, 'Love and Death in *To His Coy Mistress*', in Richard Machin and Christopher Norris, eds., *Poststructuralist Readings of English Poetry* (Cambridge, 1987), 105–21.
10. Gilles Sambras, 'Sexe et politique: Les Oiseaux de proie d'Andrew Marvell', *Imaginaires: Revue du Centre de Recherche sur l'Imaginaire dans les Littératures de Langue Anglaise* 7 (2001), 59–74.
11. Bodleian Library MS Don b.8, 283–4.
12. Paul Hammond, 'Marvell's Sexuality', *The Seventeenth Century* 11 (1996), 87–123.

13. Samuel Johnson, 'Life of Cowley', in his *Lives of the English Poets*, ed. Birkbeck Hill, 3 vols. (New York, 1967), 1:20.
14. See Smith's note for lines 29–30 of *The Mower against Gardens* (*Poems*, 134).
15. Donald Friedman, *Marvell's Pastoral Art* (Berkeley, 1970); or the excerpt of that argument published as 'Knowledge and the World of Change: Marvell's "The Garden"', in Harold Bloom, ed., *Modern Critical Views: Andrew Marvell* (New York, 1989), 77–100.
16. *Upon Appleton House*, XXIV.
17. John Rogers, 'The Enclosure of Virginity: The Poetics of Sexual Abstinence in the English Revolution', in Burt and Archer, eds., *Enclosure Acts*, 229–50.
18. *Short Memorials of Thomas Lord Fairfax, Written by Himself* (London, 1699), 86.
19. See Ovid, *Fasti* V:183ff.; and Maggie Kilgour, 'Eve and Flora' (*Paradise Lost* V.15–16), *Milton Quarterly* 38 (2004), 1–17. For *Flora meretrix*, see Ann B. Shteir, 'Flora primavera or Flora meretrix? Iconography, Gender, and Science', *Studies in Eighteenth Century Culture* 36 (2007), 147–68.
20. Catullus, *Carmina*, II:62, in *The Poems of Catullus: A Bilingual Edition*, trans. Peter Green (Berkeley, 2005).
21. Victoria Silver discusses the connections between regicidal fantasy and the figure of the young girl in 'The Obscure Script of Regicide: Ambivalence and Little Girls in Marvell's Pastorals', *English Literary History* 68 (2001), 29–55.
22. John Gerard, *The Herball, or, Generall Historie of Plantes* (London, 1597), 42.
23. Janet Levarie, 'Renaissance Anacreontics', *Comparative Literature* 25 (1973), 221–39.
24. William Kerrigan, 'Marvell and Nymphets', *Greyfriar* 27 (1986), 3–21; Jonathan Crewe, 'The Garden State: Marvell's Poetics of Enclosure', in Burt and Archer, eds., *Enclosure Acts*, 14–32. When this passage was complete, I was delighted to come across Catherine Robson, *Men in Wonderland: The Lost Girlhood of the Victorian Gentleman* (Princeton, 2001), which makes a similar argument about Victorian masculinity.
25. Diane Purkiss, *Literature, Gender and Politics During the English Civil War* (Cambridge, 2005), Introduction, 5ff.; and Walter Ong, 'Latin Language Study as a Renaissance Puberty Rite', *Studies in Philology* 56 (1959), 103–24.
26. Cf. Homer, *Iliad* VI:460ff.
27. On the significance of breasts and breastfeeding see Kathryn Schwartz, 'Missing the Breast', in David Hillman and Carla Mazzio, eds., *The Body in Parts: Fantasies of Corporeality in Early Modern Europe* (New York, 1997), 147–70.
28. Steven N. Zwicker, 'Virgins and Whores: The Politics of Sexual Misconduct in the 1660s', in Conal Condren and A. D. Cousins, eds., *The Political Identity of Andrew Marvell* (Aldershot, 1990), 85–110; Barbara Riebling, 'England Deflowered and Unmanned: The Sexual Image of Politics in Marvell's "Last Instructions"', *Studies in English Literature* 35 (1995), 137–57; Denise Lynch, 'Politics, Nature, and Structure in Marvell's "The Last Instructions to a Painter"', *Restoration* 16 (1992), 82–92.
29. Purkiss, *Literature, Gender and Politics*, 178–201.
30. See Hammond, 'Marvell's Sexuality'.
31. John Cleveland, *Poems* (London, 1657), 77.

32. Thomas McGeary, '"Warbling eunuchs": Opera, Gender and Sexuality on the London Stage, 1705–42', *Restoration and 18th Century Theatre Research* 7 (1992), 1–22, for a similar point.
33. *Andrew Marvell: The Complete Poems*, ed. Elizabeth Story Donno (New York, 1972), 137; cf. Smith, *Poems*, 188.

Further reading

Jonathan Crewe, 'The Garden State: Marvell's Poetics of Enclosure', in Richard Burt and John Michael Archer, eds., *Enclosure Acts: Sexuality, Property, and Culture in Early Modern England* (Ithaca, NY, 1994), 270–89.
Michael DiSanto, 'Andrew Marvell's Ambivalence toward Adult Sexuality', *Studies in English Literature* 48 (2008), 165–82.
Paul Hammond, 'Marvell's Sexuality', *The Seventeenth Century* 11 (1996), 87–123.
Derek Hirst and Steven N. Zwicker, 'Andrew Marvell and the Toils of Patriarchy: Fatherhood, Longing, and the Body Politic', *English Literary History* 66 (1999), 629–54.
'Eros and Abuse: Imagining Andrew Marvell', *English Literary History* 74 (2007), 371–95.
Theodora Jankowski, 'Good Enough to Eat: The Domestic Economy of Woman–Woman Eroticism in Margaret Cavendish and Andrew Marvell', in Corinne S. Abate, ed., *Privacy, Domesticity, and Women in Early Modern England* (Aldershot, 2003), 83–110.
Elena Levy-Navarro, 'History Straight and Narrow: Marvell, Mary Fairfax, and the Critique of Sexual and Historical Sequence', in Richard Utz and Jesse G. Swan, eds., *Postmodern Medievalisms* (Rochester, NY, 2004), 181–92.
Sarah Monette, 'Speaking and Silent Women in *Upon Appleton House*', *Studies in English Literature* 42 (2002), 155–71.
Barbara Riebling, 'England Deflowered and Unmanned: The Sexual Image of Politics in Marvell's "Last Instructions"', *Studies in English Literature* 35 (1995), 137–57.
John Rogers, 'The Enclosure of Virginity: The Poetics of Sexual Abstinence in the English Revolution' in Richard Burt and John Michael Archer, eds., *Enclosure Acts: Sexuality, Property, and Culture in Early Modern England* (1994), 229–50.
Victoria Silver, 'The Obscure Script of Regicide: Ambivalence and Little Girls in Marvell's Pastorals', *English Literary History* 68 (2001), 29–55.
Steven Zwicker, 'Virgins and Whores: The Politics of Sexual Misconduct in the 1660s', in Conal Condren and A.D. Cousins, eds., *The Political Identity of Andrew Marvell* (Aldershot, 1990), 85–110.

6

MICHAEL SCHOENFELDT

Marvell and the designs of art

Despite the sparkling verbal wit of his poetry, Andrew Marvell is a decidedly visual poet. Indeed, one of the distinguishing features of Marvell's lyrics is their deep sensitivity to the visual, even painterly, elements of perception and representation. Regularly in his poetry, visual attributes mark ethical, psychological, or political stances. His poetry is distinguished by a remarkable responsiveness to the full range of the visual and plastic arts, from painting to sculpture and architecture.[1] Architecture in particular seems to engross him because it allows him to explore the permutations of structure and design as he meditates on the formal aspects of his own poetic work. His poetry is obsessed by the ever-shifting distinction between the aesthetics implicit in nature, frequently articulated as if it were a self-conscious work of art, and the aesthetics of human creative effort. Marvell, moreover, is fascinated by the ways that art frames and enables apprehension. His profound insight into the contingent qualities of perception complicates any simple distinction between the products of nature and the artefacts of human design. The conventions of visual representation, he seems to say, are what enable us to see the design implicit in the order of the natural world. Most important, these conventions are also what enable us to imagine the world from perspectives other than our own. Tracking the various manifestations of the visual in Marvell's poetry elucidates his singular accomplishments as a poet.

In *The Gallery*, for example, Marvell imagines the soul, the most private and inward space of an individual, as an external and comparatively public place: a picture gallery. In the poem, Marvell literalizes the poetic commonplace of the lover's heart encompassing an image of the beloved, rendering the privy chamber of the core self as an exhibition hall. Visual elements mediate the poem's affective essence; the poem opens with an invitation to the beloved to 'view' the gallery of his soul: 'Clora come view my soul and tell | Whether I have contrived it well' (lines 1–2). Clora is encouraged to pass judgement on the artful way he has 'contrived' the gallery, but the invitation to aesthetic judgement quickly becomes a referendum on the ethics of her behaviour towards him. Clora is depicted in a variety of ways, all portending either her attractiveness or her cruelty. She is 'painted in the dress | Of an inhuman murderess', and possesses a well-furnished theatre of cruelty for making her lover suffer: 'Thy fertile shop of cruel arts' (lines 9–10, 12). She maintains various 'Engines' of torture, 'Of which the most tormenting are | Black eyes, red lips, and curlèd hair' (lines 13, 15–16). Yet this is, we learn, a two-sided painting, for 'on the other side', she is voluptuous Aurora who sensuously 'stretches out her milky thighs' and is surrounded by 'wooing doves' (lines 17, 20, 23). She also appears in the nightmarish guise of an 'enchantress' who 'dost rave' over the 'entrails' of her 'restless lover', as well as 'Venus in her pearly boat', rising up out of the ocean (lines 25–34). The extended metaphor of a picture gallery allows Marvell to satirize the conventional masochism of erotic poetry, while the genre of the two-sided picture expresses the contradictions and ambivalences of eros. His internal gallery possesses a 'thousand more' pictures of her 'In all the forms thou can'st invent | Either to please me, or torment' (lines 43–4). The inescapable blend of pleasure and pain in erotic experience engenders two opposing sides of the same picture. The conclusion of the poem, though, harks back to beginnings: he remembers the way she looked when he first saw her. She was, it seems, a thoroughly pastoral mistress, 'A tender shepherdess, whose hair | Hangs loosely playing in the air' (lines 53–4). *The Gallery* indicates that a thorough depiction of the conventionally bimodal relationship requires a wide range of representations in different visual genres.

The Gallery is typical of Marvell in its use of a visual framework to designate the necessarily partial nature of any single representational mode. It is also typical of Marvell in the considered way that interior and exterior spaces are imagined to be fungible, and mutually defining. In *The Mower's Song*, he explores the connection between intellection and perception, as the Mower describes how 'My mind was once the true survey | Of all these meadows fresh and gay; | And in the greenness of the grass | Did see its hopes as in a glass' (lines 1–4). The speaker of *The Garden* famously describes how the green world he inhabits colours the mental processes through which he apprehends it: 'Annihilating all that's made | To a green thought in a green shade' (lines 47–8). Thoughts assume the hue of their object, and the visual attribute of colour asserts deeply philosophical meanings.[2] Repeatedly in Marvell, seeing enables knowledge, and vision precedes enlightenment. Apparently superficial descriptions of external features lead him to the deepest recesses of the self.

The lyric *On a Drop of Dew* focuses on the mutually constitutive nature of vision and cognition. Like *The Gallery*, *On a Drop of Dew* opens with an injunction to participate in a particularly focused kind of vision: '*See* how the orient dew ... | Round in itself incloses: | And in its little globe's extent, | Frames as it can its native element' (lines 1–8; my emphasis). As in *The Garden*, vision entails cognition. *On a Drop of Dew* displays Marvell's profound fascination with an object that absorbs and reflects and so frames the world around it. Serving like the pictures in *The Gallery* as an emblem of the soul, the dewdrop attests to the terrifying permeability of the human interior: 'Restless it rolls and unsecure, | Trembling lest it grow impure' (lines 15–16). Its shape attests to the circumambient attributes of the world from which it comes and to which it aspires to return: 'recollecting its own light, | Does, in its pure and circling thoughts, express | The greater Heaven in an heaven less' (lines 24–6). Marvell's refined capacity to read the various physical attributes of the dewdrop in deeply philosophical terms testifies to the ethically transformative power of vision.

The soul, then, can be either a transparent drop or a series of pictures at an exhibition, but in either case the ineffable is mediated through the material. Visual culture offers Marvell a wide range of metaphorical and perceptual resources as he searches for external correlatives for the deeply internal and invariably ethereal features of mind and soul. Art is the medium through which Marvell develops the sometimes disorienting but ultimately comforting doctrine that a change in perspective entails a change both in the object and in the viewer. Marvell is not just using words to describe a work of art in the revered tradition of poetic ekphrasis; rather, he uses poetry to show how all creation aspires to the status of art, and is inevitably apprehended through the parameters of art.

It is hard to know how this seemingly postmodernist notion of subjectivity becomes so pronounced in Marvell's literary world; perhaps the various changes of political perspective and position that history demanded of Marvell led him to this realization. For many writers (think of Milton), living through the turbulent seventeenth century only rigidified their political attitudes. But Marvell, dexterously adjusting to various opposing regimes, may have found that a tempestuous political world nourished his sense of the contingencies of commitment and perception. In the political poems, we can see Marvell's delight in the revelation of how proximity and distance become principles of political and ethical variation. In *The First Anniversary of the Government under His Highness the Lord Protector*, Marvell finds that Oliver Cromwell appears very different depending on one's national allegiance:

> He seems a king by long succession born,
> And yet the same to be a king does scorn.
> Abroad a king he seems, and something more,
> At home a subject on the equal floor.   (lines 387–90)

Even a commanding political figure such as Cromwell is subject to perspective, and changes according to the angle from which he is viewed. Indeed, in *A Poem upon the Death of his Late Highness the Lord Protector*, Marvell compares Cromwell to a fallen 'sacred oak', whose height can only be fully measured when it has fallen: 'The tree erewhile foreshortened to our view, | When fall'n shows taller yet than as it grew' (lines 261, 269–70). The ironies that imbue Marvell's *Horatian Ode upon Cromwell's Return from Ireland* derive in large part from such studied shifts in perspective and allegiance. In the *Horatian Ode*, Marvell is intrigued by the way that history becomes art, as the death of Charles resolves itself into a 'memorable scene' of high tragedy: 'That thence the royal actor borne | The tragic scaffold might adorn, | While round the armèd bands | Did clap their bloody hands' (lines 53–6). Here political events are perceived through the genres of art. Marvell, moreover, leaves us to question whether this surprising turn to the dramatic arts occurs because of an innate theatricality in the monarchy and person of Charles I, or because of the covertly constitutive pressure that genre exerts over the narratives of history. Throughout this remarkable poem, and indeed, throughout his political career, Marvell manages diplomatically to question or confirm positions and hierarchies via sudden shifts of genre and perspective.

One of the central reasons for the particular attraction of the visual arts to Marvell is their capacity to deploy proximity and distance as principles of political and perspectival distortion. In the poem *Eyes and Tears*, Marvell's speaker remarks on how 'the self-deluding sight, | In a false angle takes each height" (lines 5–6). Here he indicates how strong passion modifies one's perspective – another lesson that may originate in Marvell's experience of political zeal – just as the tears of grief literally distort vision by refraction. Marvell's poems, then, ruminate on the power and limitations of vision, and use the appurtenances of visual art to do so. They explore the capacity of perspective, frame and genre to alter at once the viewer and the object viewed.[3] In fact, one reason Marvell is so interested in the dialogue form – his comparatively small corpus includes poems entitled *A Dialogue, Between the Resolved Soul, and Created Pleasure*, *A Dialogue between the Soul and Body*, and *A Dialogue between Thyrsis and Dorinda* – is that this form allows him to convey several legitimate sides of an issue at once. Marvell knows that all experience is at best partial, like the two-sided painting in *The Gallery*; it can be flipped over and examined from a different perspective, which will yield in fact a different object. Marvell also knows that art establishes the parameters of what we are able to see, and how we see it. His poetry is engaged in establishing an elaborate geometry of perception and position, demonstrating that to move through time or space is to change both the object and the subject of perception. As such, it challenges the idea that any single perspective could have an exclusive claim on the truth.

His attitude to the metamorphic powers of perspective is probably best illustrated by his detailed account of the way that perspective modulates our views of the conventional contrast between nature and art. The speaker of *The Mower against Gardens* endorses an orthodox preference for the purity of nature over the aesthetic corruption of formal gardens:

> Luxurious man, to bring his vice in use,
>   Did after him the world seduce:
> And from the field the flowers and plants allure,
>   Where Nature was most plain and pure.
> He first enclosed within the gardens square
>   A dead and standing pool of air.   (lines 1–6)

Gardening, the human effort to impose pattern on nature, is imagined as the violation of an inherently pristine milieu. 'And flowers themselves were taught to paint', laments the Mower, suggesting that the corruptions of human cosmetics are connected to the central practices of the visual arts (line 12).

Marvell's fascination with the relations between perception and perspective render his account of the relationship between nature and art more complex than the Mower's complaint would allow. Nature, Marvell suggests, is mediated by art, and is frequently apprehended through its genres, but never subordinate to it.[4] Marvell indeed loves to describe natural scenes through the language of the visual arts, as if this were the only vocabulary for articulating their beauty. The poem *Upon the Hill and Grove at Bilbrough, To the Lord Fairfax*, opens with an imperative to 'See' how the hill seems like a carefully planned work of art, only better:

> See how the archèd earth does here
> Rise in a perfect hemisphere!
> The stiffest compass could not strike
> A line more circular and like;
> Nor softest pencil draw a brow
> So equal as this hill does bow.
> It seems as for a model laid,
> And that the world by it was made.   (lines 1–8)

Human design provides the aesthetic criteria for the speaker's praise of the natural landscape. Bilborough, moreover, offers a visual correlative of the admirable conduct of its new owner, Lord Fairfax:

> *See* then how courteous it ascends,
> And all the way it rises bends;

> Nor for itself the height does gain,
> But only strives to raise the plain.
>
> Yet thus it all the field commands,
> And in unenvied greatness stands.
>
> (lines 21–6; emphasis mine)

The political and ethical language flatters Marvell's patron, even while articulating a pattern of ideal aristocratic behaviour. If seen correctly, the hill is like a work of art, exemplifying the humble yet dominant demeanour of its owner. It bends to the plain below even as it commands the field.

Marvell, then, is deeply interested in the way that aesthetic patterns and forms express codes of ethics and allegiance. This interest is developed at great length in Marvell's magnificent country house poem *Upon Appleton House, To My Lord Fairfax*. The poem repeatedly manifests its ethical lessons through the lens of architectural aesthetics. The opening lines of the poem establish a close connection between the estate's particular aesthetic form and its owner's ethical conduct: 'Within this sober frame expect | Work of no foreign architect' (lines 1–2). The repudiation of foreign design involves a rejection of exotic affectation and preference for modest vernacular features. The source of its aesthetic, moreover, is an ethical realm opposed to the grandeur of architecture; it is 'Humility alone [which] designs | Those short but admirable lines' (lines 41–2). As in *Upon the Hill and Grove at Bilbrough*, praise of the estate is a tribute to the estate's owner, Thomas Fairfax, whose aesthetic and ethical choices it reflects and embodies. Just as 'beasts are by their dens expressed' (line 11), so is Fairfax manifested in his estate. This is an aesthetic in which form truly does follow function: 'what needs there here excuse, | Where ev'ry thing does answer use?' (lines 61–2). The poem, moreover, aggressively criticizes architectural solipsism, the kind that would be practised by an architect 'Who of his great design in pain | Did for a model vault his brain' (lines 5–6).

After telling us in great detail what the house and the estate are not, Marvell affirms the house's distinctive conformity with the natural world that surrounds it:

> But all things are composèd here
> Like Nature, orderly and near.   (lines 25–6)

Marvell oxymoronically asks a term from human art – 'composèd' – to depict the estate's ostensibly 'natural' aesthetic. Overall, the estate attests not so much to the superiority of nature over art as to the pre-eminence of artful nature over presumptuous art:

But Nature here hath been so free
As if she said, 'Leave this to me'.
Art would more neatly have defaced
What she had laid so sweetly waste;
In fragrant gardens, shady woods,
Deep meadows, and transparent floods.　　(lines 75–80)

Just as the house is built in conformity to nature, so does nature flourish in conformity with the most rarefied principles of Vitruvius, the great Roman architect. The trees become columns, each of which 'in as loose an order grows, | As the Corinthian porticoes'; 'arching boughs' connect them (lines 507–8). The speaker paradoxically discovers a kind of sanctuary from the pressures of history and society in the woods that absorb the monumental aesthetic of political architecture. The speaker, moreover, describes the dappled shadows on the ground in terms that engross his cultural inheritance: 'What Rome, Greece, Palestine, ere said | I in this light mosaic read' (lines 581–2). 'Mosaic' is a wonderfully rich term here, at once invoking the piecemeal pattern formed by the leaves and light, the first five books of Moses, and the use of small pieces of stone to construct a picture. Continually, Marvell asserts the value of nature by likening it to objects of deliberate design. The easy opposition between nature and art keeps being asserted in terms that cause it to break down, since nature is invariably apprehended through the conceptual frames of visual art.

When Marvell describes the meadows and river on the estate as they are seen from a distance, he employs a deliberately disorienting set of perspectival changes. Marvell playfully imagines how the view of the meadow and its inhabitants changes with perspective and scale:

And now to the abyss I pass
Of that unfathomable grass,
Where men like grasshoppers appear,
But grasshoppers are giants there:
They, in their squeaking laugh, contemn
Us as we walk more low than them:
And, from the precipices tall
Of the green spires, to us do call.　　(lines 369–76)

The grasshoppers and men reverse positions in a hierarchy based on size, and the meadow becomes like a body of water in which it seems the men would drown.

No scene that turns with engines strange
Does oft'ner than these meadows change.
For when the sun the grass hath vexed,

> The tawny mowers enter next;
> Who seem like Israelites to be,
> Walking on foot through a green sea.
> To them the grassy deeps divide,
> And crowd a lane on either side.   (lines 385–92)

The poem takes great pleasure in these tricks of the eye, as the landscape metamorphoses through a change in position. At the same time, these ocular sleights prepare one to accept a critical lesson of political and aesthetic experience: that where one stands determines what one sees.

Indeed, some of the most self-consciously political statements in the poem occur in stanzas that endow the estate with a kind of intrinsic theatricality. As one striking vista yields to another, Marvell's descriptive language mixes the languages of politics and aesthetics, the vocabularies of faction and vision:

> This scene again withdrawing brings
> A new and empty face of things;
> A levelled space, as smooth and plain,
> As cloths for Lely stretched to stain.
> The world when first created sure
> Was such a Table rase and pure.
> Or rather such is the *toril*
> Ere the bulls enter at Madril.
>
> For to this naked equal flat,
> Which Levellers take pattern at,
> The villagers in common chase
> Their cattle, which it closer rase;
> And what below the scythe increased
> Is pinched yet nearer by the beast.
> Such, in the painted world, appeared
> Dav'nant with th'universal herd.   (lines 441–56)

Marvell manages in a few lines to advance a wide range of artistic and cultural practices via the metaphorical apprehension of nature: the machinery of theatrical illusion, the flat canvas of oil painting, and the level arena for bullfighting. The levelled space invokes a blank canvas prepared for the famous Dutch portrait painter Sir Peter Lely, particularly appropriate since the estate provides such a knowing portrait of its owner. Yet the level plain can also be viewed as an inspiration for the revolutionary politics of the Levellers, whose aspirations to 'equal' rights the aristocratic Fairfax would likely have condemned. The rancour of political faction is perhaps suggested by the implied violence of the bullring. Finally, the 'painted world' of William Davenant's ambitious but incomplete epic *Gondibert* is invoked somewhat contemptuously as an image of the villagers chasing their cattle across the meadow. Absorbing both Leveller and royalist aesthetics, the meadow, like the estate and its lord, dampens the vehemence of such political extremes.

Indeed, the entire scene briefly resolves into a 'landskip' (the Dutch word that would soon become 'landscape' designating a painting representing natural scenery), before Marvell plays more optical tricks; the villagers and their cattle

> seem within the polished grass
> A landskip drawn in looking-glass.
> And shrunk in the huge pasture show
> As spots, so shaped, on faces do.
> Such fleas, ere they approach the eye,
> In multiplying glasses lie.
> They feed so wide, so slowly move,
> As constellations do above.
>
> Then, to conclude these pleasant acts,
> Denton sets ope its cataracts;
> And makes the meadow truly be
> (What it but seemed before) a sea.   (lines 457–68)

Marvell allows the dramatic arts to trespass on the estate; the 'pleasant acts' of changing natural scenery invoke the elaborate machinery of the Renaissance court masque. As Marvell had observed a bit earlier in the poem, 'No scene that turns with engines strange | Does oft'ner than these meadows change' (lines 385–6). The flood, moreover, makes the meadow, which had been likened to a sea, into an actual body of water. Things in Marvell's poems are always in the process of becoming either something else or themselves through the medium of visual art.

Marvell, then, is captivated by the ways in which the ostensibly firm contrast between art and nature is repeatedly eroded. In *The Mower's Song*, he explores the way that the meadows become heraldry, the symbolic representation of human social distinction based on lineage: 'And thus, ye meadows, which have been | Companions of my thoughts more green, | Shall now the heraldry become | With which I shall adorn my tomb' (lines 25–8). Marvell in fact likes to conclude poems as he does here, by watching aspects of nature assume the forms and materials of art. In *The Nymph Complaining for the Death of her Fawn*, the speaker describes how the nymph's loss will transform her into marble – a conventional image of the capacity of extravagant grief to stupefy those who experience it. But Marvell embellishes the conventional image, likening her marmoreal being to a sculpture artfully engraved by her tears:

> First my unhappy statue shall
> Be cut in marble; and withal,
> Let it be weeping too: but there
> Th'engraver sure his art may spare;
> For I so truly thee bemoan,
> That I shall weep though I be stone:
> Until my tears, still dropping, wear
> My breast, themselves engraving there.   (lines 111–18)

In both *The Mower's Song* and *The Nymph Complaining*, Marvell allows the fiercest grief to resolve itself in terms of the most rarefied aesthetics.

The Picture of Little T. C. in a Prospect of Flowers also employs the genres of visual art, but to very different effect. It is first of all a self-conscious poetic equivalent of a painting of a child amid flowers. The word 'Prospect', in particular, designates a kind of landscape, particularly next to the term 'Picture'. The poem, moreover, possesses an almost painterly attention to colour, describing 'golden days! | In the green grass' (lines 2–3). The speaker knows that 'wanton Love' will one day 'under her command severe, | See his bow broke and ensigns torn' (lines 14–15). The imagination of the future erotic power of the child reveals the full rationale for the poem's aspiration to painting: the speaker wants to preserve this moment since the passage of time threatens T. C. and him with change. The speaker wants to 'parley with those conq'ring eyes, | Ere they have tried their force to wound' (lines 18–19). The experienced speaker knows the power of erotic vision to wound, and hopes like the speaker of *Upon Appleton House* to find some protection in the sanctuary of nature, asking that he 'be laid, / Where I may see thy glories from some shade' (lines 23–4). The poem ends with a kind of supplication to T. C., hoping that her comparatively innocent plucking of flowers will not anger 'Flora', who might in turn 'Nip in the blossom all our hopes and thee' (lines 36, 40). The practices of painting offer the fantasy that the fetching visual tableau of this fleeting moment might be captured and preserved.

Marvell's sense of the visual, then, entails a careful attention to surfaces, and to the evanescence of beauty. He is intrigued by the way that visual art, and particularly architecture, can be used to reveal the hidden principles of design in apparently random materials. In an overtly political poem, *The First Anniversary of the Government under His Highness the Lord Protector*, Marvell shrewdly employs principles of architectural tension to describe the precarious stability achieved by the balance of contrary forces under the 'protecting' roof of Cromwell, the Lord Protector:

> The commonwealth then first together came,
> And each one entered in the willing frame;

> All other matter yields, and may be ruled;
> But who the minds of stubborn men can build?
> No quarry bears a stone so hardly wrought,
> Nor with such labour from its centre brought;
> None to be sunk in the foundation bends,
> Each in the house the highest place contends,
> And each the hand that lays him will direct,
> And some fall back upon the architect;
> Yet all composed by his attractive song,
> Into the animated city throng.
>   The common-wealth does through their centres all
> Draw the circumf'rence of the public wall;
> The crossest spirits here do take their part,
> Fast'ning the contignation which they thwart;
> And they, whose nature leads them to divide,
> Uphold, this one, and that the other side;
> But the most equal still sustain the height,
> And they as pillars keep the work upright;
> While the resistance of opposèd minds,
> The fabric as with arches stronger binds,
> Which on the basis of a senate free,
> Knit by the roof's protecting weight agree.   (lines 75–98)

Marvell here depicts the 'wondrous order and consent' by which 'Cromwell tuned the ruling Instrument' (lines 67–8). Later in the poem we learn that the construction and maintenance of the state demands a continual process of architectural preservation, at least as creative and arduous as the effort involved in the original construction:

> 'Twas heaven would not that his pow'r should cease,
> But walk still middle betwixt war and peace;
> Choosing each stone, and poising every weight,
> Trying the measures of the breadth and height;
> Here pulling down, and there erecting new,
> Founding a firm state by proportions true.   (lines 243–8)

Architecture provides Marvell with an account of the world that is at once aesthetic and architectonic. Invoking the ancient tradition of *concordia discors*, the idea that the most profound and beautiful harmonies spring from discord, Marvell suggests that the stability of the state emerges from a careful balancing of tensions within the state.

In the poem *Tom May's Death*, a poem that is likely by Marvell, the poet criticizes May's effort to use Roman models to judge English events; he terms May a 'Foul architect that hadst not eye to see | How ill the measures of these states agree' (lines 51–2). May, the speaker suggests, not only violates decorum, the matching of the appropriate style to a fitting subject, when he 'by Rome's example England lay' (line 53); he also makes a serious political miscalculation. Marvell repeatedly invokes the principle of decorum as both an aesthetic and a political practice in some of his late political satires. *Clarendon's Housewarming* (another poem of disputed authorship often associated with Marvell) uses the generic machinery of the country house poem to mock the grandeur of the recently constructed mansion of Edward Hyde, Charles II's chief minister. No 'sober frame', Clarendon House is the polar opposite of Appleton House. Clarendon is 'Pharoah', building his magnificent structure at the expense of the nation: 'He cared not though Egypt's ten plagues us distressed, | So he could to build but make that policy law' (lines 39–40). The aesthetic inspiring Clarendon House is indulgence and pretension, not sober humility. Describing an estate that places individual gain and political grandiosity ahead of country, the poem reveals political corruption through the language of aesthetic excess.

Art and architecture, then, provide Marvell with a way of offering political judgements at an oblique angle; as the author of *Clarendon's Housewarming* shrewdly observes, 'all buildings must censure abide' (line 101). Working in a milieu and genre established by the royalist poet Edmund Waller, Marvell (and perhaps others) uses the visual arts as a medium to satirize contemporaneous political developments. In *Instructions to a Painter, for the Drawing of the Posture and Progress of his Majesties Forces at Sea*, Waller had presented the Duke of York's victory of 3 June 1655 as a symbol of the high motives that led to the war, and the heroic conduct that won the war. In the process, he inaugurated a minor genre of 'advice to a painter' poems, in which poets used the visual arts to comment on contemporaneous political developments.[5] In his contribution to this genre, *The Last Instructions to a Painter*, Marvell investigates the proper decorum of representation for the deeply impoverished and profoundly non-heroic age in which he lives.

> But ere thou fall'st to work, first painter see
> It ben't too slight grown, or too hard for thee.
> Canst thou paint without colors? Then 'tis right:
> For so we too without a fleet can fight.
> Or canst thou daub a signpost, and that ill?
> 'Twill suit our great debauch and little skill.
> Or hast thou marked how antique masters limn
> The alley-roof with snuff of candle dim,
> Sketching in shady smoke prodigious tools?
> 'Twill serve this race of drunkards, pimps and fools. (lines 3–12)

The poem develops an explicit contrast between such tittering obscenity and the unfailingly heroic style of Peter Paul Rubens:

> Here, painter, rest a little, and survey
> With what small arts the public game they play.
> For so too Rubens, with affairs of state,
> His lab'ring pencil oft would recreate. (lines 117–20)

'Small arts' is a perfect phrase for the bankrupt modes of representation suffusing the deeply diminished political world of the Restoration.[6] The poem culminates in a parodic praise of the theoretically fruitful marriage of painting and poetry:

> Painter, adieu! How well our arts agree!
> Poetic picture, painted poetry!
> But this great work is for our monarch fit:
> And henceforth Charles only to Charles shall sit.
> His master-hand the ancients shall outdo,
> Himself the poet and the painter too. (lines 943–8)

It is conventional for eulogy to suggest that the honoured object supplies its own best praise; Marvell deliberately distorts this gesture, mockingly suggesting that only Charles could paint his own portrait, or compose his own poem of praise. It is as if the very media of representation have gone awry in the corrupt and misshapen political world of the Restoration.

Throughout his poetry Marvell displays a deep engagement with the materials and practices of visual art and design. His poetry is a multimedia performance. But this is never an art explored simply for art's sake; Marvell, rather, is deeply interested in the ethics of aesthetics, in the ways that various modes of aesthetic representation assume or support or challenge various social and political values. He is in fact a verbal architect, but one as interested in embellishment as in structure, and who uses embellishment to explore the mysteries of structure. His absorption with architectonics, moreover, is never static; it is always accompanied by a correlated fascination with the dynamic tensions that underpin architectural stability. Fascinated by the metamorphoses produced by changes in perspective and scale, he writes poetry distinguished by the imperative, at once visual and cognitive: 'See'. Marvell knows well that vision is an always partial but nonetheless crucial way of knowing the world. In spectacularly witty poetry, he uses the genres of visual art to assert the ultimately unknowable qualities of the world such art aspires to reproduce. Art, he suggests, teaches us how to see, and teaches us how partial and inadequate our vision is. In a politically turbulent time, such lessons may have been necessary, and even consoling.

NOTES

1. Rosalie Colie, '*My Ecchoing Song*': *Andrew Marvell's Poetry of Criticism* (Princeton, 1970), 106. The book contains perhaps the fullest account available of Marvell's deep engagement with the visual arts.
2. As Donald Friedman remarks, 'Marvell plays upon the division within our visual and mental functions, a division which is nevertheless underpinned by the connections and similarities between seeing and knowing' ('Sight and Insight in Marvell's Poetry', in C. A. Patrides, ed., *Approaches to Marvell: The York Tercentenary Lectures* (London, 1978), 328).
3. On contemporaneous theories of landscape and perception, see James Turner, *The Politics of Landscape: Rural Scenery and Society in English Poetry 1630–1660* (Cambridge, MA, 1979); and Chris Fitter, *Poetry, Space, Landscape: Toward a New Theory* (Cambridge, 1995).
4. Nuanced accounts of Marvell's attitude to nature are available in Donald Friedman, *Marvell's Pastoral Art* (Berkeley, 1970,) and Robert Watson, *Back to Nature: The Green and the Real in the Late Renaissance* (Philadelphia, 2007).
5. Annabel Patterson, *Marvell and the Civic Crown* (Princeton, 1978), offers an illuminating discussion of the satirical tradition of the speaking picture.
6. James Turner suggests that the poem 'parodies the artistic elevation of royal desire in order to destroy the visual fixation that kept subjects like Pepys half in love with monarchy' ('The Libertine Abject: The "Postures" of *Last Instructions to a Painter*', in Warren Chernaik and Martin Dzelzainis, eds., *Marvell and Liberty* (Basingstoke, 1999), 236).

Further reading

Paul Alpers, *What Is Pastoral?* (Chicago, 1996).

Warren Chernaik, *The Poet's Time: Politics and Religion in the Work of Andrew Marvell* (Cambridge, 1983).

Stuart Clark, *Vanities of the Eye: Vision in Early Modern European Culture* (Oxford, 2007).

Rosalie Colie, '*My Ecchoing Song*': *Andrew Marvell's Poetry of Criticism* (Princeton, 1970).

William Empson, *Some Versions of Pastoral* (London, 1935).

Chris Fitter, *Poetry, Space, Landscape: Toward a New Theory* (Cambridge, 1995).

Donald Friedman, *Marvell's Pastoral Art* (Berkeley, 1970).

Judith Haber, *Pastoral and the Poetics of Self-Contradiction: Theocritus to Marvell* (Cambridge, 1992).

Jean Hagstrum, *The Sister Arts: The Tradition of Literary Pictorialism and English Poetry from Dryden to Gray* (Chicago, 1958).

J. B. Leishman, *The Art of Marvell's Poetry* (London, 1966).

Diane McColley, *Poetry and Ecology in the Age of Milton and Marvell* (Burlington, VT, 2007).

Henry V. S. Ogden and M. S. Ogden, *English Taste in Landscape in the Seventeenth Century* (Ann Arbor, MI, 1955).

C. A. Patrides, ed., *Approaches to Marvell: The York Tercentenary Lectures* (London, 1978).

Annabel Patterson, *Marvell and the Civic Crown* (Princeton, 1978).

Steven Pincus, *Protestantism and Patriotism: Ideologies and the Making of English Foreign Policy 1650–1668* (Cambridge, 1996).

Claude J. Summers and Ted-Larry Pebworth, eds., *On the Celebrated and Neglected Poems of Andrew Marvell* (Columbia, MO, 1992).

James Turner, *The Politics of Landscape: Rural Scenery and Society in English Poetry 1630–1660* (Cambridge, MA, 1979).

Robert Watson, *Back to Nature: The Green and the Real in the Late Renaissance* (Philadelphia, 2007).

Steven N. Zwicker, *Lines of Authority: Politics and English Literary Culture,1649–1689* (Ithaca, NY, 1993)

7

PHIL WITHINGTON

Andrew Marvell's citizenship

'This day £36 13s 4d is taken out of the iron chest and paid unto Mr Edmond Popple for the use of his brother Andrew Marvell Esquire given him by this board for his service in the last session.'[1] So was recorded in the minute book of the Common Council (or 'Bench' or 'Board', as it was also wont to style itself) of Kingston-upon-Hull on 3 December 1663. It is an everyday and unremarkable moment of civic business that nevertheless encapsulates many of the themes of this essay. This is true in terms of both what it reveals about Andrew Marvell's citizenship and also what, on closer viewing, it leaves unsaid. Most obviously, it hints at the prominent part that Marvell's urban background, education and identity played in his civic persona: a provincial urbanity that was constitutive of – rather than an alternative to – his metropolitan and national political consciousness, but which has been largely neglected, or at least underplayed, by critics and historians. Second, it indicates the importance of family and friendship in structuring Marvell's civic associations and responsibilities. Edmond Popple was at once Marvell's brother-in-law and a prominent burgess of Kingston-upon-Hull who sponsored his 'brother' to be made a freeman of Hull in 1658 (a prerequisite of standing for parliamentary election) and who acted as his financial broker with the Board thereafter. A similar conflation of familial and political affiliation can be found in many other of Marvell's most important civic associations.

   Less obvious from the entry is that, since as early as the parliamentary elections of March 1661 (when Marvell retained his seat under the newly restored monarchy of Charles II), serious factional and ideological differences had spoiled the relationship between Marvell and his fellow MP for Hull, Colonel Anthony Gilby – differences that reflected tensions both nationally and locally. Nor would it be obvious that, since the first sitting of what was to become known as the Cavalier Parliament, Marvell and his friends had been thoroughly outpoliticked by the loose alliance of royalists, courtiers, soldiers, episcopalians, and like-minded Hull burgesses to which Gilby belonged.

Indeed, far from being the relentless defender of England's liberties and free-doms (as many hagiographers and historians have claimed), Marvell had been close to losing his parliamentary place only nine months earlier for absconding without warning to the Netherlands – an act consistent with his marginalization from the political process of Restoration. In the meantime his 'brother' Edmond Popple had become a beleaguered figurehead for local dissenters in the face of rampant monarchism and clericalism that few – Marvell included – seemed to know how to resist.

None of which is to suggest, as is often the case in discussions of Marvell's 'political identity', that his citizenship was especially elusive or unfathom-able.' On the contrary, this essay argues that Marvell's citizenship, like his religion, was relatively straightforward and consistent once he became fully embroiled on a practical level in the politics of his city and nation. Indeed it goes as far as to suggest that, in terms of the strength of his underlying convictions, in his obsessive reflections on the craft of politics, and in his use of his superlative rhetorical skills for the good of the nation (as he saw it), Marvell embodied a particular tradition of civic humanism as it had devel-oped in England over the previous hundred or so years. What we do find in Marvell is, however, a constant tension between an ideal of citizenship as both a culture of public life and a method of personal decorum, and the reality of the circumstances in which he found himself embroiled. This tension between theory and practice is, of course, one that all publicly minded people must confront to some degree or other. However, for Marvell the paradox seems especially accentuated, and accounts for the power of his illicit criti-cisms of the ruling regime.

The following discussion deals with the related issues of citizenship as an ideal and citizenship as practice. It sketches the tradition of civic humanism inherited by Marvell as it developed in England from the first half of the sixteenth century. It outlines the institutions through which this political culture was established and disseminated and shows how a precocious son of an East Yorkshire clergyman could be exposed to its tenets. It also unpacks some of its core values and the manner in which they were adopted and articulated by Marvell in the course of his public life. These core values include in the first instance his investment in the Ciceronian virtues of *pru-dence* and *civility*: the objective set of conditions that for English humanists should characterize not merely political processes but also social relations more generally, and the cultivation of personal skills through which and by which people should participate in those relationships. Second, these core values encompass Marvell's belief in the authority of reasonable *discourse* – both written and oral – over arbitrary power and status in any public decision-making process or debate. This is not to say that Marvell believed that everyone should be free to say what they want. Rather he shared the humanist conviction that it was through rational discussion by qualified and informed parties that issues of public concern should be broached and resolved. Third, they include his powerful sense of *place* – in particular his respect for corporate privileges and powers (most obviously cities and parliaments) and their centrality to the condition and, indeed, sanctity of the 'nation' (Marvell's favourite word for the English polity after 1660).

In establishing the basic tenets of Marvell's political philosophy this chapter also considers the social contexts of his citizenship. Marvell's standing as a writer has generally encouraged critics to focus on his literary output as evidence of his civic activism and beliefs. There are good reasons for this. The politically engaged writer who uses his or her skills for the good of the commonwealth was a central figure of English humanist lore from the early sixteenth century onwards.[3] In his orations, satires, histories and polemics Marvell acted upon the reason and sensibilities of the reading public quite as effectively as Thomas Elyot, Thomas Smith, Thomas Middleton, or, indeed, his patron John Milton. It nevertheless remains the case that Marvell only embraced anonymous polemic once the autonomy, civility and discursive capacity of England's urban and parliamentary institutions appeared to be in jeopardy.[4] He was a citizen before he was a satirist and polemicist. And he became a polemicist to preserve his citizenship.

John Pocock long ago argued that the most likely way for early modern Englishmen to develop a heightened civic consciousness was through religion and law. Although he was accomplished in both, Marvell was neither a minister nor a lawyer. Nor did he operate in the field of courtly and aristocratic politics – another source of civic consciousness – although he acquired powerful patrons and 'friends' in both the Cromwellian and Caroline administrations. A more likely way to understand Marvell's citizenship is through his role as humanist 'secretary'. In the 1650s Marvell served both the households of great men (in a way reminiscent of Thomas Hobbes and John Locke) and the English Commonwealth (in the way that Samuel Pepys subsequently administered the 'King's Service'); certainly many of his attitudes resonate with the persona of the discreet counsellor and man of business. However, the context that distinguishes Marvell from (for example) Hobbes and Pepys, and which offers the key to understanding his political philosophy, becomes apparent when the early modern meaning of 'citizen' is properly considered and historicized.

From a properly historicized perspective it is not anachronistic to style Marvell a citizen only because he was a freeman of Hull. As late as the nineteenth century it was this particular form of urban inhabitancy and participation that the English sense of 'citizen' (and its synonyms 'burgess' and 'freeman') described.[5] It referred specifically to the householders who were formally enfranchised to urban corporations (in return for the economic and political privileges located there) and the men – such as Marvell – whom they employed to solicit their 'business'. One of the consequences of the spread of civic humanism was that this apparently restrictive and archaic sense of the citizen was invigorated and imbued with many of the assumptions associated with classical citizenship. Local office-holders in many different kinds of community, from the rural parish upwards, experienced the same kinds of pressures and opportunities, so much so that the later Tudor and early Stuart regimes have been styled a 'monarchical republic'. Within this context the civic potential of towns and cities, with their concentration of civic resources and especial governmental needs, was especially pronounced. As a result, from an early age Marvell would have learnt that urban citizenship entailed a concern for the larger 'commonwealth' (as it was styled at the time) that, while certainly encompassing the public good of the local urban community, nevertheless transcended the narrow limits of the town hall. A key practical mechanism in this reciprocal relationship between town and nation was the role of boroughs in electing the House of Commons: in crude terms 80 per cent of sixteenth- and seventeenth-century MPs were elected by burgesses (though electoral procedures varied from place to place).[6] It follows that the immediate context for understanding Marvell's citizenship in the early modern sense of the term is his role as Hull's parliamentary representative in particular, and his civic friendships and affiliations more generally.

Marvell and civic humanism

'The word of God: The society of good men: and the books of the Ancients. There is one way more, which is by diversion, business, and activity; which are also necessary to be used in their season.' Marvell suggested these 'diversions' to Sir John Trott in the later 1660s as a way of coping with the death of Trott's son, Marvell's friend (*Letters*, 299). They also nicely encapsulate the foundations, or perhaps raw materials, of Marvell's conception of citizenship. This was an ideal that was intellectually derived from Protestantism and humanism; that encouraged individuals – citizens – to act as well as think for the commonwealth and public good; and which valorized virtuous, participatory, and free 'societies' over hierarchical authority based simply on birth or wealth. However, Marvell's citizenship was not a rigorous philosophy of the kind associated with canonical figures such as Hobbes, Milton, or Locke: as many critics and historians have frustratingly found, he cannot be categorized easily as 'Hobbesian', 'republican', or 'Whig'. This is in part because Marvell never explicated his ideas in systematic fashion – they become apparent inadvertently, in the shape of letters to mayors and friends or exercises in panegyric and polemic. It is also because Marvell, perhaps more obviously than any other public figure of the later seventeenth century, was heir to a long period of cultural change in England which encouraged the adoption of particular assumptions and sensibilities rather than adherence to a particular creed (though those assumptions and sensibilities could become integrated into more clearly delineated political ideologies).

Broadly speaking this process of cultural change was twofold. The dimension most familiar to modern readers is the 'long reformation' – the various cycles of evangelical activism and conservative reaction that ripped through England from the 1520s to the 1690s and transformed so much more than church liturgies in their wake. William Lamont has shown where Marvell stood in relation to this tradition, which Marvell experienced first-hand through his clergyman father: he can be found 'in a very clearly defined wing of Protestant nonconformity', somewhere in the vicinity of the moderate Presbyterian Richard Baxter, and opposed not merely to the imperialism of 'Popery' but also tyrannical bishops and 'unreasonable' Independents at home.[7] A cultural development just as important, though until recently less recognized, was the establishment and dissemination of an indigenous tradition of civic humanism over the same 'long' period. Its roots were in the fifteenth century: it was then that the word that encapsulated its trajectory – 'commonweal' or 'commonwealth' – first entered the English vernacular, and when many of the institutions and technologies that were to drive it – grammar schools, corporations, the printing press – developed their early modern shape. The process gained momentum in the sixteenth century; its touchstones might be regarded as the foundation of St Paul's School in London in 1509 and the publication of Thomas More's *Utopia* in 1516. The first a humanist institution, the second a humanist text, each were palimpsests for the humanist transformations in education and print during the generations that followed.

The social extent to which civic humanism was disseminated has received a good deal of recent attention from historians and literary critics. This might seem surprising. St Paul's was, after all, a school for England's metropolitan elites, *Utopia* a Latin pastiche of Plato packed with clever in-jokes. Yet to think about *The Best State of a Commonwealth and the New Island of Utopia* for a moment: it was translated by Ralph Robinson into the vernacular in the 1550s, the 1551 edition appearing during the reign of the arch-Protestant Edward VI and the 1556 edition under his equally strident Catholic sister, Mary. Ironic or not, many of its 'commonwealth' themes had already became prevailing tropes and slogans of the era. These included the responsibility of governors to their people, the epistemological authority of the ancients, the use of learning and counsel for pragmatic ends, the relationship between civility, virtue and the public good, the dangers of private and selfish interests, and identification of the unprecedented social and economic problems currently facing England (in the sixteenth century). This was true for statesmen: disagreements among Tudor historians as to which decade was most committed to 'commonwealth' policies should not obscure how Thomas Cromwell, Protector Somerset and William Cecil all framed their governance in its terms. It was also true for proselytizers and rebels: evangelical reformers and Norfolk insurgents talked to the same purpose – commonwealth – even if they meant and pursued it in different ways. In the meantime, a generation of humanist writers looked to serve, profit and entertain their commonwealth in manuscript and, increasingly, print: not in Latin, like More, but in the vernacular, like Thomas Elyot, Thomas Smith, and dozens of others.

That this trickle should turn into a veritable flood from the later sixteenth century was in large part due to the rise of the urban-based grammar school. St Paul's and grammars like it served as a template for the wholesale restructuring and expansion of education in the sixteenth and seventeenth centuries along humanist lines. Legislation passed in Henrician and Edwardian parliaments saw religious schools either disbanded or reformed (often under the control of urban corporations) and a large number of new grammars founded (usually as adjuncts to urban corporations). The result was a remarkably centralized curriculum based on classical texts that brought the 'new learning' – in particular Cicero – not merely to the nobility and gentry but also to the 'middling sorts' (as the great Elizabethan pedagogue Richard Mulcaster described his favourite class of student). Moreover it did so explicitly to serve the commonwealth and public good. Many scholars have warned that the rhetoric of commonwealth which accompanied these changes should not be taken at face value; clearly, moreover, a humanist education facilitated personal gain and cultural distinction as well as social betterment (though as the humanist Thomas Smith observed in the 1540s, private- and common-wealth did not have to be mutually exclusive). Social historians have also rightly noted that this 'revolution' in education was hardly comprehensive: it excluded the majority of women, labourers, and rural villagers. It was nevertheless more penetrative than anything seen before, and the proportion of educated Englishmen in 1640 was not to be superseded until the early twentieth century.[8] More to the point, Marvell was just such an Englishman. Marvell was not only educated at Hull Grammar School (where his father served as a master) but also won an exhibition from the Common Council to study at Trinity College, Cambridge. Like William Shakespeare, Ben Jonson, and John Lilburne (none of whom went to university) and John Milton (who did), Marvell was an archetypal product of the early modern grammar school system: a clever, middling, urban beneficiary of a humanist education.

If this highlights the continuities of Marvell's citizenship then it is also worth dwelling on its urban and corporate qualities. At the general level, transformations in schooling and publishing were implicated in other infra-structural developments that were indicative of England's burgeoning urbanism: for example, the exponential growth in metropolitan and provincial litigation; the spectacular expansion of the metropolis; and the emergence of an English 'corporate system', whereby the number of incorporated cities, boroughs and towns almost quadrupled in the hundred years after 1540. As a result of this process urban centres (Hull among them) were not only granted significant privileges and resources. They were also encouraged to regard themselves as 'little commonwealths' serving their own and the greater good – enfranchised communities of citizens, burgesses and freemen endowed with the requisite civility to govern themselves, their households, their towns, and, when appropriate, their country. As such it was no coincidence that Thomas More wrote *Utopia* as 'Citizen and Sheriff of the Famous City of London' or that his sixteenth-century translator, Ralph Robinson, should be another London citizen who 'Englished' the text at the specific request of citizen-friends with whom he fraternized. Likewise the school where Marvell was educated was established in 1483 by Bishop Alcock, seized by the crown in 1547, enlarged and placed under the stewardship of burgesses in the 1580s, and given wholly over to the control of the Common Council in 1604. These institutional changes reflected the conceit that there should be a close relationship between the citizenship of the council chamber and the classical curriculum in the classroom. They also meant that Marvell's education was a direct product of civic paternalism. With other urban prodigies of the period the corporate aspects of their upbringing are often difficult to trace. Shakespeare wrote only one play located in a setting which bore any resemblance to the civic community in which he grew up; Jonson largely held the civil and civic pretensions of citizens in contempt; Milton's indigenous citizenship was superseded by a more thoroughgoing classical republicanism. Marvell was different. Although he visited Hull only rarely after leaving for university the impact of his upbringing, perhaps because of his father, remained indelible.

We know this because of the remarkable series of letters that Marvell wrote to the mayors and aldermen of Hull between 1660 and 1678 in his capacity as the borough's MP. It is unlikely that any other early modern MP communicated as often with the constituency he had been elected to represent as Marvell – itself an indication that he took his civic duties extremely seriously. Two concepts recur so often and so regularly in the letters that they serve as a kind of motif for Marvell's political method. They are *prudence* and *civility*.

Prudence, alongside justice, fortitude and temperance, was one of the cardinal virtues of the medieval period. It described the skill in applying what Chaucer termed 'goodly wisdom' to practical affairs and overlapped with other personal qualities such as *discretion* and *circumspection*. 'Civility' was a more complex term describing the capacity of individuals to behave in a manner appropriate to any social situation or relationship: i.e. in ways that accorded respect and recognition to other parties and avoided giving offence and intimidation. In order to mediate the 'will' of people richer and more powerful than others, protocols of civility recognized position and status, protected those potentially vulnerable to abuse, and established bonds of reciprocity profitable to all parties.[9] When Marvell assured Oliver Cromwell in 1653 that 'the only Civility which it is proper for me to practise with so eminent a Person is to obey you, and to perform honestly the work that you have set me about', he was acknowledging an asymmetrical relationship that was nevertheless distinct from servility or, indeed, slavery (*Letters*, 291).

Like the term 'manners', civility has become anodyne over time, suggesting a simple concern for etiquette or politeness. However, in the sixteenth and seventeenth centuries it represented an elaborate ethical system to be applied both to social institutions and social actors. Civility demanded social acuity, self-awareness and control, and an inbred decorum – or 'feel for the game' – enabling the person to make the best of social situations and relationships. Your prudence in turn required reason, calculation, and knowledge on the part of the person (citizen or otherwise), allowing individual and collective decisions to be reached on an informed and rational basis. Both virtues were antithetical to impulsive and passionate behaviour and both inclined the individual to reflect, constantly, on the nature of political and social circumstances and his or her place within them. Although prudence is a quality often associated with Machiavelli, it is more likely that early modern Englishmen would have identified it with Cicero, the patron saint of England's civic renaissance and the classical writer to whom Marvell, like Machiavelli himself, was most obviously indebted.[10] That is not to say Marvell did not have his Machiavellian moments: any valorization of political calculation and pragmatism ran that risk. It remains the case that Marvell conjoined prudence with the expressly Ciceronian concept of civility and conceived it not as the bulwark of autocratic rule – or indeed personal gain – so much as the guarantor of the public good and national interest. This was a strikingly Ciceronian conceit in an era that wore its scepticism and self-interest on its sleeve. While there were many contexts in which Marvell would have been exposed to Cicero, one of the earliest and most formative would have been the grammar school. While Cicero was central to England's school curriculum, it was likewise a Ciceronian outlook that humanist reformers had aimed to instil into the procedures and practices of governance – urban government included. With Marvell they succeeded on both counts.

When invoked as often as they are by Marvell, prudence and civility can be taken as the calling card of the early modern civic humanist. There is only space here to give a few examples of Marvell's use of the terms. In November 1660 Marvell and his fellow MP John Ramsden warned Mayor Richardson that the advice 'we shall give you we remit unto your own prudence'; that political decisions were usually questions 'either in Law or in conscience or in prudence'; and that on this occasion 'the whole stress lies upon your prudence'. Five months later Marvell declared to Richardson that 'The bonds of civility betwixt Colonel Gilby' – the MP recently elected in the place of Ramsden – 'and myself' were 'unhappily snapped in pieces, and in such manner that I cannot see how it is ever possible to knit them again'. In 1668 Marvell reported approvingly that Lord Bellasyse, although passionate about a dispute that had arisen between the burgesses and the garrison stationed in Hull, 'according to the prudence with which men must always handle a mixed business ... inclines to that way for removing the stumbling block'. Marvell also assured the burgesses that, at a meeting to resolve the problem, the military chiefs used 'all the civility imaginable to you ... there were twenty good things said on all hands tending to the good fame, reputation and advantage of the Town'; later he complimented the mayor (civilly) that 'I cannot but add one word of that esteem which I have for your prudence in the conduct of this whole business'. In 1670 Marvell commented, 'These things I have been thus careful to give you a plain account of, not thinking a perfunctory relation worthy your prudence', adding (prudently) 'but must in exchange desire you will not admit many inspectors into my letters'. Three years later he told a correspondent that Samuel Parker's *Bishop Bramhall's Vindication of Himself* (1672), which provoked Marvell to write *The Rehearsal Transpros'd* (1672), 'is the rudest book, one or other, that ever was published (I may say) since the first invention of printing'. In 1675 he ruminated that 'for when there is a necessity[,] Prudence or God's Providence steps in by more extraordinary methods' and in 1676 observed 'It is a Tribute due from one in my Station to your Prudence to inform you from time to time of things that pass in Parliament.' In the meantime he told Mayor Shires that 'I have received so courteous and civil a Letter from you that it warms my very heart and I shall keep it as a mark of honour always to lie by me amongst whatsoever things I account most precious and estimable' (*Letters*, 10–11, 26, 80, 84, 111, 312, 152, 174, 164).

Marvell's letters suggest not only that he valued prudence and civility above all other virtues, but that he expected the political culture in which he worked to do the same. He can be found advising Hull's mayors how to 'do' politics prudently and civilly; they can be found returning the favour, the bench asking their MPs 'to proceed according to their prudence and discretion'.[11] Marvell also judged the behaviour of others – whether dissolute noblemen, 'rude' ecclesiastics, or ineffectual courtiers and statesmen – on these terms. As important, the letters themselves are exemplary exercises in prudent and civil correspondence: to the puzzlement of some later critics, who have been surprised by the circumspect tone of the missives, Marvell not only preached prudence and civility but also performed them in his prose.[12] Like Cicero, he valued prudent and civil rhetoric over 'loquacious folly'. This reflected Marvell's more general, and humanist, concern for *discourse*: civic life was as much a discursive process as a realm of action whereby prudent decisions were reached – or should be reached – through civil modes of counsel, argument and debate. One of Marvell's central criticisms of the Restored regime, and the reason he began to supplement his parliamentary duties with that of anonymous pamphleteer, was the decreasing discursive efficacy of England's representative body. That Charles II began to observe debates in the House of Lords was merely the tip of the iceberg in terms of the emasculation of parliamentary process. A culture of bribes, placemen and intimidation – not to mention overfamiliarity and complacency – strangled debate and led Marvell to ask his favourite nephew (the son of Edward Popple) in March 1670: 'In such a Conjuncture, dear *Will*, what probability is there of my doing any Thing to the Purpose?' As he explained in his *Account of the Growth of Popery and Arbitrary Government*, his fellow MPs had become 'like so many good fellows met together in a public house to make merry'. As a result, 'the use of so public a counsel is frustrated, there is no place for deliberation, no persuading by reason'.[13] Marvell's pessimism contrasts sharply with the palpable glee that characterizes his letters to Hull's Bench between 11 April 1678 (written two months after *An Account* was published) and his final letter to the Bench on 6 July 1678. Precipitating the change in tone was a new Speaker for the House of Commons. One of the roles of Speaker was, of course, to regulate parliamentary debate; the election of Sir Robert Sawyer, who allowed discussion that had previously been curtailed, released a Pandora's Box of civic energy. Marvell was able to report how the Commons had heard 'a long Narrative of Fact from the Committee concerning Popery'; how 'the House is very busy'; how debates about the 'presence and counsel' of the king continued from one day to the next; how debates 'endured till toward nine at night'; how supply and foreign policy were 'long debated' and the 'debate took up the whole day'; how the Chancellor's speech was debated 'thoroughly'; how 'they entered into a great debate of looking into the Privy Seals for secret service'; how debates 'rose' as if from nowhere and 'several debates' followed debates followed 'free conferences' (*Letters*, 302, 221, 222, 223, 224, 226, 233, 237).

Prudence, civility and discourse were clearly not the preserve of corporate citizens. Rather they signified a more general tradition of civic humanism in which corporate citizens participated, and which Marvell was especially consistent in reproducing within the context of Restoration political culture. What distinguished Marvell's citizenship as especially 'corporate' was his powerful sense of place. This is true in terms of his accentuated localism, N. H. Keeble observing that 'the one personal sentiment to emerge clearly from the constituency letters is the writer's attachment to Hull'.[14] However, it is also true in the more abstract sense of urban communities like Hull forming body politics with their own incorporated 'soul', extensive institutional and architectural resources, and a particular position and role within the larger body of the nation. In the words of John Barston, the town clerk of Tewkesbury who in 1576 wrote the first vernacular treatise on the concept of society, corporate towns formed a 'special kind of society and fellowship of one people, gathered together in one town, which resembles the beginning of all civility, and is the lively [precedent] of behaviour to the rustic and ruder sort'.[15] As Henry Ireton forcefully argued in the Putney Debates seventy years later, 'he that has his livelihood by his trade and by his freedom of trading in such a corporation – which he cannot exercise in another – [. . .] is tied to that place, for his livelihood depends upon it'. As a result, 'that man has an interest – has a permanent interest there, upon which he may live, and live a freeman without dependence'. Urban freedom was, in effect, a kind of property with political as well as economic benefits and obligations – a place that gave the citizen not only independence but also a 'local and permanent interest in the kingdom'.[16] The power of place and propriety – and the civility, independence and interest that flowed from it – was a general attribute of early modern political culture. What was particular about the conception of place with which Marvell grew up in Hull was that it was rooted not so much in a culture of 'possessive individualism', as is usually argued for rural free-holders and country gentlemen, as one of associational life: 'society', as Barston conceived it. The citizen-householder was prosperous, civil and free precisely because of his collective commitments and resources: the corporate community made the citizen and vice versa.[17]

Marvell and Restoration politics

This spatial imperative of corporate citizenship was second nature to Marvell: as he told Hull's burgesses, 'I reckon your bench to be all but as one person' (*Letters*, 111). It is illustrated by the way he approached one of the most important issues facing the restored regime in the early 1660s: how to organize the militia. The militia was a specific kind of civic resource which only larger cities and boroughs, usually with 'county' status, regarded as constituent of their place. The militia was especially significant for Hull both in terms of the port's strategic position facing the Low Countries (with which the English were intermittently at war) and the burgesses' role in precipitating the outbreak of civil war in 1642, when Charles I was forcibly denied access to the town.[18] Marvell was appointed to the parliamentary committee charged with dealing with the problem in 1660 and he made his attitude clear to Mayor Richardson on 17 November. He hoped 'to see the whole army disbanded &, according to the [Militia] Act ... your Town once more ungarrisoned, in which I should be glad & happy to be instrumental to the uttermost'. This predilection reflected less war-weariness or disdain for militarism and more a heightened civic sensibility. Marvell explained that 'I cannot but remember, though then a child, those blessed days when the youth of your own town were trained for your militia, and did methought become their arms much better than any soldiers that I have seen there since'. Now that 'we are about a new Act of regulating the Militia that it may be as a standing strength but not as ill as a perpetual Army to the Nation', he encouraged Richardson 'to signify to me anything in that matter that were according to your ancient custom and desirable to you' (*Letters*, 2). Marvell was clearly suspicious of standing armies and garrisons; that suspicion was tantamount to a deep investment in civic independence, custom, and jurisdictional integrity.

If Marvell's prudence was not Machiavellian then his appreciation of the citizen-in-arms clearly was. He may well have learnt it from his father who, aside from his ministerial and pedagogic duties, was also heavily involved in helping the burgesses maintain the defences of Hull until his accidental death in 1641.[19] In late 1660 it quickly became apparent that civic militias were under threat. Powerful interests – including leading figures among the East Riding gentry; the new Lord Lieutenant, Lord John Bellasyse; and royalist soldiers under the patronage of the Duke of York – had no intention of allowing burgesses in Hull either to go 'ungarrisoned' or to muster their militia autonomously. Marvell helped make the Hull militia separate from that of the East Riding, so negating the influence of local gentry but increasing the authority of the Lord Lieutenant, Bellasyse. However, Marvell failed to close the garrison. In the meantime the well-connected Hildyard family requested that the Bench return the Manor House in Hull to their possession. This large structure had been converted into a garrison during the civil wars and given to the Bench as recompense for damages (fiscal and physical) suffered by the town. Sir Robert Hildyard was an East Riding gentleman, his brother Henry lived in Surrey, and encouraged by burgesses in the town they now looked to take their property back. On receiving their request in

November 1660 Mayor Richardson immediately handed the matter over to 'our representatives in Parliament'.[20]

The response of Marvell and his fellow MP John Ramsden revealed a palpable sense of place. First, they were frustrated that certain (unnamed) burgesses 'in occasional discourse' with the Hildyard brothers had apparently engineered the claim on the Manor House: it was a political act that undermined the civic community as a homogenous body. The two men now warned Richardson to 'be very private in what we shall write unto you ... That in doing our duty to you, we may not incur the displeasure of any'. Second, the MPs reiterated the imperative of place that should nevertheless inform civic decision-making. They hoped that 'you are as tender of whatsoever belongs to the Town, as you would be of your own private possessions' and reminded Richardson that 'having the Manor House, you are now entire within yourselves': 'in this the possession is not peculiar to a man's self, but the interest of a whole corporation'. Third, they outlined the basis on which the burgesses should come to a decision. This was prudence; in particular 'what reason in prudence is there for you to give a perpetual station & garrison in your Town (for such is the Manor House) to a family who have been and will be always, whether you restore it or not, the greatest instruments of continuing you a Garrison[?]'. Finally, Marvell and Ramsden indicated their preferred course of action. If the Board complied with the request from Hildyard 'it may be executed and concluded by some other persons'. If the Board sought to preserve the spatial integrity of the town by refusing to relinquish the Manor House then 'we shall willingly Serve you therein' (*Letters*, 10–11).

As well as illuminating Marvell's corporate sensibility, the incident and its aftermath also represent an early indication of the course Restoration politics was to take. The Hull Bench ignored the advice of Marvell and Ramsden and sold the Manor House for £300. Not only was the garrison retained but the governor, Colonel Anthony Gilby (a client of the Duke of York), defeated Ramsden in the parliamentary elections of March 1661 and the soldiery were extravagantly feted by the Bench.[21] It was noted earlier that the 'bonds of civility' between Marvell and Gilby soon snapped. They were subsequently able to represent their borough in distant but prudent tandem, fulfilling Marvell's prediction that 'though perhaps we may sometimes differ in our advice concerning the way of proceeding yet we have the same good ends in general' (*Letters*, 26). However, in the years immediately following the election – the crucial period that saw the construction of the Clarendon Code (the sequence of legislation by which the Restoration regime was established) – the 'way of proceeding' was very much that of Gilby rather than Marvell. This is true in terms of the parliamentary legislation passed and which impacted directly on Hull. The 'bill of Corporations' (as Marvell described it) was 'an unpleasing business' that enabled commissions of soldiers and gentry to purge corporations of both office-holders elected in the Cromwellian era and citizens refusing to renounce the Solemn League and Covenant (*Letters*, 33). (The Covenant was the 1643 agreement between Scottish Covenanters and English parliamentarians to rid the islands of 'Popery'. It became one of the symbols of dissent after 1660.) The Corporation Act was passed in conjunction with the more infamous Act for Universal Conformity, which reasserted epis-copalian authority in England's rural and urban parishes. Hull lost its leading minister and three aldermen because of the legislation.[22] Gilby's pre-eminence is also apparent in Marvell's personal relationship with a town that was clearly riddled with faction and politicking, the governors of which increasingly looked to its garrison as the best source of political patronage. The writing was on the wall by July 1661, when the Bench 'put to the vote whether Mr Marvell shall be desired to undertake the solicitation of the Town's business about the renewal of the Town's charter'. It was 'carried in the affirmative': Marvell clearly retained support, despite his enemies. However, for the com-petence of a town 'solicitor' to be debated (and recorded) in this way reflects the intense politicking in the corporation.[23] Marvell's relationship with the Bench, increasingly influenced by the opposing faction, deteriorated thereafter. In October, Gilby and not Marvell was presented with his 'knight's penny' for serving as MP, and in November the Manor House was sold. 7 November 1661 was a particularly bad day for Marvell. A series of orders by the Bench praised Gilby rather than Marvell for making Hull's militia separate from the East Riding (despite Marvell initiating the policy); presented plate to Gilby's wife 'as a gratuity for her husband's respect to this town' (he had returned his October fee); and replaced the moderate Presbyterian John Shaw with the conformist William Ainsworth as master of the borough's hospital. Last but not least, 'This day Milton's book against the portraiture of his Sacred Majesty being by order of His Majesty amongst other books to be burnt the said book was this day burnt in the Common Hall of this town'.[24] Milton was, of course, Marvell's old friend whom Marvell had (possibly imprudently) defended in the House of Commons a year earlier. Milton may well have been an unpopular figure in Hull in any case: another republican, his friend Robert Overton, governed the garrison in the 1650s and no doubt left sour memories, especially among the community's Presbyterians. For all that, neighbouring York had also experienced republican governors and retained a significant Presbyterian presence; there is no record of the same symbolic violence there. The book-burning indicated the factional intensity of Hull and the manner in which Marvell, for all his support in the town, was marginalized.

It was in this somewhat ostracized state that Marvell temporarily escaped his civic duties in May 1662 by leaving for Holland without previously warning the Bench. His removal proved too good an opportunity for his enemies to ignore, Bellasyse and Robert Hildyard encouraging the burgesses to 'proceed against him' and 'endeavour a new choice'.[25] Marvell returned in time to save his place and witness his brother-in-law, Edmond Popple, embroiled in a significant struggle with the Bench. Popple was elected alderman on 2 July 1663, a place that the Bench would not allow him to fill without swearing against the Solemn League and Covenant. Popple refused 'the office and the oath' twice, each time explaining that he could 'take the oath set down for regulating corporations but cannot suffer the declaration for renouncing the covenant'. After seeking legal advice the Bench reluctantly began negotiations with Popple for a fine; they also inscribed the oath against the Solemn League and Covenant in the minute book and saw that all office-holders took it. Again, this was not a measure introduced in York. Popple agreed to pay £150 on 27 November 1663 in four instalments. Sixteen days later, in a significant gesture, he paid the fine in full: his debt to the Bench was paid and he was relieved from holding office (and so reneging on the Covenant). The depth of the divisions that the conflict reflected was revealed on 7 January 1664, when the election to replace Popple as alderman was boycotted by the burgesses, who were clearly not entirely supportive of the position taken by the Bench.[26]

By the end of 1663, therefore, Marvell was representing a civic community the governors of which were ostentatiously hostile to Milton and the Covenant and closely aligned to the garrison, gentry and bishops. The initial struggle for the Restoration effectively lost, Marvell resorted to prudence and civility on his return from Holland, working efficiently alongside Gilby in the Commons and encouraging the burgesses to remain 'friends' with 'Gentlemen your neighbours' even as relations became increasingly – and inevitably – strained by the events and revelations of the 1660s and early 1670s (*Letters*, 84). Even then, though, the partisan preferences of the Bench were entrenched: when Marvell ventured to recommend the Earl of Sandwich as a replacement High Steward in 1670 the Bench ignored him and elected Bellasyse instead (*Letters*, 106). The choice, it transpired, was imprudent. Bellasyse was Catholic and it must have been with some satisfaction that Marvell watched him excluded from this and his other offices by the 1673 Test Act, even more that the burgesses subsequently approached Marvell to broker with the Duke of Monmouth to take the position. Marvell could report in November 1677 how 'using words of great civility to your selves and the Town, [Monmouth] told me that he would be ready to gratify you in any expedient you should propose' (*Letters*, 199). The worm had to some extent turned.

Although Marvell's civic idealism did not equate with political reality, his practical experience of citizens was not limited to the Hull Bench. On the contrary, Marvell found solace in at least three overlapping friendship networks in the years after 1660. The most obvious of these was with his 'brothers' and 'cousins' in the Society of Trinity House in Hull. As well as regulating shipping into the port, the Society proved a sanctuary for burgesses like Edmond Popple who were disenchanted with the Bench and its political orientation. Marvell was not only extremely active in London on behalf of the 'worthy society' but also maintained close links with the equivalent body in Dartmouth; it is also telling that although Marvell made no mention to the Bench of his trip to Holland, he was keen to reassure the Society of his intentions. Edmond Popple had nominated Marvell for freedom of the borough in the 1650s and remained his closest ally in the town. The strength of kin that this suggests is poignantly expressed in Marvell's letters to his nephew, William Popple, a London citizen and wine merchant based in Bordeaux. William was a writer and polemicist in his own right, authoring numerous poems and plays, translating Locke's *Letter on Toleration* from the Latin in 1689, publishing *A Rational Catechism* (1687), and taking a significant interest in Marvell's literary estate. While a factor in Bordeaux he served as a conduit not only for Marvell's familial affections but also for the MP's expressly imprudent and uncivil observations about the condition of English politics.

If the Popples of Hull and Bordeaux were one source of civic consolation for Marvell then the Thompson brothers in the city of York were another. The Thompsons originated from the East Riding, which might explain their friendship with Marvell. Three of the sons of the patriarch Richard Thompson – Henry, Stephen, and Edward – apprenticed as wine merchants in the households of Henry and Leonard Thomson (no relation to the Thompsons), leaders of York's mercantile and civic elite before and during the mid-century troubles. Although the Thomson brothers relinquished their interest in civic politics at the Restoration, it was continued, along with their wine business, by their erstwhile apprentices: Henry, Edward and Stephen all served as Lord Mayor and Sir Henry was an MP for York from 1673. Marvell's letters to Edward and Henry reveal an unusual familiarity; Edward is always addressed as 'mon tres cher ami' ('my very dear friend') and Sir Henry was clearly privy to Marvell's famously secretive drinking circle (*Letters*, 305, 315). Moreover, as with Edmond and William Popple this was the companionship of politically like-minded citizens. At the Restoration the citizenry in York chose an alternative political course to the burgesses in Hull: there was no burning of Milton's books nor reneging on the Covenant; dissenters were protected by the civic authorities and the garrison was distrusted; strategic buildings were not sold (indeed Henry Thompson purchased the fortified Clifford's Tower in order to keep the corporate body 'entire'). More to the point, Sir Henry and Edward Thompson were leading progenitors of what can be legitimately described as nascent Whiggism within the city.

The same can be said, finally, of Marvell's friends and kinsmen among the London citizenry – in particular Richard Thompson (identified by Marvell's early editor H. M. Margoliouth as the younger brother of Sir Henry and Edward) and Richard's cousin Edward Nelthorpe, of whom Marvell was especially fond. Both Richard and Nelthorpe were frenetically active in the metropolitan politics of the 1670s, leading the campaign of London's Common Council against the Court of Aldermen, agitating for Parliament to be dissolved, and playing a leading role in the coffeehouse culture that the court attempted to censor. Their activities were irreparably complicated at the end of 1677 when the joint-stock company they had formed went bankrupt and they were declared outlaws by the House of Commons. As a result Thompson and Nelthorpe were excluded from civic office and forced into hiding to avoid their creditors. It was in this company that Marvell's satirical and polemical writings were spawned and in which, somewhat extraordinarily, he eventually located his household. For the last six months of his life Marvell and his 'help-meet' who was soon to present herself as his literary executor and as Mrs Mary Marvell lived not so much in a private house as in a nexus for itinerant and indebted citizens.

Conclusion: commonwealth and nation

Marvell's experience of corporate and parliamentary politics was a source of frustration. His alternative civic networks, built around powerful bonds of male friendship and kin, provided degrees of ideological and affective sustenance that contributed in a much more obvious fashion to the critical opinions articulated in his polemics. These opinions were rooted in a set of assumptions fostered by a tradition of civic humanism that reached back well into the sixteenth century: to a proud if imperilled genealogy of 'commonwealth'. This might seem a strange claim to make for a man who used the term 'commonwealth' only twice in his collected correspondence, and then in derogatory fashion. On 20 November 1669 he reported 'that [Colonel] Ludlow was in England that Commonwealths men flock about the town & there were meetings said to be where they talked of new Models of Government'. Five days later he recalled how Westminster was rife with rumours 'that there was some great & evil design on foot, & many old Army common welths & Council of States men and Outlaws & foreigners about town' (*Letters*, 90, 91). The point to remember is that the *word* 'commonwealth' was damaged goods after 1660. Appropriated as the moniker of the regimes of the 1650s, it had become separated from the *concept* of commonwealth as it had developed under the care of humanist and Protestant reformers in the sixteenth and early seventeenth centuries. After 1660 the idea of the collective good of the people that was distinct from and served by sovereign authority needed a new semantic home; for Marvell this was without doubt the 'Nation'.

To give just a few examples: in June 1663, just after his mysterious trip to Holland, he almost inadvertently distinguishes between 'the service of the King and the Nation'. The following decade Marvell reassured Mayor Foxley that 'in the more general concerns of the nation [I] shall god willing maintain the same incorrupt mind and clear conscience, free from Faction or any self-ends, which I have by his Grace hitherto preserved' (the reassurance is ironic: Foxley had been instrumental in outpoliticking Marvell in 1661). By January 1678 Marvell could sign a letter to the burgesses of Hull 'New years day 1678 which I wish happy to you and the Nation'. This followed more than a decade pondering and discoursing 'the State of the Nation', the 'Safety of the Nation', 'the true Interest of the Nation', 'the peace and safety of the nation', 'the apprehensions of the Nation'; and so on (*Letters*, 37, 172, 202, 163, 182, 195, 162, 186, 184). This national sensibility was never meant to diminish the power of the 'state', whether republican, Cromwellian, or monarchical. On the contrary, Marvell was well aware that for England to survive and flourish as a Protestant and commercial nation in the global conditions of the later seventeenth century its citizens required a central administration that was creditable, rational and, most important, effective both militarily and diplomatically. It was only then that the interests of the nation could be advanced and defended. While Oliver and Richard Cromwell had delivered or promised many of these qualities, it was quickly evident that the restored Stuarts could not. By the time Marvell wrote *An Account of the Growth of Popery and Arbitrary Government*, his polemical masterpiece, it seemed clear the court of Charles II was uncivil and imprudent, that the discursive capacity of the nation had been denuded, that the integrity of its institutions – its places – had been jeopardized. As such, the regime represented precisely the antithesis of the civic humanist values that Marvell held dear: it exemplified not so much the florescence of Ciceronian values in English guise as the unmediated exertion of arbitrary and tyrannical 'will'.

NOTES

1. Hull City Archives (HCA), BRB4, f. 55.
2. Conal Condren and A.D. Cousins, 'Introduction', in Condren and Cousins, eds., *The Political Identity of Andrew Marvell* (Aldershot, 1990), 4–8.

3. Mike Pincombe and Cathy Shrank, 'Introduction', in Pincombe and Shrank, eds., *The Oxford Handbook of Tudor Literature* (Oxford, 2009).

4. Annabel Patterson, *Marvell: The Writer in Public Life* (Harlow, 2000), 25–7.

5. Reinhart Koselleck, *The Practice of Conceptual History: Timing History, Spacing Concepts* (Stanford, 2002), 216.

6. Phil Withington, *The Politics of Commonwealth: Citizens and Freemen in Early Modern England* (Cambridge, 2005).

7. William Lamont, 'The Religion of Andrew Marvell: Locating the Bloody Horse', in Condren and Cousins, eds., *Political Identity*, 151.

8. Richard Tuck, *Philosophy and Government 1572–1651* (Cambridge, 1993), 2; Keith Wrightson, *English Society 1580–1680* (London, 1982), 191–4.

9. Jennifer Richards, *Rhetoric and Courtliness in Early Modern Literature* (Cambridge, 2003).

10. Annabel Patterson, *Marvell and the Civic Crown* (Princeton, 1978), 15–17.

11. HCA, BRB4, f. 367.

12. N. H. Keeble, '"I would not tell you any tales": Marvell's Constituency Letters', in Condren and Cousins, eds., *Political Identity*, 111–34.

13. Cited in Patterson, *Marvell: The Writer in Public Life*, 27.

14. Keeble, 'Marvell's Constituency Letters', 118.

15. John Barston, *The Safeguard of Societie* (1576), B1r.

16. Andrew Sharp, ed., *The English Levellers* (Cambridge, 1998), 110.

17. Jonathan Barry, 'Civility and Civic Culture in Early Modern England: The Meanings of Urban Freedom', in Peter Burke, Brian Harrison and Paul Slack, eds., *Civil Histories: Essays Presented to Sir Keith Thomas* (Oxford, 2000), 181–96.

18. HCA, BRB4, f. 309.

19. HCA, BRL19, 20, 21.

20. HCA, BRB4, f. 336.

21. HCA, BRB4, ff. 396; 351; 313, 378.

22. HCA, BRB4, ff. 357–9, 369–70, 371–2, 376

23. HCA, BRB4, f. 373.

24. HCA, BRB4, f. 399.

25. HCA, BRL669; BRB4, ff. 503, 34.

26. HCA, BRB4, ff. 522, 526–27, 528, 551, 553, 556, 561.

Further reading

Jonathan Barry, 'Civility and Civic Culture in Early Modern England: The Meanings of Urban Freedom', in Peter Burke, Brian Harrison and Paul Slack, eds., *Civil Histories: Essays Presented to Sir Keith Thomas* (Oxford, 2000), 181–96.

   'Bourgeois Collectivism? Urban Association and the Middling Sort', in Jonathan Barry and Christopher Brooks, eds., *The Middling Sort of People* (Basingstoke, 1994), 84–112.

Christopher Brooks, 'Apprenticeship, Social Mobility, and the Middling Sort, 1550–1800', in Jonathan Barry and Christopher Brooks, eds., *The Middling Sort of People* (Basingstoke, 1994), 52–83.

Patrick Collinson, *Elizabethan Essays* (London, 1994), especially 'De Republica Anglorum: Or, History with the Politics Put Back' and 'The Monarchical Republic of Queen Elizabeth I'.

Mark Goldie, 'The Unacknowledged Republic: Office-holding in Early Modern England', in Tim Harris, ed., *The Politics of the Excluded, c. 1500–1850* (Basingstoke, 2001), 153–94.

John F. McDiarmid, ed., *The Monarchical Republic of Early Modern England* (Aldershot, 2007).

Markku Peltonen, *Classical Humanism and Republicanism in English Political Thought 1570–1640* (Cambridge, 1995).

Jennifer Richards, *Rhetoric and Courtliness in Early Modern Literature* (Cambridge, 2003).

Cathy Shrank, *Writing the Nation in Reformation England, 1530–1580* (Oxford, 2004).

Paul Slack, *From Reformation to Improvement: Public Welfare in Early Modern England* (Oxford, 1999).

'Great and Good Towns, 1540–1700', in Peter Clark, ed., *The Cambridge Urban History of Britain, Vol. II, 1540–1840* (Cambridge, 2000), 347–76.

Robert Tittler, *The Reformation and the Towns in England: Politics and Political Culture, c. 1540–1640* (Oxford, 1998).

Phil Withington, *The Politics of Commonwealth: Citizens and Freemen in Early Modern England* (Cambridge, 2005).

'Public Discourse, Corporate Citizenship and State Formation in Early Modern England', *American Historical Review* 112 (2007), 1016–38.

8

ANDREW McRAE

The green Marvell

To write about nature and the environment in Marvell's poetry is to risk accusations of simple-mindedness. For nature is rarely – if ever – just nature for Marvell. In the tradition of pastoral poetry, the natural world provides an avenue, with its own rich and highly stylized stock of imagery, for reflecting on wider issues of human life, ranging from love and sexuality through to matters of state. Indeed, in the context of the mid seventeenth century, as other essays in this volume repeatedly remind us, politics infiltrated all poetic kinds, imprinting its own logic and symbolism even upon apparently uncommitted texts. In Marvell's estate poem *Upon Appleton House, To My Lord Fairfax*, for example, 'the tallest oak', brought down by the 'feeble stroke' of a woodpecker, is also King Charles I, executed by the stroke of an axe just a few years before the poem was written (lines 551–2). But sometimes it is worth stating the obvious. While a tree may carry many associations within a poem, there is surely some value to be derived from considering it *as a tree*. Moreover, there is arguably some cause, given Marvell's repeated attention to the natural environment, to engage with the insights of the emergent body of 'eco-criticism', which is committed to exploring the ways in which ecological discourses shape and inform literary texts.

This approach, like so many others one might take to Marvell, comes hedged with caveats. Marvell is not a programmatic poet. Hence, just as it is notoriously difficult to ascribe coherent political arguments to his works, it is fruitless to try to position him as some kind of pre-modern environmental campaigner. Marvell is much more elusive than that; as Donald M. Friedman states, he is not so much a presenter of arguments as 'an observer of the process of thought itself'.[1] Furthermore, it must be acknowledged that the modern environmental movement is a relatively recent creation, and has the most shadowy of origins in the early modern period. There was no such thing as a study of ecology in seventeenth-century England, and to read Marvell in the light of this discipline's insights risks the crude interpretative errors of anachronism. These caveats, however, also indicate the value of

Marvell's work in this context. For, while he was not a scientist or theorist, his poems contain some of his century's most sensitive reflections on relations between humanity and the natural world. They repeatedly centre attention on particular natural environments and their inhabitants, clarifying in the process some of the period's critical debates about uses and abuses of the land. And they reveal a mind grappling its way towards new kinds of appreciation of the natural environment.

The present discussion aims, above all, to contextualize Marvell's 'green thought'. Rather than reading his poems in search of modern ecological perceptions, it is arguably more valuable to situate these works in relation to seventeenth-century perceptions and discourses. This goal dictates the structure of the chapter, which moves from a consideration of the meanings of environment and environmentalism in Marvell's time, through to more specific engagement with particular poems. The key texts here are hardly surprising; although Marvell drew upon a stock of natural imagery throughout his career, certain works attend more rigorously to the environment. These include the group known as 'the Mower poems', as well as the century's most remarkable poetic exploration of a particular rural estate, *Upon Appleton House*.

Environment and environmentalism in Marvell's England

Some ways of perceiving the world can become so pervasive that it is a struggle to think our way out of them. When approaching the seventeenth century, however, it is important to appreciate that this was a culture with only a rudimentary interest in what we understand as ecology. The modern mantra that decisions taken by individuals about uses of the earth's resources will affect the entire planet, for instance, was alien within this context. But what else was it possible to think? How else could contemporaries of Marvell make sense of the natural world and the position of human beings within it? What intellectual models, and what other discourses, were available to them? Once we start asking such questions, we might discover some sophisticated ways of making sense of the world. Crucially, though, we might also discover that 'ecological' ideas and images are almost impossible to isolate. Rather, they were richly enmeshed with other strands of thought, from the religious to the economic.

When average men and women in early modern England looked upon the land, it is fair to say that their most pressing considerations were those concerning ownership and use. By contrast with a modern structure of absolute property, most land in early modern England was laid open to multiple claims. Hence, while estates had identifiable landlords, their rights to use the land as they wished were often heavily circumscribed by the competing rights of others. These could range from rights of tenancy through to more specific rights of usage, including rights of grazing, rights to collect firewood, and rights of passage. Uses of the land were similarly governed by sedimentary layers of experience and ideology, which lent further shape to local society. According to the prevailing theory of agricultural land management, or 'husbandry', the manorial estate was like 'a little commonwealth', to be managed in a way that would support its various inhabitants.[2] For landlords this model could place a powerful constraint on individualism, positioning the lord as a mere steward, responsible for those beneath him and ultimately answerable to God. For those beneath the lord and directly involved in working the land, the natural world was a site at once of community and labour, though rarely an entirely reliable place of belonging. The notion of 'home', as Don E. Wayne has shown in his reading of Ben Jonson's poetry, was a bourgeois construction, unavailable to the rural masses.[3] Moreover, local environments themselves assumed the status of texts, inscrutably holding within them the threats of harvest failure and dearth, and thus constantly demanding interpretation. Almanacs and a range of books on husbandry, along with rich sedimentations of local lore, instructed farmers on how to observe the signs of nature, and as a result maintain a precious and precarious state of order.

These structures, however, were under acute pressure in the early modern period. Indeed a range of factors, including rising prices and population, propelled efforts to transform social and spatial relations in the English countryside. In many respects the definitive change was the enclosure of common land: the act, put simply, of eradicating the traditional grid of customary rights and replacing it with recognizably modern structures of property. While much of England remained unenclosed in Marvell's lifetime, and while many acts of enclosure proceeded relatively unproblematically, some elicited violent protests, and served to crystallize radically opposed perceptions of rural society. For enclosing landlords, the land was their 'own', to manage and rearrange as they chose. For those losing customary rights, however, even if they received some form of compensation, enclosure could be experienced as a form of dispossession which rendered them fundamentally placeless. Hence a recurrent image in agrarian complaint literature, from the time of Sir Thomas More's *Utopia*, is of husbandmen being transformed into vagrants as villages are cleared for sheep pastures. Most enclosure riots were thus essentially conservative, aiming to restore a lost order. In regions where uses of the land were also being transformed, such as areas of fenland which were drained and therefore appropriated for conventional forms of agriculture, some of the protests were particularly intense. In such instances the process of change – or, as the reformers preferred to say, 'improvement' – involved not merely changes in property relations but fundamental transformations in relations between individuals and places.

By the time that Marvell was writing, however, there was also an established strand of protest literature which dared to imagine a world in which relations between humans and the land were not determined by property. The idea of communism, famously entertained by More in *Utopia*, filtered through subsequent generations, identifiable on the fringes of agrarian protests. In the Oxfordshire Rising of 1596, for example, one of the leaders was said to have 'intended to kill the gentleman [sic] of that countrie, and to take the spoile of them', as the first step towards a national revolution.[4] Shakespeare mimicked such contemporary voices when he staged the historic rebellion of Jack Cade in *2 Henry VI*. In the words of Cade's followers: 'it was never merry world in England since gentlemen came up' (IV.ii.6–7). In the climate of religious radicalism that gripped the nation in the 1640s and 1650s, such arguments acquired a greater degree of sophistication. Gerrard Winstanley, who led a group that styled itself the True Levellers (though they became known popularly as the Diggers), declared boldly that 'The Earth … was made to be a Common Treasury of relief for all', and that structures of property were distorting this divinely ordained structure. Winstanley represented the earth as a 'mother' to all of humanity, which should not be hindered from 'giving all her children suck'. He sought to realize this vision by establishing a community on common land at St George's Hill, Surrey, which he and his followers aimed to farm through 'righteous labour, and the sweat of our browes'.[5] This audacious and short-lived exercise attracted the interest of Marvell's patron, the parliamentary general Sir Thomas Fairfax, and is most likely recalled in the reference to 'Levellers' in *Upon Appleton House* (line 450).

Scientific thought of the period reassessed human uses of the land in somewhat more practical ways. Again, though, approaching the early modern period with modern preconceptions of an intellectual discipline would be misleading. For science, almost as much as Winstanley's politics, was to a considerable degree forged out of other discourses and practices, particularly those of religion. This helps to explain the attraction of the philosophy of vitalism or animist materialism, which appears to have informed some of Marvell's work. Vitalism 'holds in its tamest manifestation the inseparability of body and soul and, in its boldest, the infusion of all material substance with the power of reason and self-motion'.[6] This movement prompted a wide range of speculation on different kinds of systems – paradigmatically the human body, but also natural environments, and even artificial structures such as those of the state – and the connections between them. More influential, in the long run, was the movement that has become known as the 'scientific revolution', or the 'new philosophy', that drew its inspiration above all from Francis Bacon. For Bacon, the pursuit of empirical knowledge about nature was a moral duty, entirely in accord with the teachings of religion. In particular, he liked to cite Proverbs 25:2: 'It is the glory of God to conceal a thing: but the honour of kings is to search out a matter.'[7] The subsequent movement of enquiry, which reached its peak a generation after Bacon's death, at the time when Marvell was most active as a poet, valued investigation over received wisdom, reform over custom.

All these various developments of Marvell's era – which we might reasonably try to isolate and label as religious, economic, scientific, political, and so on – contributed to a culture within which human uses of natural resources were exposed to unprecedented scrutiny. Underpinning this culture was a definitive concern for sustainability. As the nation's growing population placed increasing demands on resources, almost all the debates outlined above were drawn in some way to the question of how to manage the increasingly problematic relation between humanity and the natural world. Some scholars have argued, as a result, that the modern conception of ecology can be dated to this period.[8] While this offers a stimulating approach, we must constantly remind ourselves that any perception of ecology was richly intertwined with other discourses. Indeed, one might suggest, it was moulded out of those discourses.

Marvell's nature: 'plain and pure'

When considering any of these issues in Marvell's poetry, the word that demands immediate consideration is 'nature'. Attention to Marvell's use of this word – notoriously knotty as it is in any era – may in fact offer a way of unpicking this poet's complex representations of relations between humans and the natural world. A range of influences press upon this word: from the contemporary debates outlined above, to the literary resources of the pastoral mode. As Friedman has argued, the effort of nineteenth-century critics to position Marvell as 'a worshipper of nature who had somehow hit upon the Wordsworthian mode of apprehension in the middle of the seventeenth century' was unquestionably misguided.[9] Yet it is nonetheless fair to argue that Marvell, in his famously interrogative poetry, was questioning seventeenth-century understandings of nature. He brings different models, with their conflicting voices, into a state of creative tension, and reaches as a result towards some strikingly novel perceptions.

The tradition of pastoral literature weighed heavily on Renaissance poets. After the model of Virgil, pastoral was appreciated as the classic vehicle through which to announce a poetic career, and in the sixteenth and seventeenth centuries it became one of the most overworked of modes.[10] Pastoral is a capacious category, encompassing many different ways of representing the natural world. One ancient strand of pastoralism, particularly influential in the seventeenth century, gravitates towards an idyllic vision of easy harmony between humanity and a nurturing environment. By comparison, Virgil had established a model, in his *Eclogues*, of a more equivocal nature poetry, which questions the place of humans within the natural world just as it scrutinizes Roman politics. In Marvell's work, similarly, the idyllic vision is consistently invoked but always problematized: threatened, typically, by the exigencies of the contemporary world. For instance, the innocent speaker of *The Nymph Complaining for the Death of her Fawn* boasts of an enclosed and secret space:

> I have a garden of my own,
> But so with roses overgrown,
> And lilies, that you would it guess
> To be a little wilderness. (lines 71–4)

The mode of direct address is carefully chosen. Marvell's point is that the nymph's addressees are so corrupted by experience of the world that not only can they not find her private garden, but they could not recognize its perfection if they did. But even here the vision is exposed to scrutiny. The fawn has been shot by 'wanton troopers riding by' (just as England had been violated in Marvell's time by the agents of civil war), and the nymph stands fundamentally helpless as she clutches variously at religious and legal arguments against them (line 1). Taking a cue from eco-criticism, one might even suggest that her own pronounced ownership of the animal – 'my fawn' (line 2) – exposes her claim against the troopers as essentially a matter of property. The pastoral myth, therefore, cannot quite be made to stick to the English landscape, for all the efforts of the speaker.

This poem, like many of Marvell's works, centres attention on a garden. Although the preferred style of gardens in seventeenth-century England, by modern standards, was relatively contrived and ornate, the garden represented to early modern eyes nature at its most refined. As Bacon wrote: 'God Almighty first planted a garden. And indeed it is the purest of human pleasures.'[11] Marvell's *The Garden*, which is his most intent reflection on gardens, opens as a quintessential celebration of pastoral *otium* (meaning freedom from business, or ease):

> How vainly men themselves amaze
> To win the palm, the oak, or bays;
> And their uncessant labours see

Crowned from some single herb or tree,
Whose short and narrow vergèd shade
Does prudently their toils upbraid;
While all flow'rs and all trees do close
To weave the garlands of repose.

Fair Quiet, have I found thee here,
And Innocence thy sister dear!
Mistaken long, I sought you then
In busy companies of men.
Your sacred plants, if here below,
Only among the plants will grow.
Society is all but rude,
To this delicious solitude.   (lines 1–16)

The governing conceit here plays upon the use of particular plants – 'the palm, the oak, or bays' – as symbols of achievement in particular spheres of human activity (military, civic and poetic, respectively). The poem, by contrast, dares to imagine a world in which even structures of symbolism give way to the essential qualities of plants themselves. Withdrawal from society enables the speaker to discover not only 'Quiet' and 'Innocence', but an engagement with the 'sacred'. As all readers of this poem discover, however, this vision cannot be sustained. His description of himself 'Stumbling on melons' and 'fall[ing] on grass' comically invokes the Fall in the Garden of Eden (lines 39–40); the rejection of sexuality ('Two Paradises 'twere in one | To live in Paradise alone' (lines 63–4)) feels prudish and sterile; and the closing admiration of 'the skilful gard'ner' who has fashioned 'flow'rs and herbs' into the form of a sundial introduces time, art and labour into the world of the poem at a single stroke (lines 65–6). In the process, the pastoral myth of harmony with nature is deftly unpicked.

This notably ambivalent examination of the garden is pursued, from a more distinctive perspective, in *The Mower against Gardens*. This poem stages Marvell's version of the art/nature debate, which had become a staple of the pastoral tradition. His speaker (to whom I will return in the following section) adopts an extreme position, figuring gardens as artificial perversions of nature:

Luxurious man, to bring his vice in use,
  Did after him the world seduce:
And from the fields the flowers and plants allure,
  Where Nature was most plain and pure.   (lines 1–4)

The garden is here posited as a product of a lascivious and rapacious humanity. The sexual overtones are sustained throughout, developed in particular detail when the Mower attends to the contemporary debate over grafting:[12]

> And yet these rarities might be allowed
>   To man, that sov'reign thing and proud;
> Had he not dealt between the bark and tree,
>   Forbidden mixtures there to see.
> No plant now knew the stock from which it came;
>   He grafts upon the wild the tame:
> That the uncertain and adult'rate fruit
>   Might put the palate in dispute.   (lines 19–26)

For the Mower, there is an essential purity to the 'wild', which is 'tame[d]' – or, more pointedly given the poem's sexualized discourse, 'enforced' (line 31) – by the act of grafting. By contrast, he insists, 'Nature' remains 'willing' to 'dispense', to everyone, its 'wild and fragrant innocence' (lines 33–4).

The human imposition upon the natural form of a tree – evident here in the image of the grafting gardener dealing mysteriously 'between the bark and tree' – clearly weighed upon Marvell's imagination. In *Upon the Hill and Grove at Bilbrough, To the Lord Fairfax*, for instance, written on an estate held by Fairfax, Marvell figures his patron's wife as 'the deity of a sacred grove' situated at the heart of the estate, and Fairfax himself as 'her devotee'.[13] Fairfax, the poem claims, often 'retired' to the grove:

> And on these oaks engraved her name;
> Such wounds alone these woods became:
> But ere he well the barks could part
> 'Twas writ already in their heart.   (lines 45–8)

By comparison, in *The Garden* the speaker takes a step further from human referents, stating: 'Fair trees! Where'se'er your barks I wound, | No name shall but your own be found' (lines 23–4). Yet the problem, for each poem, is that not only the definition of property rights and the act of carving a name, but even the process of giving a name, is acknowledged as a product of human culture. And human culture, for all the fundamental urge in each poem for a sense of identification with these other, arboreal inhabitants of the garden, is acknowledged as essentially violent in its engagement with nature.

In a number of other poems, Marvell's effort to imagine essential natural forces beyond the appropriating hand of humanity leads to a preoccupation with roots. In both *Upon Appleton House* and *The Garden*, the physical point at which a tree's root emerges from the ground is chosen as a site of connection with place. In the former, the scene is ostensibly one of angling; however, the imagery transfigures the speaker into the landscape:

> Oh what a pleasure 'tis to hedge
> My temples here with heavy sedge;
> Abandoning my lazy side,
> Stretched as a bank unto the tide;
> Or to suspend my sliding foot,
> On the osier's underminèd root,
> And in its branches tough to hang,
> While at my lines the fishes twang!   (lines 641–8)

The playful mysticism of this passage is swapped in *The Garden* for a more forthrightly ecstatic vocabulary:

> Here at the fountain's sliding foot
> Or at some fruit-tree's mossy root,
> Casting the body's vest aside,
> My soul into the boughs does glide.   (lines 49–52)

Elsewhere, imagining roots within the ground informs perhaps his most moving image of the sympathy between humanity and nature, as he describes not only 'the flow'r with'ring' in response to the death of Oliver Cromwell's daughter (and, by implication, to that of Cromwell himself, which followed shortly), but also pictures 'The sad root' which 'pines in secret under ground' (*Poem upon the Death*, lines 55–6). The former image is a textbook study in pathetic fallacy; the latter is more distinctive and personal. The Mower reminds us elsewhere that even roots may not be beyond the acquisitive grasp of culture; the tulip's 'onion root', he laments, may be 'sold' for the price of 'a meadow' (*The Mower against Gardens*, lines 15–16). Yet his desire to identify a source, or site, of natural vitality with which to identify is as much the poet's as his own.

Much critical attention has been devoted to the action of the poet's mind in *The Garden* as, in a state of ecstasy, it creates

> Far other worlds, and other seas;
> Annihilating all that's made
> To a green thought in a green shade.   (lines 46–8)

Debate has focused particularly on the relation of human creativity to natural processes of growth. Critics have struggled, for instance, to position the verb, 'Annihilating', as suggestive of transcendence and omnipotence rather than destruction and obliteration.[14] Undeniably, though, the connection between the poet's concentration on a definitive quality of nature – greenness – and a sense of creative release is pivotal. The word 'green' punctuates Marvell's poems, signifying a vital nexus of ideas and emotions which underpins so much of his work. This includes, variously, associations of youth, growth and creativity; however, above all else, it centres upon nature, glimpsing in this instance a primal sense of harmony between the poet and this particular green place. Indeed, there is unquestionably something distinctive about this poet in his effort not only to think his way through existing conceptions of nature, but also to imagine principles and even physical sites which are beyond the appropriating hand of human culture. Equally characteristic, however, as this discussion has demonstrated, is his appreciation of the ultimate futility of this exercise. Human culture is acknowledged, time and again, as universally violent and acquisitive, inscribing its meanings and values upon the natural environment.

The mower

As other chapters in this volume demonstrate, Marvell's poetic canon is characterized by subtle shifts of voice and manipulations of personae. Acts of interpretation, as a result, involve wrestling with insubstantial, and often inconsistent, voices. One such figure is the mower. The group of four pieces that are known collectively as 'the Mower poems' is comprised of three entirely in the Mower's voice and one written in the third person but structured nonetheless around the Mower's speech. In one of the four he is named as Damon, but in the others he is merely 'the Mower'. Beyond this group, Marvell invites points of comparison with *Upon Appleton House*, which locates a lengthy mowing scene within a particular place. This attention to mowers and mowing is arresting, especially if the poems are situated in relation to the pastoral tradition, which traditionally employs shepherds as at once protagonists and emblems of a particular kind of engagement with nature. Moreover, Marvell's attention to the mower functions not just on a literary plane but also contextually, scrutinizing the uses and meanings of the land through the imagined consciousness of a labourer.

Marvell's mower is defined by his labour. While an economic historian might well say something similar about shepherds, their textual history was utterly different; the shepherd of pastoral literature was typically an exemplar of *otium*, as contrasted with engagement in the business of life in the city and at court. In some strands of the pastoral tradition, moreover, his association with leisure led to authorial assumptions that the shepherd was truly a figure of the gentleman or nobleman. He might thus be translated into an owner of flocks rather than a hired hand, while the pastoral mode might be exploited as a vehicle through which 'to insinuate and glaunce at greater matters'.[15] Pastoral is thereby disentangled from the actual business of a contemporary landscape and its economy; at its extremes, as William Empson has argued, it aestheticizes economic relations, 'imply[ing] a beautiful relation between rich and poor'.[16] But Marvell is concerned to undo this process. There was some precedent for his project, since the ploughman had an established presence in

English cultural history, linked especially to a literature of agrarian complaint.[17] The mower, though, was effectively free of literary associations, yet very clearly located in the English rural economy. Men were employed as mowers on daily rates of pay for roughly two months of the year, usually combining this employment with various other forms of work.[18] They were thus easily associated with the heavy labour of summer, and by implication with wider social and economic relationships. The villagers who exercise their customary rights to graze their cattle on the fields of Nun Appleton, for instance, may in actuality have been the same people who had recently mown those fields (*Upon Appleton House*, lines 451–4).

Within this context, Damon's determined self-definition is immediately arresting: "'I am the mower Damon, known | Through all the meadows I have mown'" (*Damon the Mower*, lines 41–2). Some critics are struck by Damon's simplicity or naïvety, especially when compared to some of the sophisticated shepherds of the pastoral tradition. Such readings attend to Damon in the manner of a character in a play, and follow the overt narrative of his thwarted love for the shepherdess Juliana.[19] But it might be worth, for the moment, trying to set this narrative aside, and to focus instead on that essential claim to an identity and integrity founded upon labour and place. At one point he even lays claim to a form of property in the land:

> What, though the piping shepherd stock
> The plains with an unnumbered flock,
> This scythe of mine discovers wide
> More ground than all his sheep do hide.
> With this the golden fleece I shear
> Of all these closes every year.
> And though in wool more poor than they,
> Yet am I richer far in hay. (*Damon the Mower*, lines 49–56)

One way of interpreting this passage is to argue that, by staging the Mower's deluded claims to ownership of the product of his labour, the poem is complicit in the period's entrenched exploitation of wage labour.[20] This is without doubt compelling; for all his infamous political equivocation, Marvell was no socialist. But it is perhaps equally valid to identify the Mower's 'organic immersion' in his environment, by virtue of his role in cycles of life and death that bind human beings to the natural world.[21] As Marvell figures Damon imagining the landscape nurturing him in his labour the sun, for instance, 'lick[ing] off my sweat' at noon, or 'the ev'ning sweet' providing 'cowslip-water' in which to bathe his feet (lines 45–8) – he examines a form of engagement with nature equally valid, though also equally contrived and illusory, to that of the ecstatic speaker in *The Garden*.

Yet it is entirely characteristic of Marvell's verse that such images are not allowed to stand unchallenged. Mowing is acknowledged in these poems as an act of violence, imposing forces of culture upon both land and labourer. In one stanza of *Damon the Mower*, for instance, the narrative voice interrupts Damon's speech to observe his indiscriminate sweeps of his scythe:

> While thus he threw his elbow round,
> Depopulating all the ground,
> And, with his whistling scythe, does cut
> Each stroke between the earth and root,
> The edgèd steel by careless chance
> Did into his own ankle glance;
> And there among the grass fell down,
> By his own scythe, the mower mown.   (lines 73–80)

What does it mean to strike 'between the earth and root'? This is another of those Marvellian images that defies efforts of visual realization, working instead through an emotional power of suggestion. It recalls the violence of grafting, or carving upon trees, suggesting not natural cycles but rather interruptions to 'the natural flow of growth and sustenance'.[22] And Damon himself is not only brought down himself by this violence, but figured in another poem as at once physically and psychologically uprooted: 'so displaced | That I shall never find my home' (*The Mower to the Glow-worms*, lines 15–16). While the agent of this displacement is Juliana, the authorial act of loosening the Mower from his proclaimed unity with the landscape bears wider connotations. Indeed, it is entirely characteristic of these poems that such claims, whether made by mowers or gardeners, should be exposed not only to an ironic scrutiny, but even to a degree of ridicule.

The 'calm beauty' that critics have identified in the Mower's speech is therefore situated within an altogether more complicated social and economic context.[23] Rural environments are places of beauty and abundance, within which labourers as well as landlords, Marvell suggests, may experience momentary sensations of integration with natural processes. Yet they are at the same time sites of labour and exploitation, violence and deracination. The Mower poems are not consistent, nor do they move towards a sense of resolution; they rather allow different voices, images and perceptions to jostle within the space of a text, making various claims upon the reader's attention. Crucially, this process resists critical efforts to identify an argument that might, however anachronistically, be labelled 'green'. Discourses of nature are altogether too rigorously enmeshed with those of rural economy to support such interpretative strategies.

The estate

Marvell's most detailed poem of place takes the manorial estate as its subject. *Upon Appleton House* is generally positioned as a belated, and characteristically unconventional, contribution to the early Stuart genre of the country house poem. This genre's most influential products, pieces such as Jonson's 'To Penshurst' and Thomas Carew's 'To Saxham', manage acts of panegyric on patrons by centring attention on their estates. The estate thus exemplifies, for the poet, the moral and ethical qualities of its owner. Marvell's poem adapts this model to the more problematic subject of his patron's retirement, at the age of thirty-eight, from his command of the Parliamentary forces in the nation's civil wars to his Nun Appleton estate in Yorkshire. Numerous studies of the poem, as a result, have attended to its fraught politics. But *Upon Appleton House* is also distinctive in its length (776 lines) and its detailed survey of the estate as a geographical unit, as the poet moves outward from the house, through the gardens, fields and into the surrounding woods. Ken Hiltner reminds us that the word 'ecology' literally translates from the Greek as 'the "account" (*logos*) of the "house" (*oikos*)'.[24] Working within the parameters of this definition, one might argue that Marvell offers in this poem one of his century's most important exercises in ecological poetics.

The country house poem typically insists upon the order and harmony of its subject, positioned in contrast to architectural and moral excesses evident elsewhere in the country. Marvell extends this trope into an essay on proportion:

> Why should of all things man unruled
> Such unproportioned dwellings build?
> The beasts are by their dens expressed:
> And birds contrive an equal nest;
> The low-roofed tortoises do dwell
> In cases fit of tortoise-shell:
> No creature loves an empty space;
> Their bodies measure out their place.   (lines 9–16)

The analogy with animals, characteristically pastoral, is initially challenging for any attempt at an eco-critical reading, since the house, and the estate on which it stands, bears only the most tenuous relation to a bird's nest or a tortoise's shell. Yet, if we can once accept the social politics of Marvell's implication that a great lord by his very nature will require a great estate, the argument might be seen as a key to the poem's appreciation of ecology. For 'nature', as Raymond Williams has taught us, is never a politically innocent word.[25] In this poem, nature is thus not the 'plain and pure' principle that the

Mower espouses, but a force which can be brought into agreement with human structures of ownership and use. 'But all things are composed here', he declares, 'Like Nature, orderly and near' (lines 25–6).

Nun Appleton is represented thereafter as a working estate. Indeed the poem merges elements of pastoral with others derived from georgic, the literary mode committed to descriptions of agricultural cycles. But Marvell's version of georgic is markedly equivocal, all too aware of the demands that human culture makes of the land. Suitably for a poem set in summer, though also tellingly within the Marvellian canon, the central image of labour is one of mowing. The 'tawny mowers' of this poem, however, 'Who seem like Israelites to be', distinctly lack the sensitivity of Damon:

> With whistling scythe, and elbow strong,
> These massacre the grass along:
> While one, unknowing, carves the rail,
> Whose yet unfeathered quills her fail.
> The edge all bloody from its breast
> He draws, and does his stroke detest;
> Fearing the flesh untimely mowed
> To him a fate as black forbode.
>
> But bloody Thestylis, that waits
> To bring the mowing camp their cates,
> Greedy as kites, has trussed it up,
> And forthwith means on it to sup:
> When on another quick she lights,
> And cries, 'He called us Israelites;
> But now, to make his saying true,
> Rails rain for quails, for manna, dew.'   (lines 393–408)

The essential violence of the act of mowing is here accentuated by the accidental death of a bird. What is for Fairfax a source of fodder that will sustain his herds of cattle through the winter, and for the mowers a site of paid labour, is for the rail a habitat. In its resolution of this struggle over a natural resource, the poem is typically inscrutable. 'Thestylis' is an ironically pastoralized name given to one of the women supporting the male mowers in the meadow. Her interjection into the narrative unsettles the troubled and judgemental tone, positing instead a kind of crude peasant wisdom. And this cannot easily be dismissed. Acts of 'bloody' destruction, the poem acknowledges, underpin human engagements with the natural world. Cloaking them in biblical terms, as Thestylis does, is a comic act of opportunism; the metamorphosis of a lamented victim into a snack, however, is figured by the poem as a quintessential act of human culture.

The poem's concern with the uneasy relation between usage and destruction is developed in a subsequent scene set in the estate's wood. Although this passage is principally pastoral in mood, as the poet describes himself listening to the song of stock doves and treading carelessly on a bed of 'gelid strawberries', the period's debate over woodland management provides an insistent subtext (line 530). This 'double wood of ancient stocks', the poem suggests, might have provided 'Fit timber' even for Noah (lines 489, 485–6). In Fairfax's time, as the demands of war were ravaging the nation's resources, causing concern in particular about the viability of timber stocks, it could obviously have provided a supply fit for any number of uses. The wood's forester ('holt-felster', or keeper of the woods), however, is not a man but a hewel, or green woodpecker:

> But most the hewel's wonders are,
> Who here has the holt-felster's care.
> He walks still upright from the root,
> Meas'ring the timber with his foot;
> And all the way, to keep it clean,
> Doth from the bark the woodmoths glean.
> He, with his beak, examines well
> Which fit to stand and which to fell.   (lines 537–44)

Humans, we recall from other poems, cannot help but meddle with trees. This poem's hewel, by contrast, truly manages the wood, surveying tree trunks from the roots upwards, and 'glean[ing]' woodmoths from the bark in order to protect the trees. Yet, as the poem's diction discloses, this is little more than an ecological fantasy. Indeed the act of 'Meas'ring' and also the classification of 'fit[ness]' – echoing the earlier endorsement of the wood's 'Fit timber' – acknowledge equally the thrifty gaze of a true forester. The wood is thus positioned as a site within which the competing demands of the estate's various species may be assessed, though not necessarily resolved.

As happens so often in Marvell's works – and as, indeed, is typical of discourse on the natural world throughout his era – pastoral myths of plenitude and harmony are therefore simply not allowed to stand. Nature is unknowable in isolation from its uses; ecology is inseparable from economy. Throughout the poem, in fact, there is an acute appreciation of pressure on resources. After the meadow has been mown, for instance, the villagers introduce their cattle:

> which it closer rase;
> And what below the scythe increased
> Is pinched yet nearer by the beast.   (lines 452–4)

The verb, 'pinched', registers with keen sensitivity the demands being placed not merely on individual blades of grass but on the wider ecological unit of Fairfax's estate. As Robert Markley argues, in this poem 'humankind is continually, if implicitly, threatening to destroy the very conditions that, through our labor, we idealize and seek to recreate'.[26] And these dangers, the poem is honest enough to acknowledge, are products of the very structures of culture that the poem is so determined to celebrate.

Claims that Marvell's poems 'create . . . an ecological way of thinking' remain contentious.[27] There is at once too great a gulf between seventeenth-century conceptions of the environment and those of our own time across which to stretch the definition of ecology, and simply too little commitment to argument in Marvell's notoriously open and interrogative verse. Nonetheless, as readers increasingly attend to issues relating to the environment and its sustainability – to what we might now refer to as 'green thought' – Marvell's poetry will rightly command attention. He writes in unique and searching ways about the natural world, the ways it is perceived by humanity, and the ways in which human culture at once draws sustenance from it and threatens to devastate it. Marvell assembles, in his poems, the perspectives and discourses that might make a rudimentary form of environmentalism possible. His own green thought, however, like so much about the man and his work, remains elusive.

NOTES

1. Donald Friedman, 'Andrew Marvell', in Thomas N. Corns, ed., *The Cambridge Companion to English Poetry, Donne to Marvell* (Cambridge, 1993), 278.
2. John Norden, *Surveiors Dialogue* (1610), 27.
3. Don E. Wayne, *Penshurst: The Semiotics of Place and the Poetics of History* (Madison, WI, 1984).
4. Edwin F. Gay, 'The Midland Revolt and the Inquisitions of Depopulation of 1607', *Transactions of the Royal Historical Society*, new series, 18 (1904), 238.
5. *The Works of Gerrard Winstanley*, ed. George H. Sabine (Ithaca, NY, 1941), 252, 265, 260.
6. John Rogers, *The Matter of Revolution: Science, Poetry, and Politics in the Age of Milton* (Ithaca, NY, 1996), 1.
7. Charles Webster, *The Great Instauration: Science, Medicine and Reform 1626–1660* (London, 1975), 341.
8. Diane Kelsey McColley, *Poetry and Ecology in the Age of Milton and Marvell* (Aldershot, 2007); Ken Hiltner, *Milton and Ecology* (Cambridge, 2003).
9. Donald M. Friedman, *Marvell's Pastoral Art* (Berkeley, 1970), 124.
10. Sukanta Chaudhuri, *Renaissance Pastoral and Its English Developments* (Oxford, 1989).
11. Francis Bacon, *Essays*, ed. John Pitcher (London, 1985), 197.
12. On this debate, see Rebecca Bushnell, *Green Desire: Imagining Early Modern English Gardens* (Ithaca, NY, 2003), 148–60.

13. *Poems*, 207, lines 43–4n.
14. See especially Jonathan Crewe, 'The Garden State: Marvell's Poetics of Enclosure', in Richard Burt and John Michael Archer, eds., *Enclosure Acts: Sexuality, Property, and Culture in Early Modern England* (Ithaca, NY, 1994), 274; Friedman, *Marvell's Pastoral Art*, 167; Friedman, 'Andrew Marvell', 285.
15. John Fletcher, *The Faithfull Shepheardesse* (1610?), sig. ¶2v; George Puttenham, *The Arte of English Poesie* (1589), ed. Gladys Doidge Willcock and Alice Walker (Cambridge, 1936), 38.
16. William Empson, *Some Versions of Pastoral* (London, 1986; originally published 1934), 11.
17. Andrew McRae, *God Speed the Plough: The Representation of Agrarian England, 1500–1660* (Cambridge, 1996), 23–57.
18. Rosemary Kegl, '"Joyning my Labour to my Pain": The Politics of Labor in Marvell's Mower Poems', in Elizabeth D. Harvey and Katharine Eisaman Maus, eds., *Soliciting Interpretation: Literary Theory and Seventeenth-Century English Poetry* (Chicago, 1990), 95.
19. See, e.g., Linda Anderson, 'The Nature of Marvell's Mower', *Studies in English Literature* 31 (1991), 131–46.
20. Kegl, '"Joyning my Labour to my Pain"'.
21. Rogers, *The Matter of Revolution*, 62.
22. Friedman, *Marvell's Pastoral Art*, 135.
23. Susan Snyder, *Pastoral Process: Spenser, Marvell, Milton* (Stanford, 1998), 54.
24. Hiltner, *Milton and Ecology*, 26.
25. Raymond Williams, *Keywords: A Vocabulary of Culture and Society* (London, 1976), 219–24.
26. Robert Markley, '"Gulfes, Deserts, Precipices, Stone": Marvell's "Upon Appleton House" and the Contradictions of "Nature"', in Gerald MacLean, Donna Landry, and Joseph P. Ward, eds., *The Country and the City Revisited: England and the Politics of Culture, 1550–1850* (Cambridge, 1999), 100.
27. McColley, *Poetry and Ecology*, 14.

Further reading

Rebecca Bushnell, *Green Desire: Imagining Early Modern English Gardens* (Ithaca, NY, 2003).

Sukanta Chaudhuri, *Renaissance Pastoral and Its English Developments* (Oxford, 1989).

Donald M. Friedman, *Marvell's Pastoral Art* (Berkeley, 1970).

Anthony Low, *The Georgic Revolution* (Princeton, 1985).

Diane Kelsey McColley, *Poetry and Ecology in the Age of Milton and Marvell* (Aldershot, 2007).

Andrew McRae, *God Speed the Plough: The Representation of Agrarian England, 1500–1660* (Cambridge, 1996).

Robert Markley, '"Gulfes, Deserts, Precipices, Stone": Marvell's "Upon Appleton House" and the Contradictions of "Nature"', in Gerald MacLean, Donna Landry and Joseph P. Ward, eds., *The Country and the City Revisited: England and the Politics of Culture, 1550–1850* (Cambridge, 1999), 89–105.

Susan Snyder, *Pastoral Process: Spenser, Marvell, Milton* (Stanford, 1998).

Keith Thomas, *Man and the Natural World: Changing Attitudes in England, 1500–1800* (London, 1983).

James Turner, *The Politics of Landscape: Rural Scenery and Society in English Poetry 1630-1660* (Oxford, 1979).

Robert N. Watson, *Back to Nature: The Green and the Real in the Late Renaissance* (Philadelphia, 2006).

Raymond Williams, *The Country and the City* (London, 1973).

9

JOAD RAYMOND

A Cromwellian centre?

Marvell returned in 1647 from travels in Europe, where he had, according to a later employment reference written by John Milton, learned some Dutch, French, Italian and Spanish. He also learned to fence. In Italy he may also have acquired grounding in political theory, judging by a later allusion to him as 'a notable English Italo-Machiavillian'.[1] His first recorded action on his return was to sell some property in Cambridgeshire. All told, on his return he may have been well suited for a literary-political career in 1650s Britain.

During the republican decade he found employment first as a tutor working for the scions of powerful men – for Mary Fairfax, daughter of Sir Thomas Fairfax, commander-in-chief of the army in England and Ireland, and subsequently for William Dutton, ward of Lord Protector Oliver Cromwell – then as Latin Secretary to Secretary of State John Thurloe, and finally as MP for Hull. His life trajectory moves from personal associations and perhaps influence, as can be traced in the careful reflection of Fairfax's own interests, concerns and library in the meditative poem *Upon Appleton House, To My Lord Fairfax*,[2] to institutional status and authority. His writing during this period observes a more complex pattern. In contrast to the 1660s and 1670s, his literary output involved poetry rather than prose (though it cannot be said with any degree of certainty how many poems he wrote in these years). He is concerned with land and the nation, with political argument, political vocabularies, news, allegiance and loyalty. Yet, for all his pursuit of employment in the republican regime, his poems do not speak in a direct way of commitment or loyalty, or at least of the poet's commitments. They are at once exquisite demonstrations of technique and heuristic exercises. Most remained unpublished: *The First Anniversary of the Government under His Highness the Lord Protector* was printed as an anonymous pamphlet in 1655, in the guise of a piece of pro-Protectorate propaganda, advertised in the official government newsbook, and he penned songs performed at the wedding of Cromwell's daughter. Otherwise there is little evidence that his republican-period poetry was read or coloured perceptions either of the poet or of contemporary events.

When Robert Boulter and Mary Marvell, the poet's widow, collaborated over the 1681 volume *Miscellaneous Poems*, their initial plan had been to include Marvell's political poetry from the 1650s. The volume was an element in a Whig publishing campaign, seeking to capitalize on Marvell's reputation as a prose writer.[3] Doubts while the volume was at press, perhaps caused by a resurgence of anti-dissenter sentiment, led to the sudden decision to remove the three poems about Cromwell: *An Horatian Ode upon Cromwell's Return from Ireland*, *The First Anniversary* and *A Poem upon the Death of O. C.* The publishers may have been concerned that their inclusion would result in the censorship of the whole volume. The poems were cancelled from most copies of *Miscellaneous Poems*, surviving in only two copies and a manuscript transcription. Not until Edward Thompson's edition of 1776 were the poems unreservedly published, and reunited with Marvell's other poetry. This history forced the three poems into each other's company. They were made to constitute, through the retrospective actions of a posthumous publication history, a trilogy of poems about Cromwell. This trilogy moves – in what is perhaps the customary reading – from a hesitant and ambivalent declaration of interest, through an official and stolid support, to a personal expression of grief.

Scholarly criticism of Marvell over the past three decades has emphasized that his own views are hard to detect in his poems. His poems are a tissue of allusions, experiments with voices, profoundly rhetorical. Despite the use of the first person in the lyrics, they seldom express what Paul Hammond describes as the 'grammar of commitment'.[4] Yet the fierce intelligence with which Marvell engages with the geometry of political identity, allegiance and constitutions compels his readers to seek the associations between his poems and their contexts, and so to his own involvement in politics, however hard to pin down. The Cromwell trilogy is the keystone of accounts of Marvell's political identity prior to his career as an MP, but it is an 'accidental triptych'.[5] Not only does each speak to a different political moment, but each is, to a striking degree, also not a poem about Cromwell. Just as Marvell shuns speaking his own views, at least in any direct way, Cromwell is in his poems an aspect of political circumstance, and a figure for the difficulties of political engagement and the nature of historical change. For all his indefatigable unyieldingness, this is a pliable Cromwell.

An Horatian Ode upon Cromwell's Return from Ireland was for much of the twentieth century the object of exemplary criticism, that is, criticism that sought to demonstrate the nature of poetry or at least the correct way of reading poetry. In particular, the *Horatian Ode* was a testing ground for 'aesthetic' and 'historical' modes of literary criticism. In the 1920s, T. S. Eliot did much to revive Marvell's reputation, while inventing a literary history and an aesthetic that explained Eliot's own position in the pageant of literary tradition. Subsequently, a debate between Cleanth Brooks and Douglas Bush in the late 1940s and early 1950s (straddling the tercentenary of its composition in the summer of 1650) explored the complexities of the *Horatian Ode*'s presentation of Cromwell and Charles, and disputed its political allegiances and the role of intention and historical context in interpretation.[6] The *Horatian Ode* then became a testing ground for the New Criticism and, later, for various historicisms. John Wallace's deft study of Marvell's politics, *Destiny His Choice: The Loyalism of Andrew Marvell* (1968), presented a poem entangled with the terms of the Engagement Controversy and the dilemmas of allegiance following the regicide.[7] Wallace's Marvell articulates a conditional commitment to Cromwell, without irony or ambivalence but with a great deal of realpolitik, and Wallace argued with an unprecedented density of historical evidence and understanding. Annabel Patterson, who has stimulated much interest in Marvell's writing and has done more than anyone to (re-)establish Marvell as a poet of political engagement, argues that the *Horatian Ode* is committed to a Protestant imperial vision, rooted in classical precedent.[8] Subsequent critics, including Robert Wilcher and Blair Worden, have been more inclined to find traces of royalism in the poem, usually more sentimental than constitutional.[9] David Norbrook has allied its political complexities to the sublime aesthetics of republican literary culture.[10] John Creaser, comparing Marvell's prosody with Milton's, finds in the *Horatian Ode* an interplay between a disciplined framework and metrical and syntactical expressiveness that reflects the poet's notions of liberty, as well as his uncertainty about the virtues of the republic and its military champion.[11] While the *Horatian Ode* induces fascination, the density of the contexts that have been brought to bear upon it, the subtlety of its echoes, and the complexity of its argument suggest that far from being the 'well-wrought urn' of New Criticism – perfect, self-contained and unchanging – it is a text that resists timelessness and insists on an intoxicating contemporaneity.

The *Horatian Ode* has well-marked formal boundaries. Its stanzaic form, alternating couplets of iambic tetrameter and trimeter, is both unusual and strictly enforced. It has a cogent rhetorical structure, falling into six sections: an exordium, an encomium, a digression, a history, a deliberation on the future and a conclusion. These progress logically. The exordium addresses a 'forward youth', who is commended to pursue an active life in this time of public responsibility; there follows an encomiastic portrait of Cromwell; then, by way of digression, a portrait of Charles that ends with his execution; next, a forensic section on history compares the British republic to the Roman; this turns to a deliberative passage on the future that predicts and praises prospective conquests and envisages a 'climacterick' role for a British empire in world history; the conclusion offers advice to Cromwell that is implicit counsel to other citizens. These sections correspond to stages of an argument in which the speaker explores the circumstances of post-regicide Britain, and advises those who would be civic-minded to submit to Cromwell in expectation of future victories.

The praise of Cromwell has been read as ironic, and the *Horatian Ode* as a lament for the dead king. Charles I is portrayed as a foil, noble and passive, to Cromwell's embodiment of morally ambivalent force:

> He nothing common did, or mean,
> Upon that memorable scene;
> > But with his keener eye
> > The axe's edge did try.   (lines 57–60)

The sentiment that critics experience in reading about the regicide, at least in some parts of the world, hardly corresponds to Marvell's steely gaze. If the poem is read in the context of 1649 royalism, with its fetishization of the king's book *Eikon Basilike*, and the rapid construction, in pamphlets, broadsides and newsbooks, of the legend of the royal martyr, what is most powerful in these lines is Marvell's indifference. Marvell expresses no horror at the event, and any distaste is politely restrained. He omits to mention the heir to the throne, who was a unifying motif in royalist writing after January 1649. The king he describes is decorous, but he is going to his death, and consigning himself, along with the theatricality he embodies ('That thence the royal actor born | The tragic scaffold might adorn', lines 53–4), to history. Nature, the poet tells us, with a Machiavellian amorality, 'must make room | Where greater spirits come' (lines 43–4), and Cromwell is evidently a greater spirit. The encounter between the king's eye and the axe dramatizes, by metonymy, the shift from the old regime to the new. Yet the lines have more in common with journalism than with royalist elegy, express or covert. On the scaffold, while delivering his final, scripted speech, Charles twice warned off a man on the scaffold from touching the axe. *A Perfect Diurnal*, one of the several newsbooks that printed the official news of the execution, reports him as saying: 'Hurt not the Ax that may hurt me',[12] He was concerned that interference with the axe would dull its edge, resulting in a more painful, and perhaps less decorous execution. Marvell's king's eye is sharp with wisdom and the knowledge that he represents an older, more chivalric order, but also with anxiety. Marvell would most likely have learned this detail, and many others that shape and texture the poem, from reading the newsbooks. So would almost all of the poem's potential readership, as the king was inaudible to those not on the scaffold. There is in these lines a clever homophonic pun in 'axe' on '*acies*', the Latin for eyesight and a sharp edge, but there is also an attention to the details of history, as reported in the news, and to the power of journalism to capture history in the making. One of the most characteristic features of Marvell's poetry is its ability to contain both of these at the same time.

Marvell's praise of Cromwell may be oddly diffident, and too many of its locutions ('If we would speak true', 'his highest plot', 'ruin the great work', 'Justice against Fate complain') susceptible, with a little pressure, to uncomplimentary interpretation, but this is to say no more than that it is difficult praise. That is certainly the tenor of the concluding couplet – 'The same arts that did gain | A pow'r must it maintain' – which closes the case study in power explored in the poem. The *Horatian Ode* is, ultimately and significantly, not an encomium of Cromwell. The poet unambiguously counsels support of the commonwealth, and offers admiration of its military hero, but does so provisionally, on the understanding that allegiance can be withdrawn under less auspicious circumstances. The materials from which the ode is drawn – the generic transformations from Horace's odes, Lucan, Machiavelli – mark it as a republican poem of sorts, engaged in the effort to renovate literary culture, or at least develop a mode of writing capacious enough to respond to the stunning events of the preceding years.[13] Yet the voice in which it is spoken is not Marvell's but that of a persona Marvell creates to explore the grounds of political allegiance in the summer of 1650. It is a poem that praises Cromwell, but not a poem written in praise of Cromwell. It is a republican poem, but not in the sense that it advocates republicanism.

The poem published as *The First Anniversary of the Government under His Highness the Lord Protector* in 1655 had its title changed, in the abortive printing of 1681, to *The First Anniversary of the Government Under O. C.* The shift acknowledged the fading context of the Instrument of Government, but it also emphasized the man rather than the office, and hence the individual above the constitution that defined and limited his role. The poem is meditative in form, exploring the circumstances and events of the first year of the republican government based on a written constitution introduced by the Council of State in December 1653, under which Cromwell assumed the title of 'Lord Protector'. Marvell probably wrote the poem in December 1654 and January 1655. It is composed in couplets of iambic pentameter, and though the number of irregular stresses is unusually high for Marvell, and the sentences long and prosaic, the couplets are almost all closed, most with a heavy rhyme. While the form is disciplined and controlled, in contrast to the *Horatian Ode* the structure is muted. The poem has been described as fragmentary or disunified, and while some critics have searched for concealed rhetorical structures,[14] others have been willing to attribute its apparent incoherence to the damage done to poetry by assuming political commitments.[15] This may be because interpretations that claim the poem presents

Cromwell as a Davidic king, as a modern Augustus, as a candidate for the crown, as a biblical judge, or as a millennial hero, focus too exclusively on Cromwell, contrary to the complex perspectives of the poem.[16] The organizing principle of the poem is, as with the 'forward youth' of the *Horatian Ode*, the individual who is called upon to discover allegiances and commitments in contemporary political circumstances:

> And well he therefore does, and well has guest,
> Who in his Age has always forward prest:
> And knowing not where Heavens choice may light,
> Girds yet his Sword, and ready stands to fight;   (lines 145–8)

This individual – close to but not identical with Marvell himself – commends the constitution, and praises Cromwell as the central figure within that constitution, and not without some apprehensiveness. The poem is not a panegyric for Cromwell, though it was always vulnerable to being read as one because of the very difficult line that Marvell negotiates between the written constitution and the military leader. It is rather a deliberation on the constitution, its fortunes over the preceding year, and its immediate prospects, a deliberation that results in a demonstrative affirmation.[17]

The poem begins with praise of Cromwell as a leader not susceptible to human years, contrasting this with the earthly limitations of kings. A second section turns from Cromwell to Amphion, the legendary founder of Thebes, and a long simile in which the new constitution is described through a compelling musical–architectural metaphor. There then follows a deliberation on the role of the individual in this new state, including the lines quoted above, in which the poet plays with the possibility of the millennium, before firmly rejecting it (we must, he insists, accept and engage with affairs as they stand). This then leads, logically, though discomfortingly, into the narration of Cromwell's riding accident in 1654, in which the poet contemplates the death of the Lord Protector, presenting it as commensurate with a fall in nature. As this dark fantasy is dispelled, relief turns into a passage praising Cromwell for his interest in the public good, manifested in his taking up the office of Lord Protector, despite his reluctance; this is then juxtaposed against an attack on Fifth Monarchism, the millenarian political movement that Marvell probably thought most immediately threatened the fragile balance of power, including the promise of religious toleration included within the constitution. The conclusion puts praise in the mouths of foreign princes, Cromwell's natural enemies, who admire and fear Cromwell from a distance, before the final four couplets sign off in the poet's own supplicating voice, ending with the comparison of the Protector to the angel of Bethesda.[18]

Marvell subordinates the praise of Cromwell to his – or his speaker's – admiration of the constitution. Amphion's building is a carefully calibrated description of the Instrument of Government:

> The common-wealth does through their centres all
> Draw the circumf'rence of the public wall;
> The crossest spirits here do take their part,
> Fast'ning the contignation which they thwart;
> And they, whose nature leads them to divide,
> Uphold, this one, and that the other side;
> But the most equal still sustain the height,
> And they as pillars keep the work upright;
> While the resistance of opposèd minds,
> The fabric as with arches stronger binds,
> Which on the basis of a senate free,
> Knit by the roof's protecting weight agree.   (lines 87–98)

Marvell acknowledges the conflict within the country, but claims that this conflict binds together – echoing the 'brotherly dissimilitudes' in Milton's *Areopagitica* (1644) – the tripartite government, consisting of Parliament, Council of State and Lord Protector.[19] The terms of Marvell's praise identify the arrangements of the constitution. The legislative power lay in triennial parliaments, and the executive in the Council of State and the office of Lord Protector. The Lord Protector's office was elective, not hereditary. The forty-two clauses of the Instrument of Government placed significant limitations on the Protector's prerogative: he was not by any means a king by another name. One area of unlimited authority, however, was in international relations, in treating with foreign rulers, and in declaring war and peace (though here, as in other powers, he required the consent of a majority of the Council of State). Accordingly the Cromwellian court, usually restrained and understated, was more ceremonial when entertaining ambassadors. This is where Marvell's praise of Cromwell is most unlimited, and his deployment of the perceptions of foreign princes recognizes both government practice and constitutional provision.[20] Despite this caution, Marvell intimates the tension between constitution and the political realities. With the benefit of hindsight it is easy to be cynical about the disparity between a written constitution limiting Cromwell's authority and the leviathan figure who would brush it aside when he found it impractical. Warning of this possibility became evident within days of the publication of Marvell's poem when Cromwell dismissed the first Protectorate Parliament on 22 January 1655, irritated with its continued debating of the terms of the constitution.[21] Marvell's Cromwell always threatens to erupt through the constitution:

> For to be Cromwell was a greater thing,
> Than ought below, or yet above a king:
> Therefore thou rather didst thyself depress,
> Yielding to rule, because it made thee less.   (lines 225–8)

Herein perhaps is a warning, but otherwise the poem optimistically limits Cromwell to the terms of the constitution.

In praising the Protectorate's constitution, and Cromwell the man in terms of the office of Lord Protector, while nonetheless recognizing the tension between the individual and the political arrangements, Marvell engages with the political languages that characterized public, political discourse from late 1653 through early 1655; he speaks them, and reworks them, thinks through them. He echoes and overthrows Fifth Monarchist argument; he reworks political theory interpreting and contesting the Instrument of Government (or 'Government' as it was then most commonly termed); he encounters royalist polemics accusing Cromwell of tyranny or royal ambitions. He is thoroughly, entirely engaged with the world of pamphlets and newsbooks that lies beyond the poem. The same can be said of the *Horatian Ode*, though in *The First Anniversary* the sublimation of the language of reporting and polemic is less complete, and Marvell speaks to that world, and not just of that world. This ability to absorb the world of cheap print and turn it into something else, to blow hot sand into exquisite form, is a foundation of Marvell's aesthetics. This world has offered a focus to modern scholarship of seventeenth-century literature, though the role of pamphlets and newsbooks in shaping literary history and aesthetics needs further investigation. However, there was something acutely ephemeral about the context of *The First Anniversary*, beyond its trafficking with texts that were rapidly discarded and dismissed. The political moment of which it spoke was a brief one. It began with the inauguration of the new government – an event that further divided republicans into compromisers and outright opponents of Cromwell, forcing the former into coalition with other groups – and it ended with Cromwell's dismissal of the parliament; this period extended from 16 December 1653 to 22 January 1655. Shortly after the poem's publication its fragile balance seemed outdated, and the terms of the debate about the constitution and its provisions shifted to accommodate new arguments about prerogative. Later in 1655 the Council of State introduced a new layer of regional governance in the form of the military rule of the Major Generals, overturning the attempt by the Instrument of Government to separate army, religion and civil government.

In September 1657 Marvell was appointed Latin Secretary to John Thurloe. His personal association with Cromwell at this time is reflected in two songs he wrote for the marriage of Cromwell's third daughter, Mary, in November. Marvell's songs, both in pastoral settings, were probably performed at a musical entertainment celebrating the wedding. They were published in the 1681 *Miscellaneous Poems*. Cromwell was not expunged from the volume: also to survive the last-minute cancellations was the Latin epigram *In Effigiem Oliveri Cromwell*, which celebrates how all enemies flee Cromwell's image, while citizens enjoy quiet leisure (*otia*) under it, and another Latin epigram, *In eandem Reginae Sueciae transmissam*, to accompany a portrait of Cromwell sent to the Queen of Sweden.[22] Perhaps the quasi-Caroline form of the songs, and the social exclusivity of the Latin, ensured that these could survive the 1681 purge: they do not have the political intensity and interrogation of allegiance that the three longer poems manifest.

On 3 September 1658 Cromwell died. Over the coming months Marvell wrote an elegy for him, and on 23 November he followed the funeral procession: the plan for the event shows him walking with the other secretaries for foreign tongues, including Milton and Samuel Hartlib.[23] In the interim, following the abandonment of the rule of the Major Generals, Cromwell had declined the offer of the crown in February 1657 (he had done so previously in 1653, before accepting the title Lord Protector), and in June 1657 the Second Protectorate Parliament had introduced a substantially revised constitution, under the name of the 'Humble Petition and Advice'. This constitution reintroduced an upper house, gave the Protector the right to nominate his heir, and broadened his prerogative. It inaugurated a period of government closer to traditional monarchy in power and ceremonialism. Cromwell reassured the army officers, sincerely, that he did not like the title of king. Nevertheless poetry followed the gravity of court ceremony, and the patterns of constitutional change, and tended to portray Cromwell as a king, or not to rise to the challenge of finding new terms in which to praise him that distinguished him from monarchy and monarchical culture.[24] His burial at Westminster Abbey, and the elegies celebrating his life and death, reinforced this trend.

Marvell's *A Poem upon the Death of his Late Highness the Lord Protector* twice failed to be published. It was originally promised in January 1659 when the publisher Henry Herringman entered in the Stationers' Register a volume entitled *Three Poems to the Happy Memory of the Most Renowned Oliver, Late Lord Protector of this Commonwealth, by Mr Marvell, Mr Driden, Mr Sprat*. When this materialized later in 1659, Marvell's contribution had been replaced with a poem by Edmund Waller, and the volume was issued under the imprint of William Wilson. Marvell's poem is more complex than those in this volume and, because less conventionally elegiac, more bound to the political questions arising from Cromwell's death, which may explain its withdrawal. *A Poem upon the Death* was also withdrawn from the 1681 volume, though the first 184 lines are extant in a single copy (with the title *A Poem upon the Death of O. C.*), while the full text was transcribed in another copy of the *Poems*, and with the title given above, apparently from another source with significant variants. When the 1776 edition appeared this manuscript version was used; this text therefore has some authority. There is reason, then, as with *The First Anniversary*, to accept as authoritative the title that refers to Cromwell's office rather than his initials. *A Poem upon the Death of his Late Highness the Lord Protector* is nonetheless, in some ways, a personal poem, and one that has been interpreted as expressing a commitment to the man rather than to a political position.

Marvell combined praise for Cromwell as an individual with admiration of his achievements. The poem describes a ruler undefeated and seemingly invulnerable, who succumbs to grief over the death of his second daughter, Elizabeth (who died in August 1658). The imagining of Cromwell's death in *The First Anniversary* becomes a dress rehearsal for the actual event: nature groans, the skies open, and thunder roars in anticipation: 'Nature it seemed with him would Nature vie; | He with Eliza, it with him would die' (*A Poem upon the Death*, lines 133–4). The stars, that had blessed him all along, are left able only to choose an auspicious time for his death. Hence he dies on 3 September, the anniversary of his famous victories at Dunbar and Worcester, and his ghost is imagined presiding over the defeat of a Spanish army at Flanders (by a French army, albeit with some English troops) on the very day of his death. The praise, which situates Cromwell as an international force with cosmic backing, very much extends that driving the latter sections of *First Anniversary*. However, Marvell soon turns to a less formulaic vision of Cromwell's might:

> He first put arms into Religion's hand,
> And tim'rous Conscience unto Courage manned:
> The soldier taught that inward mail to wear,
> And fearing God how they should nothing fear. (lines 179–82)

Cromwell emerges as the deserving hand of Providence, and Marvell wants to record as well as approve Cromwell's leadership of a *praying* army. He is 'Heaven's favourite!' (line 157). He is praised too for his ability to keep in balance, though not to reconcile, opposing forces in the commonwealth:

> What prudence more than human did he need
> To keep so dear, so diff'ring minds agreed?
> The worser sort, as conscious of their ill,
> Lie weak, and easy to the ruler's will;
> But to the good (too many or too few)
> All law is useless, all reward is due.   (lines 217–22)

This harks back to the Amphion passage in *First Anniversary*, in which the Instrument of Government and the Protector are praised for creating a stable balance of contrary forces. Here, however, it is Cromwell's prudence, and his care even for his zealous and intractable subjects, that receive the poet's admiration.

After this juxtaposition of conventional and unconventional shades of panegyric there is a more radical departure, and a dramatic shift in tone and decorum:

> I saw him dead. A leaden slumber lies
> And mortal sleep over those wakeful eyes:
> Those gentle rays under the lids were fled,
> Which through his looks that piercing sweetness shed;
> That port which so majestic was and strong,
> Loose and deprived of vigour, stretched along: (lines 247–52)

The transformation underscores what makes this unusual among the myriads of seventeenth-century elegies: the poem is moving, and breaks the generic and classical expectations for a personal testimony, but only after Cromwell has been praised as a providential hero, and a leader who breaks the moulds of leadership. The shift into the first person brings into view the same catalyst that binds *An Horatian Ode* and *The First Anniversary*: the individual who deliberates upon the circumstances of the moment, and must find a means to express allegiance or active virtues in that moment. Here, however, the voice lingers on grief, and Cromwell's body offers a kind of *memento mori*, one that resonates with the future of the community as well as those that survive him. The speaker dwells on the death and (as in Milton's elegy 'Lycidas') a false hope that the corpse holds on to a trace of life:

> Yet dwelt that greatness in his shape decayed,
> That still, though dead, greater than death he laid;
> And in his altered face you something feign
> That threatens death, he yet will live again.   (lines 257–60)

After accepting the plain reality of death, the speaker finds a more settled and sustained consolation in Oliver's son, Richard, who succeeded to the title Lord Protector, while the father treads 'the bright abyss' (line 290), and, more substantially, in the way the image of Oliver, his honour, praise and name, will console English soldiers in future ages.

The weekly newsbook *Mercurius Politicus*, edited by Marchamont Nedham, published an obituary for 'His most Serene and Renowned Highness' (exactly the same formula Dryden used in his elegy). The obituary, probably written by Nedham, also shares a vision with Marvell. In promoting

the interests of Jesus Christ among the soldiery and people of Britain, writes
Nedham, Cromwell's

> spirit knew no bounds, his affection could not be confined at home, but brake
> forth into forein parts, where he was by good men universally admired as an
> extraordinary person raised up of God, and by them owned as the great
> Protector and Patron of the Evangelical Profession. This being said, and the
> World it self witness of it, I can only adde, That God gave him Blessings
> proportionable to all the virtues, and made him a Blessing to us, by his wisdom
> and valor to secure our Peace and Liberty, and to revive the antient renown of
> our Native Country.

Nedham also marked the historical significance of the date, and concluded
with the succession of Richard Cromwell.[25] Like *An Horatian Ode* and *First
Anniversary*, then, Marvell's elegy imaginatively engages with the news culture of the day, distilling its elements into something new.

The shock of the monosyllabic eyewitness testimony – 'I saw him dead' – is
its stark directness, its confrontation of death face to face. It is a risky piece of
poetic virtuosity. But it also, and surprisingly, correlates to other forms in
which Cromwell's death was represented.

> On Monday the 18 instant, the Representation of the person of his late Highness
> in Effigie, will be exposed to publick view at Somerset-house upon a Bed of
> State, vested with his Robe of Estate, a Scepter placed in one hand, a Globe in the
> other, and a Crown laid on a Velvet Cushion a little above the head, after the
> antient and most becoming Ceremony of the preceding Princes of this Nation
> upon the like occasion; which point of Honor is the more due to his memory, by
> how much he advanced the honor of our Country by his incomparable Actions,
> beyond the example of any that swayed the Scepter of this Land before him.[26]

This is how *Mercurius Politicus* reported Cromwell's lying in state. In death
the crown that he had spurned in life was assigned to him, though he was
distanced and perhaps insulated by the velvet cushion. A wooden effigy with a
wax mask was displayed rather than the corpse itself, because of concern over
the speed of decomposition. The body had already been secretly interred in
Westminster Abbey earlier, probably on 4 or 5 September.[27] We do not know
which image of death Marvell testified to in his stirring line. The effigy was
carried in a procession to Westminster Abbey on 23 September, and it was
this procession that Marvell participated in. This suggests that it was the
effigy, rather than the corpse, to which Marvell was a witness. Nedham, who
probably walked near Marvell in the procession, reported on the death of
Cromwell with a complex mix of affect and politics not dissimilar to the
elegy's mode. The fact of Cromwell's mortality was shocking, and the uncertainty over the future was articulated through descriptions of the body,

representations that exposed the disparity between his heroic actions and his frail, fatigued corpse. Marvell's elegy converges with the public language of reporting at precisely the point where it seems most intimate and affective.

The poem presents, without any resolution, the gulf between Cromwell's superlative virtues and powers, and the reality of his vulnerability, and it is this catachresis (a strained metaphor that misapplies a word or compares discordant things; a rhetorical device associated with metaphysical poetry) that is moving and imaginatively reaching. Yet Marvell's elegy is not a 'metaphysical' poem, if there is such a thing, any more than is *The First Anniversary*; it yokes together Oliver as person and Cromwell as providential force so we can see the distance between them. The product of this yoking is an expression of historical wonder. The personal dimension, the shocking 'I saw him dead' is, as for the newsbooks, only one element in its formula. The sentiment is coupled with historical analysis, though the two never quite resolve into an argument, and the aesthetics of the poem lodge partly in that gap. Marvell's praise of Cromwell's achievements in the elegy continues to focus on his foreign conquests, as in the Ode and *The First Anniversary*. It was perhaps this imperial vision that persuaded Marvell to support Cromwell through the 1650s.[28] If the doubtfully attributed *A Dialogue Between the Two Horses* is Marvell's it extends this viewpoint into the Restoration. In it Charles II's horse declares to Charles I's:

> I freely declare it, I am for old Noll.
> Tho' his Government did a Tyrants resemble,
> Hee made England great and it's enemies tremble.[29]

This reflects more widespread perceptions. Pepys observed in 1667 how 'everybody doth nowadays reflect upon Oliver and commend him, so brave things he did and made all the neighbour princes fear him'; he contrasted this with popular disappointment with the new king.[30] The sentiments of Pepys's interlocutors were moved by English ignominy in the second Anglo-Dutch war; this also occasioned Marvell's satirical *Last Instructions to a Painter*, in the background of which Cromwellian glory may shimmer. The catachresis of the elegy is compounded by Marvell's style, awkward and reticent. The problem lies in his syntax, not only carefully inverted but also, at times, unclear:

> What prudence more than human did he need
> To keep so dear, so diff'ring minds agreed?
> The worser sort, as conscious of their ill,
> Lie weak and easy to the ruler's will;
> But to the good (too many or too few)
> All law is useless, all reward is due.

> Oh! ill-advised, if not for love, for shame,
> Spare yet your own, if you neglect his fame;
> Lest others dare to think your zeal a mask,
> And you to govern only heaven's task.   (lines 217–26)

Even when the manifest sense has been extracted, much remains unclear, though without the logic of *The First Anniversary* or the artful dualities of *An Horatian Ode*. Various motives can be assigned to this: the poem was written in haste (or even is incomplete), performs the choking of grief or the demise of poetry with its hero, but such readings can only be speculative.[31]

For all of its timeless capturing of the experience of a moment, in other respects the elegy was time-bound. It concludes with praise of Cromwell's successor Richard, whom, as *Mercurius Politicus* reported, the Privy Council unanimously appointed Lord Protector, according to the terms of the Humble Petition and Advice, hours after Oliver's death. Marvell politicly acknowledges that Richard's career has been obscure, but promises that he will revive his father's virtue, for 'A Cromwell in an hour a prince will grow' (line 312). Referring to the storm that preceded the Protector's death, the elegy concludes:

> Cease now our griefs, calm peace succeeds a war,
> Rainbows to storms, Richard to Oliver.
> Tempt not his clemency to try his power,
> He threats no deluge, yet foretells a shower.

The suggestion that these words are critical of Richard is untenable. In poetic terms, however, the lines stumble, and, while doubtless complimentary, their reticence contrasts with the complex positiveness of Marvell's praise of Oliver. They are not so much ambiguous as vague, especially as the couplet concluding the poem. They may caution Richard's (republican) enemies against seeking to undermine him; they may warn Richard of difficult times ahead.[32] While the storm that precedes Oliver's death is interpreted as a disruption of nature, sympathetic to human affairs, this (later) rain is evidently political, and emphasizes how much smaller a soul Richard represents. Yet the window in which Marvell's praise made sense was a narrow one. Richard ruled peacefully and with cooperation for several months. Richard's first and only parliament met on 27 January, a week after Herringman registered his volume of elegies. Parliament debated the succession and the terms of the constitution, and an anti-protectoral, republican party in parliament began to develop links with army officers discontented with conservative and anti-tolerationist moves. Richard failed to broker peace between parliament and army, and when the army dissolved the parliament at the end of April he lost power, though he held on to some of the properties and trappings of his office. He formally resigned on 25 May. Marvell's praise of

Richard as Oliver's fitting successor must have been written before April, and its publication after this date would have been inappropriate or untimely. It may be that Marvell withdrew his poem from Herringman's volume of elegies for this reason. Today, knowing the unfortunate Richard's transitory political career, its immediate future makes the poem seem even more closely bound to the hour of Oliver's death. Like *The First Anniversary*, then, *A Poem upon the Death* became obsolete shortly after its composition, the former losing its timeliness even more swiftly, though not before it had been published.

During the 1650s Marvell also wrote three poems for, or addressed to, his other employer, Sir Thomas Fairfax: *Epigramma in Duos Montes Amosclivum et Bilboreum. Farfacio*; *Upon the Hill and Grove at Bilbrough, To the Lord Fairfax*; and *Upon Appleton House, To My Lord Fairfax*, all written in 1651 and published in 1681. While these clearly circle around the common themes of person and place, retreat and engagement, and the future of the country (though, unlike the Cromwell poems, without a strong providential element), they present no evident progression, and unlike the Cromwell poems, they have not been read as a sequential triptych. The temptation to read the three cancelled Cromwell poems as a trilogy is strong, but thereby to find a progression from ambivalence, through political support to personal commitment is to pressurize them into a narrative that they do not support. The weakness of the reading of each poem associated with this narrative becomes more apparent when they are detached from that narrative and read in their precise immediate historical moment. Their attachment to and engagement with their distinct historical moments renders them discontinuous. Each of the poems is also *not* about Cromwell in a different, significant way.

There are ways in which Marvell nonetheless pursues a developing pattern through the three poems. *An Horatian Ode* contains echoes of Lucan's *Civil War*, *The First Anniversary* contains echoes of both Lucan and the *Horatian Ode*, and *A Poem upon the Death* contains echoes of all of these. Motifs echo through them too: showers, vines, horses, suns, hunting. This intertextuality, and their shared poetic language, knits Marvell's poems together. There is a sense in which the Cromwell that emerges from this – indefatigable, like lightning, tree-blasting, providential and time-defying – is a figure in a triptych, but the continuity lies in a series of formal connections, rather than a biographical narrative. It is not Marvell's affections or personal allegiances or commitments we see expressed in the poems. He is a poet of many, ethereal voices. Among the other Cromwell poems, we can find one in which Marvell presents himself as none other than Cromwell himself:

> Cernis quas merui dura sub casside rugas;
> Sicque senex armis impiger ora fero;

Invia Fatorum dum per vestigia nitor,
Exequor et populi fortia jussa manu.

[You see what wrinkles I have earned beneath a cruel helmet; thus an old man I actively confront warfare; while I press forward through the pathless tracts of the fates and with my troops follow through the sturdy orders of the people.][33]

The verses accompanied (or were written to accompany) a portrait of Cromwell sent to Queen Christina of Sweden in 1654, and give a voice to that picture. If the poem did indeed arrive in Sweden, then it was in some sense authorized as Cromwell's own speech, part of the cultural trade in international diplomacy. It is the familiar Cromwell from Marvell's poems: he performs the people's orders, active, denying age, a force of, and to contend with, fate. Cromwell has resigned himself to Marvell's view of him. Its wry voice speaks to the other Cromwell poems, reminding us of Marvell's playfulness, even when he writes most seriously.

NOTES

1. W.H. Kelliher, 'Andrew Marvell', *Oxford Dictionary of National Biography*, online edn.
2. Derek Hirst and Steven N. Zwicker, 'High Summer at Nun Appleton, 1651: Andrew Marvell and Lord Fairfax's Occasions', *Historical Journal* 36 (1993), 246–69.
3. Nicholas von Maltzahn, 'Marvell's Ghost', in Warren Chernaik and Martin Dzelzainis, eds., *Marvell and Liberty* (Basingstoke, 1999), 50–74.
4. Paul Hammond, 'Marvell's Pronouns', *Essays in Criticism* 53 (2003), 219–34, quotes at 234, 220.
5. The phrase is from Christopher Wortham, 'Marvell's Cromwell Poems: An Accidental Triptych', in Conal Condren and A.D. Cousins, eds., *The Political Identity of Andrew Marvell* (Aldershot, 1990), 16–52.
6. Repr. in William R. Keast, ed., *Seventeenth-Century English Poetry: Modern Essays in Criticism* (New York, 1962), 321–58; and partly in Michael Wilding, ed., *Marvell: Modern Judgements* (London, 1969), 93–124.
7. John M. Wallace, *Destiny His Choice: The Loyalism of Andrew Marvell* (Cambridge, 1968), 69–105.
8. Annabel Patterson, *Marvell and the Civic Crown* (Princeton, 1978), 59–94; and her 'Andrew Marvell and the Revolution' in N.H. Keeble, *The Cambridge Companion to Writing of the English Revolution* (Cambridge, 2001), 107–23, at 115–16.
9. Robert Wilcher, *The Writing of Royalism, 1628–1660* (Cambridge, 2001), 287–8; Blair Worden, 'Andrew Marvell, Oliver Cromwell, and the Horatian Ode', in Kevin Sharpe and Steven N. Zwicker, eds., *Politics of Discourse: The Literature and History of Seventeenth-Century England* (Berkeley, 1987), 147–80, at 150.
10. David Norbrook, 'Marvell's "Horatian Ode" and the Politics of Genre', in Thomas Healy and Jonathan Sawday, eds., *Literature and the English Civil*

War (Cambridge, 1990), 147–69; and his *Writing the English Republic: Poetry, Rhetoric and Politics, 1627–1660* (Cambridge, 1999), 245–71.

11. John Creaser, 'Prosodic Style and Conceptions of Liberty in Milton and Marvell', *Milton Quarterly* 34 (2000), 1–13; and his 'Prosody and Liberty in Milton and Marvell', in Graham Parry and Joad Raymond, eds., *Milton and the Terms of Liberty* (Cambridge, 2002), 37–55.

12. *A Perfect Diurnall of Some Passages in Parliament* 288 (29 January-5 February 1649), 2316.

13. Norbrook, 'Marvell's "Horatian Ode"', 147–69, and *Writing the English Republic*, 261–71; Nigel Smith, *Literature and Revolution in England, 1640–1660* (New Haven, CT, 1994), 276–94; Smith's editorial annotations in *Poems*; Laura Lunger Knoppers, *Constructing Cromwell: Ceremony, Portrait, and Print, 1643–1661* (Cambridge, 2000), 52–6.

14. Annabel Patterson, *Andrew Marvell* (Plymouth, 1994), 39–40; R. I. V. Hodge, *Foreshortened Time: Andrew Marvell and Seventeenth Century Revolutions* (Cambridge, 1978), 112; Steven N. Zwicker, *Lines of Authority: Politics and Literary Culture, 1649–1689* (Ithaca, NY, 1993), 87; Patterson, *Civic Crown*, 68ff.; Wallace, *Destiny His Choice*, 114.

15. S. K. Heninger Jr, 'Marvell's "Geometric yeer": A Topos for Occasional Poetry', in C. A. Patrides, ed., *Approaches to Marvell: The York Tercentenary Lectures* (London, 1978), 87; Worden, 'Andrew Marvell', 147–80.

16. Joseph A. Mazzeo, 'Cromwell as Davidic King', in *Renaissance and Seventeenth-Century Studies* (New York, 1964), 183–208; A. J. N. Wilson, 'Andrew Marvell's "The First Anniversary of the Government Under Oliver Cromwell": The Poem and Its Frame of Reference', *Modern Language Review* 69 (1974), 254–73; Wallace, *Destiny His Choice*, 106–44; Steven N. Zwicker, 'Models of Governance in Marvell's "The First Anniversary"', *Criticism* 16 (1974), 1–12, and *Lines of Authority*, 60–89; Gerald M. MacLean, *Time's Witness: Historical Representation in English Poetry, 1603–1660* (Madison, WI, 1990), 240–8.

17. Derek Hirst, ' "That Sober Liberty": Marvell's Cromwell in 1654', in John M. Wallace, ed., *The Golden and the Brazen World: Papers in Literature and History, 1650–1800* (Berkeley, 1985), 17–53; Joad Raymond, 'Framing Liberty: Marvell's *First Anniversary* and the Instrument of Government', *Huntington Library Quarterly* 62 (2001), 313–50; David Loewenstein, *Representing Revolution in Milton and His Contemporaries* (Cambridge, 2001), Chapter 5; Norbrook, 'Marvell's "Horatian Ode"' and *Writing the English Republic*; Edward Holberton, *Poetry and the Cromwellian Protectorate: Culture, Politics, and Institutions* (Oxford, 2008), 101–18.

18. Wallace, *Destiny His Choice*, Chapter 3; Raymond, 'Framing Liberty'; Raymond, *Milton's Angels: The Early Modern Imagination* (Oxford, 2010), Chapter 9.

19. *Complete Prose Works of John Milton*, ed. Don M. Wolfe *et al.*, 8 vols. (New Haven, 1953–82), II:555.

20. Hirst, 'Marvell's Cromwell in 1654', 21–3; Raymond, 'Framing Liberty', 339–40.

21. Austin Woolrych, *Commonwealth to Protectorate* (Oxford, 1982), 375.

22. Trans. Smith, *Poems*, 313.

23. British Library, Lansdowne MS 95, no. 2, ff. 1–15; also Public Record Office, SP 18/182/90, f. 2.

24. Derek Hirst, 'The Politics of Literature in the English Republic', *The Seventeenth Century* 5 (1990), 133–55; Sean Kelsey, *Inventing a Republic: The Political Culture of the English Commonwealth, 1649–1653* (Manchester, 1997); Knoppers, *Constructing Cromwell*; Kevin Sharpe, ' "An Image Doting Rabble": The Failure of Republican Culture in Seventeenth-Century England', in his *Remapping Early Modern England: The Culture of Seventeenth-Century Politics* (Cambridge, 2000), 223–65.
25. *Public Intelligencer* 141 (30 August–6 September 1658), 794–5; *Mercurius Politicus* 432 (2–9 September 1658), 802–3.
26. *Mercurius Politicus* 438 (14–21 October 1658), 918.
27. John Morrill, 'Oliver Cromwell', in the *Oxford Dictionary of National Biography*, online edn.
28. Patterson, 'Andrew Marvell and the Revolution'.
29. *Poems and Letters of Andrew Marvell*, ed. H. M. Margoliouth, rev. Pierre Legouis with E. E. Duncan Jones, 2 vols. (Oxford, 1971), 1:212. Smith rejects the attribution. Patterson inclines towards it: 'Marvell and the Revolution', 108.
30. Quoted in Barbara Kiefer Lewalski, *John Milton* (Oxford, 2000), 455.
31. Smith, in *Poems*, 303–4.
32. Holberton, *Poetry and the Cromwellian Protectorate*, 191.
33. *In eandem Reginae Sueciae transmissam*, lines 3–6, in *Poems*, 315. Translation by Nigel Smith.

Further reading

Conal Condren and A. D. Cousins, eds., *The Political Identity of Andrew Marvell* (Aldershot, 1990).

Derek Hirst, ' "That Sober Liberty": Marvell's Cromwell in 1654', in John M. Wallace, ed., *The Golden and the Brazen World: Papers in Literature and History, 1650–1800* (Berkeley, 1985), 17–53.

Edward Holberton, *Poetry and the Cromwellian Protectorate: Culture, Politics and Institutions* (Oxford, 2008).

David Loewenstein, *Representing Revolution in Milton and His Contemporaries* (Cambridge, 2001), esp. Chapter 5.

David Norbrook, 'Marvell's "Horatian Ode" and the Politics of Genre', in Thomas Healy and Jonathan Sawday, eds., *Literature and the English Civil War* (Cambridge, 1990), 147–69.

Annabel Patterson, *Marvell and the Civic Crown* (Princeton, 1978).

Joad Raymond, 'Framing Liberty: Marvell's *First Anniversary* and the Instrument of Government', *Huntington Library Quarterly* 62 (2001), 313–50.

Nigel Smith, *Literature and Revolution in England, 1640–1660* (New Haven, 1994).

John M. Wallace, *Destiny His Choice: The Loyalism of Andrew Marvell* (Cambridge, 1968).

Blair Worden, 'Andrew Marvell, Oliver Cromwell, and the Horatian Ode', in Kevin Sharpe and Steven N. Zwicker, eds., *Politics of Discourse: The Literature and History of Seventeenth-Century England* (Berkeley, 1987), 147–80.

Steven N. Zwicker, *Lines of Authority: Politics and Literary Culture, 1649–1689* (Ithaca, NY, 1993), 60–89.

10

JOHN SPURR

The poet's religion

In 1928 Pierre Legouis characterized Andrew Marvell as 'poète, puritain, patriote'.[1] Marvell is pre-eminently a poet: that is why we read him today and why he is worth the attention of a volume of this kind. His 'patriotism' – by which Legouis meant his Whiggish criticism of Charles II, his opposition to the 'potent and subtle' French king Louis XIV, his assertion of Protestant liberty, and his defence of Parliament against corruption and intimidation – is even better appreciated today than it was in Legouis's era thanks to the boom in academic studies of Marvell the politician, satirist and controversialist that culminated in the publication of the first scholarly edition of his prose works in 2003. Of Legouis's three epithets, it is perhaps the middle term, 'puritan', that is now most difficult to associate with Andrew Marvell. The dour, killjoy, fundamentalist overtones of that label seem at odds with Marvell the lyrical poet, irreverent satirist and teasing writer who by turns encourages us to seize the day, to prize 'delicious solitude', or to see our social and political betters in all their human squalour.

Certainly Marvell's public attachments – his association with Oliver and Richard Cromwell, his parliamentary career, and his polemics in defence of the Nonconformists – place him unambiguously on the godly side of the great ideological divide of seventeenth-century England. As one near contemporary summed him up, Marvell was 'a man not well affected to the Church or Government of England'.[2] But he was never spotted at any Nonconformist conventicle, never sat as a hearer of one of the capital's many preaching ministers, never made a personal confession of faith – in fact, like all MPs, Marvell attended the services at St Margaret's Westminster, received communion there, and took the required oaths of loyalty and conformity. He even denied in print that he was a Nonconformist, although this denial was characteristically convoluted and equivocal. He cautioned readers not 'to impute any errors or weaknesses of mine to the Non-conformists, nor mistake me for one of them, (not that I fly it as a reproach, but rather honour the most scrupulous:) for I write only what I think befits all men in Humanity,

Christianity and Prudence towards Dissenters' (*PW*, 1:267). Given the rumour and innuendo that swirled around all public figures, and that in Marvell's case touched upon his sexuality, temper, drinking, authorship and much else, it is noteworthy that no offhand remark or spiteful insinuation has surfaced to link him with any Nonconformist meeting or minister.

None of this has prevented scholars from attempting to discern the ideological meaning of his associations, or from combing his writings for clues to his spiritual allegiances. Such efforts are part of a perhaps questionable attempt to see Marvell 'whole' and to establish his religious identity. Yet Marvell, possessed of a fluid, subtle mind, was a man of anything but fixed identity. His was an evolving temperament: he may have had a youthful dalliance with Roman Catholicism, he may have moved some distance through Puritanism and Nonconformity to a position that we could call Socinianism, and he certainly exchanged royalism for loyalism and recognized the advantage of a single ruler over a republic. Above all, he was 'amphibious': attuned to all sides of most questions, and able to explore a position without committing himself to it. Socially and politically, he moved in a number of different circles, and yet somehow always remained aloof or semi-detached. Intellectually, he inhabited the rich world of contemporary European culture. The pagan classics, the Bible, Renaissance literature, contemporary English and European literature, the traditions of symbolism, emblem books, Hermeticism, astrology, and the experience of his travels – all resonate in his writing. In the footnotes to the authoritative edition of Marvell's poems, Hermes Trismegistus jostles with Pliny, Plotinus with Lucretius, and poets old – Lucan, Virgil, Ovid – with poets new – Spenser, Herbert, Waller and Milton. In the face of such evident eclecticism, it is little wonder that the valuable if rather heavy-handed attempts of earlier generations to find a key to Marvell's poetic or personal sensibility in Neoplatonism, Calvinism, or millenarianism have now given way to more plural and open-ended readings.

Whatever the mode of his writing, whether as poet, polemicist, or historian, Marvell tries out voices, inhabits personae, and constantly subverts any attempt to establish an authorial position. Even his letters seem all too aware of their recipients, the conventions, or the dangers of speaking too openly. As a young tutor writing to Lord General Cromwell, Marvell could only praise him for placing tutor and ward 'in so godly a family as that of Mr Oxenbridge whose Doctrine and Example are like a Book and a Map, not onely instructing the Eare but demonstrating to the Ey which way we ought to travell'. A private letter of consolation to a grieving father recommends activity as well as 'The word of God: The society of good men: and the books of the Ancients' (*Letters*, 304–5, 312–13). In a letter of news to the godly Lord Wharton, Marvell enclosed a sermon preached at court by

Edward Stillingfleet on the folly of scoffing. His covering comment is balanced between praise and criticism of both the preacher and the times: Stillingfleet's sermon was 'so polish't as indeed suited with the delicacy of his auditory rather then the notoriousnesse of the Evill. For certainly the impiety of men is growne so ranke in this kind and all others, that if Ministers instead of preaching and arguing could thunder and lighten, it were all but too little' (*Letters*, 310). Such pious sentiments are what these particular correspondents might expect to hear. Marvell gives away nothing of himself in even the most apparently intimate of his poems or letters. In short, none of Marvell's writing and none of his actions will allow a simple reading of the author's religious convictions.

A poet of religion?

It has been argued that a handful of Marvell's poems treat the speaker's relationship with God seriously enough to qualify their author as a religious poet.[3] But Marvell's poetry is only 'religious' in the sense that almost all of the imaginative writing produced within the Christian culture of seventeenth-century England was religious: it is charged with biblical language, images and allusions; it gestures towards Christian presumptions about the structures of human personality or human history. This verse operates within a context, inherited from classical and Renaissance poetry and thought, that is predominantly secular, pagan and literary. As a result, religion is poeticized: lyric and pastoral poetry take up devotion and repentance as natural themes, contrast the orders of nature and grace, or play with symbols which fuse the Christian and the classical; in this poetry, mowers in the fields bear overtones of death and the Fall, just as glow-worms, those Renaissance emblems of prudence, are simultaneously reminders of the pale light cast by human reason on spiritual questions. In the last resort, these are matters best pursued through the poetry itself.

Clorinda and Damon is an overtly Christian poem that never mentions Christianity: the religion is all in the delicate allusions, and even then it strains against the poem's erotic undertow. Clorinda urges her shepherd to 'seize the short joys then, ere they vade' (line 8), but Damon has encountered Pan, and what had once 'been enticing things' (line 17) now look very different: 'grass withers' and 'flowers fade' in an echo of Isaiah 40:8 (line 7); caves formerly seen as venues for love-making are now 'Virtue's grave' (line 10) and offer no shelter from 'heaven's eye' (line 12); all the newly devout shepherd yearns for is to cleanse his soul and sing Pan's praises.

Eyes and Tears is in the devotional genre of the 'tear poem', which had been developed in English by overtly religious poets such as Southwell, Donne,

Crashaw and Vaughan to explore the relationship of nature, grace and penitence, but Marvell empties it of almost all spirituality. Bar one conventional stanza on the weeping Mary Magdalene and the sinner who washed Christ's feet with tears, this poem is given over to the physiological and other paradoxes of crying, to the human and the secular rather than the devotional. Similarly, *A Dialogue between the Soul and Body*, probably written around 1652, recasts a genre associated with the themes of death and judgement as a moral or philosophical essay: Marvell's poem offers nothing on sin or redemption, and no final resolution in which the soul shakes off the fetters of the human body. However, returning to the same ground later, perhaps after 1667, Marvell does take a more obviously spiritual line. *A Dialogue, Between the Resolved Soul, and Created Pleasure* celebrates the soul which 'conscious of doing what I ought' (line 24) sticks to its ideals – humility, self-mastery, and the attainment of heaven – in the face of sensual, aesthetic and intellectual pleasures: 'Earth cannot show so brave a sight | As when a single soul does fence | The batt'ries of alluring sense, | And Heaven views it with delight' (lines 45–8).

Even when addressing a directly Christian subject, Marvell appears just as much concerned with the formal properties of the verse or the poetical tradition within which he is writing as with the religious content. *An Epitaph upon Frances Jones* was carved on her memorial tablet in St Martin-in-the-Fields, London, in 1672 (and published in the 1681 *Miscellaneous Poems*). Frances, the unmarried 38-year-old daughter of Lady Ranelagh, was praised here through the paradoxical device of denying that any praise was necessary or adequate: 'Enough: and leave the rest to Fame. | 'Tis to commend her but to name' (lines 1–2). Her single state – 'a virgin chaste' – becomes an indictment of 'this age loose and all unlaced' (lines 9, 10); and her daily self-examination, an archetypal godly devotional practice, is offered as evidence that she was ready for death at any moment, 'her soul was on heav'n so bent' (line 13). The godliness to which this witty epitaph alludes so precisely is also captured in the paradox that gives the verse its form: the poem's claimed inability to offer praise is an exemplification of the self-denial that characterized the truly devout. Form serves theme in *Bermudas* (1653–4). This psalm-like poem was intended as a compliment to John Oxenbridge, an Independent divine closely associated with the colony of Bermuda (and host to Marvell and his pupil at the time), but it also reworks earlier poetical accounts of earthly paradises. A vision is offered of nature redeemed and transformed by divine grace. The poem pictures godly oarsmen singing in praise of their God whose providential care has led them to a new Eden: 'He lands us on a grassy stage; | Safe from the storms, and prelates' rage'; the metre imitates the metrical psalms so beloved of the Puritans, 'He cast (of which we rather boast) | The

Gospel's pearl upon our coast' (lines 11–12, 29–30). This is a celebration of Christian fellowship.

In his public verse, Marvell could not and would not wish to avoid the religious idiom of political life. Consider a poem like *The First Anniversary of the Government under His Highness the Lord Protector* which is chock-full of religious themes – apocalyptic and providential, anti-Catholic, pro-reformation – all of them relevant to that moment in 1654. Cromwell is a divinely appointed ruler, bent to heaven's will, and figured here as a prophet and judge, another Elijah or Gideon, through extensive use of Old Testament parallels. The violence of the poem's anti-Catholicism, its hatred of the 'monster' in 'her Roman den impure' (lines 128–9), is startling: the poet exhorts other princes to fall into step behind Cromwell as 'captain' of an anti-papal crusade, but laments their indifference, 'still they sing hosanna to the whore, | And her whom they should massacre adore' (lines 113–14). Yet we should never forget that this is propaganda, skilfully echoing Cromwell's own apocalyptic language and concerns, and putting some distance between the dangerous millenarianism of the Fifth Monarchy men and a different strain of millennial thought which waited upon Jesus Christ to set up his reign in men's hearts. It reinforces Cromwell's endorsement of liberty of conscience as a 'sober liberty', a liberty for the 'sober party' rather than the enthusiasts. So although as a piece of formal panegyric this poem cannot offer us a programmatic statement of Marvell's personal beliefs, any more than his lyrics can, it does present us with an insight into the nature of seventeenth-century politics.

The politics of religion

The politics of seventeenth-century England were the politics of religion. Religious questions formed the political agenda: they framed issues of foreign and domestic policy and defined the credibility and purpose of governments. Politicians were animated by religious ideals and motives. This was true of almost all contemporary political actors, whether godly proponents of further reformation, ecstatic sectaries intent on bringing about the apocalypse, or sober traditionalists affronted by the harm done to men and the insult offered to God by spiritual anarchy. Yet Andrew Marvell kept his motives hidden and his options open. One obvious reason for this evasiveness was that he had a career to make. Most of the 1650s he spent in search of some kind of public employment but often at some distance from the centre of national affairs. Only his appointment as Latin Secretary late in 1657 and then his election as MP for Hull in January 1659 brought him closer to power. Meanwhile his poetry explored from several angles the role of the poet in public life: 'when the sword glitters o'er the judge's head | And fear has coward churchman silencèd, | Then is the poet's time' (*Tom May's Death*, lines 63–5); other lines, however, picture the forward youth as forsaking his muse to don his armour.

Marvell's chance to do battle came in parliamentary committees after 1660. His parliamentary career as reported in his letters to Hull can seem mundane and parochial: he presented himself as an 'incorrupt mind and cleare Conscience, free from Faction or any self-ends' in the 'generall concerns of the nation' (*Letters*, 177). However in the records he repeatedly crops up sniping at the king's ministers, opposing royal policies and criticizing ecclesiastical power. At the Restoration he was busy in the efforts to create a national church under a 'moderate episcopacy' that would be broad enough to include the moderate Puritans, the Presbyterians, as well as the episcopalians. These hopes were all dashed as a hard-line episcopalian party, including the twenty-six bishops in the House of Lords, outmanoeuvred the other groups and hustled Parliament into passing the 1662 Act of Uniformity: or as he described the coup in parodic Presbyterian terms, 'Then bishops must revive, and all unfix | With discontent to content twenty-six. | The Lords' House drains the houses of the Lord, | For bishops' voices silencing the Word' (*The Third Advice to a Painter*, lines 239–42). The Uniformity Act defined the Church of England and relegated all other denominations to the category of 'Nonconformity' or 'Dissent'. Presbyterians, Baptists, Independents and Quakers now found themselves herded together as Nonconformists and subject to sporadic persecution under the so-called Clarendon Code. Marvell abhorred this legislation. In 1668 he opposed the continuation of the Conventicle Act, which banned Nonconformist religious meetings, and memorably described its successor in 1670 as 'the quintessence of arbitrary malice'. The temporary reversal of this intolerance in 1672 was very welcome, but in print Marvell was circumspect as always, presenting sobriety as the necessary condition of toleration: the king 'has thought fit to grant some liberty to all other [i.e. non-Anglican] Sober People, (and longer than they are so God forbid they should have it)' (*PW*, 1:104).

There were such sober people among Marvell's acquaintance. In the early 1660s Marvell was moving among a group of survivors from the 1640s and 1650s, Puritan types such as Anglesey, Wharton, Holles and Harley, who were old-fashioned country gentlemen with old-fashioned views. With hindsight it is clear that these 'Puritan Whigs' provided a personal, religious and political bridge between the Presbyterianism of the 1640s and 1650s and the Whiggery of the late 1670s and 1680s.[4] Now and then we catch a glimpse of Marvell's involvement with this group: he corresponded easily with Harley; stayed in Wharton's country house and was privy to the marriage plans of his children; dined with Anglesey and used the books in his library at Drury Lane.

There were, however, other sides to Marvell, and other milieux in which he moved. As a satirist, he had no compunction in guying 'Presbyter Holles' or mocking the Presbyterian values of the Duchess of Albemarle. As a sophisticated poet, he was familiar with the Duke of Buckingham and his circle, a courtly group of wits, sceptics and libertines, whose conception of religious liberty was much more far-reaching than anything dreamt of in the pious surroundings of Lord Anglesey's household or Harley's Brampton Bryan.

Marvell's most effective interventions in the religious politics of the Restoration were not in fact made by his testy contributions to parliamentary debates, but by his pen. The genre of 'Marvellian satire' is now recognized as a significant strand of opposition to Charles II's court and government. Poems by Marvell, possibly by Marvell, or inspired by Marvell's example satirized the policies and politicians of the 1660s and 1670s, and as they were passed from hand to hand in manuscript and copied into commonplace books, they gave a voice to the unease of many about the tyrannical propensities of the Stuarts. Yet concerned as they were with the Dutch war or Clarendon's peculation or Cleveland's sexuality, these verses rarely if ever have much to say directly about religion.[5] It was in his published prose works of the 1670s that Marvell offered his most explicit commentary on religious policies and clerical power in Charles II's England. The series begins with *The Rehearsal Transpros'd* (1672) and its second part, witheringly funny attacks on the churchman Samuel Parker, followed by a defence of the irenic Herbert Croft in *Mr Smirke: Or, the Divine in Mode* and the appended *Short Historical Essay* (1676), and reaches a climax of a sort with the tendentious *An Account of the Growth of Popery and Arbitrary Government* (1677). These popular publications peddled the brilliantly simple, plausible and terrifying thesis of a deep-rooted plot to impose 'popery and arbitrary government' on the Stuart kingdoms. This had all the necessary ingredients for a wildly successful conspiracy theory: enough truth in the circumstantial details, sufficient flexibility in its application, a cast of assorted villains, and a very ready audience. Just weeks after Marvell's death the fears that he had helped to sow would enflame the country in a 'Popish plot'.

'Popery' meant many things. It could refer to papal authority, Jesuit statecraft, Tridentine teaching, local variants such as the 'Grotian' or the Gallican church, or the flattery of monarchs by ambitious priests. Often it was whatever 'anti-popery', that vital component of the seventeenth-century Protestant mentality, most feared at any specific moment. Marvell's own deployments of the idea and term are no less ambiguous: compare the violent language about Rome in the *First Anniversary* with the fantasies about nuns and the possibility of a return of the old church in *Upon Appleton House, to My Lord Fairfax*. By the 1670s Marvell was unwilling to condemn Catholic views out of hand. 'Although we live under a rational jealousie always of Popery', there is no reason to reject whatever a Catholic author might assert just because he is a Catholic, for – and here Marvell unleashes a typical shaft of wit – 'in many points we agree with them, and shall in all, whensoever our Eyes shall be shut, or Theirs shall be opened' (*PW*, II:477). The attack on Roman Catholicism in *An Account* strikes its modern editor as so unconvincing that it suggests the real targets are Louis XIV and the Papacy rather than the religion or the Church of Rome.[6] Of course Marvell is famous for his dismissal of popery: 'such a thing cannot, but for want of a word to express it, be called a religion' (*PW*, II:227). But what precisely irritated him? It turns out to be 'the bold imposture of Priests' who 'by a new and anti-scriptural Belief, composed of Terrours to the Phancy, Contradictions to the Sense, and Impositions on the Understanding' have turned 'the Laity' into 'Tenants for their Souls, and in consequence Tributary for their Estates to a more than omnipotent Priesthood' (*PW*, II:229).

This kind of 'popery', the political and social hegemony of an 'omnipotent priesthood', came near to home. One of Marvell's most insistent themes is that Charles II's England was in thrall to the priests of the Church of England. This was a historical tale. A faction of bishops had emerged in the 1620s and come to dominance under Charles I and Archbishop Laud. These 'Laudians' espoused the doctrine of absolute monarchy and *iure divino* – divine right – which they claimed for both the Stuart monarchs and their own order of bishops, with disastrous consequences for the country in the 1640s. Revived at the Restoration, this strain of episcopal thinking had captured the commanding heights of church and state and, apart from a brief hiatus courtesy of the Declaration of Indulgence in 1672 and 1673, had shaped policy ever since. Marvell warned that kings should beware of self-interested bishops, especially those who preach up the divine right of monarchy. While such preaching might appear to strengthen monarchs, the danger is that these same bishops would simultaneously promote their own divine right and teach the monarch to fear his own people – 'to the end that a Bishop might sit with a Prince in a Junto, to consult wisely how to preserve him [the king] from those people that never meant him any harm' (*PW*, II:169–70). This mythology of a Laudian takeover of the Church of England became an essential part of the 'country' party or early Whig analysis of the growth of popery and arbitrary government in the 1670s. It raised some delicate questions. Was Charles II a victim or an accomplice? Was this a struggle for the soul of the English church and English Protestantism? If so, had the Church of England been captured by a corrupt leadership or had it suffered a mass defection from its earlier principles? Like other writers in this tradition Marvell varied his emphasis to suit his immediate needs: sometimes the Church of England as constituted in 1662 had turned its back on the true Protestant tradition, on international Protestantism, on the non-episcopal churches of the Continent; in other versions, the mass of the Church of England was in thrall to 'the few', 'the knot', the 'ruling party'. Behind all this loomed the urgent question, was the Church of England salvageable?

Marvell circled this issue. On several occasions, he connected the character of the Church of England to questions of church reform. In the 1660s and 1670s reform was repeatedly discussed in the press and the highest ecclesiastical and parliamentary circles, but it was a sprawling, often ill-focused debate which took in a range of problems including the church courts and the income, distribution and lay patronage of clerical benefices. Several groups had a stake: the clergy saw reform as a way of protecting the church; the advocates of a broader church believed that a reformed Church of England would be more attractive to moderate Dissenters; and Erastians thought this might be a way of curbing clerical pretensions. Marvell warmed to the theme when defending conciliatory tendencies within the church. He argued that all societies – by which he means churches – 'do in process of long time gather an irregularity, and wear away much of their primitive institution'. These defects need 'review at fit periods ... And this Reformation is most easily and with least disturbance to be effected by the Society itself, no single men being forbidden by any Magistrate to amend their own manners, and much more all Societies having the liberty to bring themselves within that compass.' Yet, sadly, many societies go unreformed by their members, says Marvell, before disingenuously claiming that no reader could suspect him of criticizing the English bishops 'who, if they would but add a little more moderation to their great prudence, might quickly mend what is to be mended' (PW, 1:331, 333).

When a church cannot reform itself the task often falls to the godly magistrate, or, as Marvell caustically observed, 'only kings can bishops exorcise' (The Loyal Scot, line 153). At several moments in his life Marvell had recognized that a single ruler was a better bet than a republic or a parliament for promoting religious reform or liberty. Sober Restoration Dissenters such as John Owen, Philip Nye and John Humfrey saw the royal supremacy as a weapon that might be used on their behalf to cut through the tangle of Anglican interest and prejudice, and there are signs that Marvell was of the same mind. In May 1668, after the failure of an initiative for parliamentary revision of the 1662 church settlement, and on the verge of a parliamentary adjournment, Lord Wharton and other peers prepared an address from the Lords 'to the King to make use of his prerogative in Ecclesiastical affayres for the better composure and union of the mindes of his protestant subjects'. The draft of the address is in Marvell's handwriting.[7] In these small political initiatives and more significantly in the public world of print, Marvell played a major part in spreading the idea that the clergy were subverting the church, and that this subversion was contributing to the growth of 'popery and arbitrary government'. This diagnosis of Stuart mis-government was based on specific policies, all detailed in the historical *Account of the Growth of Popery and Arbitrary Government*, but it drew much of its force and urgency from Marvell's deeper, personal, almost visceral, anxieties about the clergy, the church, and definitions of orthodoxy.

Marvell, the clergy, and the church

Marvell said that he would not have taken up his pen against Samuel Parker in *The Rehearsal Transpros'd* if that cleric had not betrayed the minister's office by his violent and erroneous writing. In a passage which is often read as uncharacteristically revealing, Marvell claimed that he was too conscious of his own imperfections to dilate on those of other men, 'and though I carry always some ill Nature about me, yet it is I hope no more than is in this world necessary for a Preservative; but as for the Clergy, the memory of mine own extraction, and much more my sense of the Sanctity of their function, ingage me peculiarly to esteem and honour them' (*PW*, I:241). His 'extraction' or descent was as the son of a godly minister who enjoyed 'some measure of reputation, both for Piety and Learning: and he was moreover a Conformist to the established Rites of the Church of England, though I confess none of the most over-running or eager in them' (*PW*, I:288–9). Elsewhere Marvell maintained that 'of all vocations … I have alwaies esteemed that of the Ministry to be the most noble and happy Imployment' (*PW*, II:415). But he praised the calling all the better to criticize those who took it up. Sometimes the censure was pitched as a witty aside: he would have bishops recommend the Bible to their clergy, ''Tis a very good book, and if a man read it carefully, will make him much wiser' (*PW*, II:173). Other criticisms were smuggled to his readers in the guise of a historical analogy. There was no doubt, however, that Marvell found many, if not most, clergymen of his own day to be sorely lacking in the necessary virtues of their office.

To contemporary readers, Marvell's was a powerfully anticlerical voice. 'Merry Andrew' took his place in the long literary tradition of attacks on divines and bishops going back through Milton, via the Marprelate tracts of the 1590s, to the Protestant Reformation and beyond. But his voice also spoke of the attitudes and politics of the Restoration. 'The present clergy will never heartily go down with the generality of the commons of England,' reported Pepys in 1663, because the people were now too used to their own 'liberty' and because of 'the pride and debauchery of the present clergy'.[8] The bishops were the focus of particular animosity. They were lambasted in vitriolic terms, reminiscent of the 1640s, and slanders circulated freely that they indulged in nefarious sexual practices and were guilty of gross immorality. Pepys recorded these rumours as did Roger Morrice, and these allegations were bandied about the streets in libels and lampoons and fuelled London apprentice riots in 1668.[9]

Marvell's antagonism towards bishops grew in proportion to their power. Although he took pot shots in works of the 1650s – *Upon Appleton House* refers to the 'proud' residence of the Archbishop of York and to 'its prelate great' (lines 353, 363) – it was only after 1660, and especially in the 1670s, that the attacks moved up a gear: *The Loyal Scot* denounces the bishops in the most lurid terms – 'in faith erroneous, and in life profane | These hypocrites their faith and linen stain' (lines 170–1). Worse than all the plagues of Egypt, episcopacy is a curse on the land. Marvell paints an uncompromising picture. Bishops are the embodiment of overweening ambition, tireless in their pursuit of wealth and power; they are inherently cruel, as their power depends upon stigmatizing their victims as heretics and demanding their persecution; they flatter kings all the better to lead them by the ear, and, if need be, to overawe them. 'All mischief's moulded by these state divines': they are insatiable; everyone and everything will be sacrificed to their own interest. 'No bishop? Rather than it should be so, | No church, no trade, no king, no people, no' (*The Loyal Scot*, lines 146–8). These fears and hatreds are memorably distilled into Marvell's lines on Colonel Thomas Blood's failed 1671 attempt to steal the crown jewels from the Tower while in clerical disguise. Blood 'chose the cassock, surcingle and gown, | The fittest mask for one that robs a crown. | But his lay pity underneath prevailed, | And while he spared the keeper's life, he failed. | With the priest's vestments had he put on | A bishop's cruelty, the crown had gone' (*Epigram: Upon Blood's attempt to steal the Crown*, lines 194–9).

The historical and political analysis by which Marvell justifies his anticlericalism is revealing (but whether it fully explains the visceral hatred that he seems to feel is another question). He took his readers back to the first centuries of the Christian church and to the malign influence of those bishops who persuaded Emperor Constantine and his successors to mobilize the power of the prince in support of the church. It was the bishops' 'readiness to pick a quarrel' by branding others as 'heretics' and then encouraging the secular power to prosecute the heterodox from which so many ills had sprung:

> Nor can I wonder that those ages were so fertile in what they called Heresies, when being given to meddling with the mysteries of Religion further then humane apprehension or divine revelation did or could lead them, some of the

> Bishops were so ignorant and gross, but others so speculative, acute and refining in their conceptions, that, there being moreover a good fat Bishoprick to boot in the case, it is rather admirable to me how all the Clergy from one end to 'tother, could escape from being or being accounted Hereticks.   (*PW*, II:137)

What began with one cleric denouncing another rapidly became a tool for the oppression of the laity. 'That word of Heresy misapplyed' was a favourite weapon of papal tyranny over Christians (*PW*, II:231). But this was a weapon beloved of all clergymen, even in the Protestant England of Charles II where the medieval writ *de heretico comburendo* remained available if unused. The continuing existence of this licence to burn heretics troubled many. Marvell, who attributed its survival to 'some of our Ruling Clergy' who were not prepared to part with any power they held 'over the poor Laity', sat on the parliamentary committee which eventually achieved its repeal in 1677 (*PW*, II:72).

Marvell was deeply interested in the mechanisms which defined orthodoxy and heterodoxy, and, above all, in the creeds, those statements of Christian belief drawn up by the Councils of the Early Church. The Church of England's Thirty-Nine Articles endorse the Apostles', Nicene and Athanasian Creeds as necessary and as warranted by scripture: the Prayer Book required minister and people to recite the Apostles' Creed at morning and evening prayer and the Athanasian Creed on thirteen feast days including Christmas, Easter and Whitsun. But, in reality, the creeds were controversial documents. Their attempt to capture the doctrine of the Trinity – the three persons of God the father, God the son, and God the Holy Spirit – in human language had led to fierce argument and division. The Athanasian Creed troubled many conscientious seventeenth-century Protestants, including Marvell's own father, not only because of its formulation of Christ's part in the Trinity (the 'filioque' definition) but also because of its 'damnatory clause' which asserted that any who refused this creed would be denied salvation. It was common knowledge that some churchmen avoided reading the Athanasian Creed to their congregations. Significant as the Trinitarian issue was, an even larger question preoccupied Marvell: was it legitimate to require of Christians statements of their belief? Despairing of ever formulating an exact and unexceptional creed, Marvell denounced them all as 'meer instruments of Equivocation or Persecution': the wily would take them in their own sense and the scrupulous would fall foul of the penalties for following the dictates of conscience (*PW*, II:145). If confessions of faith went beyond the words of scripture and were presented as necessary to salvation, 'this is Dangerous, and the imposing of it is unwarrantable by reason or Scripture' (*PW*, II:70). Marvell, who thought every individual should be able to give an account of their faith, assumed that scripture was the benchmark by which individuals would judge their beliefs. These questions about statements of belief and fallible human language were caught up in wider Protestant debates. Concern about the legitimacy of using non-scriptural words as a test, whether as an oath, subscription or creed, mounted across the century until it burst out in the Trinitarian controversies of the 1690s and the momentous Nonconformist split at Salters' Hall in 1719.

Although Marvell might expect every Christian to offer an account of their faith, he did not display much interest in matters of doctrine. He only ventured into doctrinal controversy once, when he intervened in a dispute between Thomas Danson and John Howe, and then supposedly only to prevent 'one Divine from offering Violence to another'. The issue between the two divines was how to reconcile the Gospel's promise of salvation to all with God's foreknowledge of human impenitency and damnation. It seemed hypocritical, insincere or even tyrannical for God to will humans to salvation and encourage them to live a good life while knowing that many would fail and suffer damnation. Although both Presbyterian, Danson and Howe were theologically poles apart. Danson would not compromise on divine sovereignty and the absolute predetermination of all human actions, while Howe followed the 'middle way' between Calvinism and Arminianism associated with Richard Baxter and others, which proposed that while some were elected to salvation (in other words, predestined for salvation), the fate of the rest was undecided. To Danson this 'hypothetical universalism' was indistinguishable from popery for it seemed to raise the possibility that some might earn their own salvation. Marvell's *Remarks Upon a Late Disingenuous Discourse* (1678) posed as a balm for the controversy – the bitterness of theological disputes 'manifest the Subtilty and Malice of the Serpent' – but they subtly and insistently took Howe's side. The whole notion that human beings had no free will, that their actions were predetermined and their eventual destination predestined, struck Marvell as irrational. In the seventeenth-century context, it was safest to proclaim these questions beyond human competence, and to praise Howe for 'his Sobriety, Simplicity, and Equality of Temper: glorifying God rather in the exercise of Practical Christian Vertues, than affecting the honour of a speculative Question' (*PW*, II:480).

If one begins to assemble the shards of evidence, certain of Marvell's preoccupations emerge. Moderation is one: 'Truth for the most part lyes in the middle, but men ordinarily seek for it in the extremities' (*PW*, II:137). Sobriety is another. And reason is a third. To Marvell, something in the nature of human beings tends towards the rational, 'for by how much any thing is more false and unreasonable, it requires more cruelty to establish it:

and to introduce that which is absurd, there must be somewhat done that is barbarous' (*PW*, II:231). Fundamentally popery is 'a reproach to human reason' (*PW*, II:231, 233). The Calvinist doctrine of universal predetermination is not to be found in scripture, and is 'so contrary if not to the whole scope and design of Divine Revelation, yet to all common understanding and genuine sense of Right Reason' (*PW*, II:446). Claims that the Holy Spirit dictated to the church councils were ridiculous: 'if so many of them when they got together, acted like rational men, 'tis enough in all reason, and as much as could be expected' (*PW*, II:148). Professor von Maltzahn has assembled a powerful case for seeing such principles as 'directed toward emancipating Christian inquiry from constitutional constraints deemed counter-productive to a free-thinking that was learned and pious, whether in the individual or in the fellowship of believers.'[10] This free-thinking was – and was seen by contemporaries and heirs to be – aligned with Socinianism, a rationalist anti-trinitarian tradition familiar to Marvell and his father, and akin to the deism that became so prominent in the decades after Marvell's death.

During his own lifetime and in his own published prose writings, Marvell was a promoter of human reason, moderation and humility, but above all he sought to demolish what he felt to be the artificial and malign distinction of laity and clergy. In *A Short Historical Essay*, he described how the bishops appropriated the word *clerus* (which had designated the laity or Christian people) and applied it to 'their inferior degrees' or lower priests. 'But if the inferior degrees were the *Clergy*, the Bishops would be the Church, although that word in the Scripture-sense is proper only to a congregation of the Faithful.' When assembled as a council of the church, the bishops then claimed to be the Catholic Church and whatever they defined as a creed was the Catholic faith and necessary to salvation:

> By which means there rose thenceforward so constant persecutions till this day, that, had not the little invisible *Catholick Church* and a People that always searched and believ'd the Scriptures, made a stand by their Testimonies and sufferings, the Creeds had destroyed the Faith: and the Church had ruined the Religion. (*PW*, II:149–50)

Creeds that destroy faith, a church that ruins religion, and a priesthood that misappropriates the name of 'clergy' to drive an artificial distinction between members of the Christian community, all amounts to a comprehensive indictment of institutional Christianity. Marvell seems to want to roll all this back, and to replace it with the Christian alone with his or her bible. It is every individual's duty to be able to give an account of his faith, says Marvell: every man must work out his own salvation with fear and trembling, with all possible aids and advice, 'but when he hath done this, he is his own Expositor [of scripture], his own both minister and people, bishop and diocese, his own council, his own conscience excusing or condemning him' (*PW*, II:145).

This is a stark and bracing vision that looks back to the sixteenth-century Reformation and forward to the Enlightenment. It could easily be equated with some definitions of Puritanism as an introspective and individualistic faith, but it would sit equally well with a stripped-down minimalist religion, devoid of content and answerable to no community, the very last station on the road to deism or indifference. Either vision might appeal to a poet whose main responsibility is to his muse. And neither might be Marvell's own position. For here, as always, the writer is at work, fencing with an opponent, making the most effective sallies, and taking care to give nothing of himself away.

NOTES

1. Pierre Legouis, *André Marvell: Poète, Puritain, Patriote* (originally published in French, Paris, 1928; a revised and abridged translation Oxford, 1965; 2nd ed. 1968).
2. James Yonge, quoted in *PW*, II:400.
3. Barbara Lewalski, 'Marvell as Religious Poet', in C. A. Patrides, ed., *Approaches to Marvell: The York Tercentenary Lectures* (London, 1978).
4. *The Entring Book of Roger Morrice 1677–1691*, 6 vols. (Woodbridge, 2007), Vol. I: *Roger Morrice and the Puritan Whigs*, by Mark Goldie.
5. But Harold Love discerns some biblical allusions; see his *English Clandestine Satire, 1660–1702* (Oxford, 2004), 113.
6. Nicholas von Maltzahn in *PW*, II:181–2.
7. *Chronology*, 106.
8. *The Diary of Samuel Pepys*, ed. Robert Latham and William Matthews, 11 vols. (Berkeley, 1970–83), IV:372.
9. Pepys, *Diary*, VIII:364; *The Entring Book of Roger Morrice 1677–1691*, 6 vols. (Woodbridge, 2007), Vol. IV: *The Reign of James II, 1687–89*, ed. Stephen Taylor, 450.
10. Von Maltzahn, 'Milton, Marvell and Toleration', in Sharon Achinstein and Elizabeth Sauer, eds., *Milton and Toleration* (Oxford, 2007), 93.

Further reading

Warren Chernaik and Martin Dzelzainis, eds., *Marvell and Liberty* (Basingstoke, 2005).
Conal Condren and A. D. Cousins, eds., *The Political Identity of Andrew Marvell* (Aldershot, 1990).
Mark Goldie, *Roger Morrice and the Puritan Whigs*, Vol. I of *The Entring Book of Roger Morrice 1677–1691* (Woodbridge 2007).

N. H. Keeble, *The Literary Culture of Nonconformity in Later Seventeenth-Century England* (Leicester, 1987).

Barbara Lewalski, 'Marvell as Religious Poet', in C. A. Patrides, ed., *Approaches to Marvell: The York Tercentenary Lectures* (London, 1978).

John Spurr, *English Puritanism, 1603–1689* (Basingstoke, 1998).

Nicholas von Maltzahn, 'Milton, Marvell and Toleration', in Sharon Achinstein and Elizabeth Sauer, eds., *Milton and Toleration* (Oxford, 2007).

II

NICHOLAS VON MALTZAHN

Adversarial Marvell

O Sir, we quarrel in print, by the book – as you have books for good manners. I
will name you the degrees. The first, the Retort Courteous; the second, the Quip
Modest; the third, the Reply Churlish; the fourth, the Reproof Valiant; the fift,
the Countercheck Quarrelsome; the sixt, the Lie with Circumstance; the
seventh, the Lie Direct.   (Touchstone, *As You Like It*, v.iv.90–6)

As Touchstone's points of honour suggest, Andrew Marvell's career in print
controversy engaged him in a culture of debate with a long and rich history. His
skill in animadversion gave Marvell most of such reputation as he enjoyed by
the end of his life. To animadvert is generally 'to turn the mind to' something,
but as a term of art 'animadversion' denotes a genre of prose polemic that
disputes a previous publication, often point by point. Other terms from
Marvell's day – such as 'answers', 'reflections', 'observations', 'defence',
'reply', 'apology', 'remarks', or even 'remarks upon remarques' – bespeak a
similar style of confutation. But as well as specificity, the animus that can
animate animadversion deserves emphasis, as when Marvell uses the term
figuratively to comment on a brawl where some 'Rusticks animadverted so
severely upon' the Earl of Rochester's followers that one of them was killed
(*Letters*, 345). The complex intertextuality we meet with in animadversions
expresses differences in often vivid or even violent dispute. Marvell could turn
on a text or an antagonist in ways that excited wonder in his readers then and
since. His flair for reversal or retort – the turning at the root of 'trope' –
distinguishes both his prose and poetry.

Specific rebuttals of polemical works form a significant part of the Marvell
canon, as they do that of his older friend and sometime colleague John
Milton. Part duel and part academic disputation, the writing of animadversions, or *adversaria* as they were more widely known across Europe, issued in
a great volume of publication in the mid to late seventeenth century, not least
in England. Indeed, the English word 'animadversion' and its cognates are
seventeenth-century coinages (*Oxford English Dictionary*, sv. *animadversal*).

Polemic might meet with polemic upon polemic, as for example with Milton's *Apology Against a Pamphlet Call'd A Modest Confutation of the Animadversions upon the Remonstrant against Smectymnuus* (1642). Marvell mocks authors who wish to be above any such fray with his amused lament that 'since Printing came into the World, such is the mischief, that a Man cannot write a Book but presently he is answered' (*PW*, 1:45, also 236–7). Bound volumes of pamphlets from that time often gather entire series of these linked interventions.

Common in such pamphlets is the quotation of the offending work, some-times very extensively and often in a distinct setting of type, only to meet that with an answer, whether reasoned argument, witty rejoinder, or vituperation: in short, everything from Touchstone's 'Retort Courteous' to 'the Lie Direct'. In Milton's *Animadversions* (1641), for example, his answers range from closely printed pages of climactic peroration to 'Ha, ha, ha'.[1] Marvell had gone to school in the controversies of the 1640s and 1650s and may well have helped the recently blind Milton with his Latin *Defensio secunda* (1654), a bravura performance by a seasoned animadverter that Marvell promised to study 'even to the getting of it by Heart' (*Letters*, 306; *Chronology*, 38). He was well equipped to put this schooling to use in the 1670s, if he had not already done so anonymously on earlier occasions. Although he terms himself 'a new unlicensed Practitioner' (*PW*, 1:234–5; see also 246), a long familiarity with the genre lies behind his inventive mastery in *The Rehearsal Transpros'd* (1672). Conscious as he was of 'the nature of *Animadversions*' (*PW*, 1:96), Marvell was quick to play with convention and then to move beyond it.

Marvell's first published work was parody; his last, in his lifetime, anim-adversion. Both genres bespeak the intimate, intricate and often adversarial character of much of his writing in between. Readily as Marvell stages debates within himself – we see this in his lyric poetry, in his correspondence and in his prose works – he is as often engaged in debate with others. Such confronta-tion is often overlooked by Kantian critical tradition and by the criticism that was constrained by a Paterian fixation on ideal beauty and later New Critical suspicions of context. In the twentieth century, it became a critical common-place that Marvell exemplified a classic 'equipoise', exhibiting 'wit's internal equilibrium'; he was seen as 'unlike Donne, and unlike Milton' in his inclina-tion 'to leave opposites carefully balanced rather than fusing them or sub-ordinating them to a higher unity'. This consensus was thought to govern even 'our reception of the political and rhetorical poems, which are so finely shaded that they manage to remain lyrics despite their occasions and the pressure of public realities'.[2] A significant correction has followed in more recent studies of these 'occasions' and the 'public realities' behind the satires and more especially Marvell's prose works, now republished (2003).

Moreover the presumed chronology of Marvell's compositions that identified his metaphysical 'equipoise' with his pre-political poetry, after which virtuous beginning that 'April mood' was thought to have been irrecoverably lost, may now be further doubted owing to Restoration datings of *The Garden* and *The Mower against Gardens*.³

Marvell's virtuosity as a controversialist proceeded from his conviction that 'in this World a good Cause signifys little, unless it be as well defended' (*Letters*, 324). But it proceeded also from his long experience of literary infighting, evident in the often elaborate intertextuality of his poetry. The legacy of Eliot's emphasis on 'tradition' has been a critical undervaluing of the adversarial aspect of Marvell's poetry, which this chapter reads as a prelude to his more obviously agonistic satires and prose works in the Restoration. His strategies in animadversion especially are anticipated in his strategies as a poet.

A key point of comparison is Marvell's suddenness in such interventions, where he seems to recall the advice of 'My Fencing-Master in Spain, [who] after he had instructed me all he could, told me, I remember, there was yet one Secret, against which there was no Defence, and that was, to give the first Blow' (*Letters*, 324). Marvell had already observed the advantage of 'the first Blow' in parliamentary practice and this aspect of the duel informs his curiosity about such pre-emptive strikes more generally (*Letters*, 314; *Chronology*, 69–70, 185–6). How to achieve a first blow that would also be the last? The decisiveness required in these interventions might test 'wit's internal equilibrium' beyond recovery. But that Marvell might intervene so decisively appears especially from his four major works of animadversion in the 1670s: *The Rehearsal Transpros'd*, and its *Second Part* (1672, 1673), *Mr Smirke: Or, the Divine in Mode* (1676), and *Remarks Upon a Late Disingenuous Discourse* (1678). These challenges surprised his contemporaries, and perhaps Marvell himself, with their deranging commitments. There was much more to these works than just the 'Mastery in fooling' that his contemporaries lamented and acclaimed (*PW*, 1:27). In what may seem the crooked timber of seventeenth-century religious controversy, we can eventually trace the grain of something nearer to the Enlightenment.

The habit of argument

Between grammar school in Hull, his years at Cambridge, and the print culture of the 1640s and 1650s, Marvell had a long education in the 'zeal of contradiction', as Bacon had faulted it.⁴ He was a master of its arts even as he came to profess some suspicion of them. Some of his skill he seems to have gained from his father, a Church of England minister whose bracing style of argument shows in letters where he relentlessly expounds biblical, logical and philological arguments against a fellow Yorkshire cleric. That correspondent soon complains that Marvell Sr's writing is 'full stufft with swellinge (I may justly retorte) snarling bitinge belchinge termes . . . All which smell ranklie of a proud (to say noe worse) and hautie spiritt.' But Marvell's indomitable father just discounts such *ad hominem* attack as 'not to the purpose' and persists in close argument and biblical self-justification.[5] Marvell and others testified to his father's 'Piety and Learning' but he may have learnt still more from 'his discourse', styled 'most facetious' (*PW*, 1:289; *Chronology*, 18, 67–8). The psychodynamic consequences of this relationship have been read into some of Marvell's later polemics, not least against clerical effrontery, in ways that might inform wider reflections on 'the highly programmed contentiousness of Renaissance . . . intellectualism'.[6]

Between the ages of 12 and 20, the young Marvell went from a menial role as subsizar at Trinity College, Cambridge, to his election to a scholarship there, winning promotion in a very competitive system where disputation featured centrally. In later describing his antagonist Samuel Parker, Marvell also describes himself:

> [he] was sent early to the *University*: and there studied hard, and in a short time became a competent Rhetorician, and no ill Disputant. He had learnt how to erect a Thesis, and to defend it *Pro* and *Con* with a serviceable distinction . . . And so thinking himself now ripe and qualified for the greatest Undertakings, and highest Fortune, he therefore exchanged the narrowness of the University for the Town . . .
>
> (*PW*, 1:74)

But the erudite theology on display in Marvell's father's writing was gaining more humanist colour in the Cambridge of the 1630s, not least at Marvell's own Trinity College, when even university disputations had become increasingly literary occasions and disputants perhaps ever more susceptible, as Marvell later observed, to 'Cavil' rather than to 'Argue' (*PW*, II:68). With the passing of the great confessional contest of Reformation and 'Counter'-Reformation, some end to which may be symbolized by the end of the Thirty Years War in the Treaties of Westphalia (1648), the theologians' arsenal of polemical techniques might further arm combatants for other battles.

From Cambridge Marvell went to London, initially in a false start that took him to 'a Booksellers Shop'. This can stand for his early immersion in the print culture of the capital, now on the eve of a great transformation. With the approach of the English Revolution, and the lapse of government controls, many more titles now issued from the London presses. But constraints on the output of the printing trade meant that these much more numerous publications needed also to be shorter, with pamphlets commonly only a sheet or two long (8 to 16 pages quarto). This further favoured the publication of controversial rather than systematic works. In London Marvell may also have had some relation to that other great school of controversy, the Inns of Court, and Gray's Inn in particular (*Chronology*, 29, 159, 179). He made longer stays in the metropolis on either side of his four years' travel to the Continent (as an aristocrat's tutor, c. 1642–6), then lived in the city from 1657 for most of the rest of his life until his death in 1678. Early evidence of his hand in prose controversy or journalism has yet to be found, much as experience of this kind is suggested by the echoes of contemporary journalism and pamphleteering in his poetry, as well as by his relation c. 1650 and after, and perhaps before, with the journalist Marchamont Nedham, and also by Marvell's later mastery of animadversion.[7]

Rather than 'wit's internal equilibrium', Marvell's greatest poetry shows his fascination with the energy of dispute, as he is drawn to the most that can be said in a case or cause. His engagement goes beyond his humanist practice in arguing both sides of a question. Here he had more 'personality' than Eliot or his disciples have conceded. Marvell had an ample sense of 'the prudence with which men must always handle a mixt businesse' (*Letters*, 81), which prudence might include self-awareness and a close consideration of personal, civic, or national interests. Such habits of self-scrutiny remain more worldly in Marvell than any more retiring religious meditation.[8] Marvell was also deeply curious about commitment and its expression. His contending passions express not neutrality, but rather the anxious volatility of someone persuaded of both sides at once. They express not disinterest but conflicted interests: hence the instabilities arising from the 'tension of competing meanings' at work in his lyrics and early political poems. Machiavelli had esteemed the robust energies of competing interests as the foundation of modern politics. Marvell, termed a 'notable English Italo-Machavillian' by one contemporary, seems to have endured the contending perspectives so famously expressed in his *Horatian Ode upon Cromwell's Return from Ireland*, drawn at once to the claim of 'ancient rights' and to that of 'industrious valour' (lines 33, 38), the world as found and the world as made, however opposed.[9]

Without hard evidence of Marvell's hand in previous prose controversy, we can in other of his works show habits of mind and of voice that anticipate his published animadversions of the 1670s. His turns of phrase often evoke some competition between perspectives, one retorting upon another. At the level of the phrase or image, some internalization of these competing interests appears in Marvell's reflexive language. This 'self'-involvement of things Marvellian has been tellingly described by Christopher Ricks: 'the self-inwoven simile is a figure which both reconciles and opposes, in that it describes something both as itself and as something external to it'. In such 'reversals transposed' has been detected a 'fatal reversibility of our actions … If little T. C. picks blossoms, she will become a blossom and be picked'.[10] A like self-harvesting appears in Marvell's Latin elegiac distichs and their English counterparts. In the Latin distichs, Marvell makes the most of the witty antithesis available with 'the expansive hexameter tightening into an increasingly regular pentameter'.[11] In the English, the effect is reproduced especially in *The Mower against Gardens*, arguably a late work, where the expansive handling of human artifice in the longer lines meets with abrupt rejoinders in the short:

> He first enclosed within the gardens square
>   A dead and standing pool of air:
> And a more luscious earth for them did knead,
>   Which stupefied them while it fed.   (lines 5–8)

Here Marvell interposes the tetrameter lines to intensify the effect of the contemporary heroic couplet, where the first line proposes a statement that is then in the second subjected to qualification or contradiction, couplet by couplet.

A skilful internalization of dialectic, or witty self-retort, animates many of Marvell's lyrics and satires. Many of these are dialogues, such as the lyric debates of his *A Dialogue, Between the Resolved Soul, and Created Pleasure* or especially *A Dialogue between the Soul and Body*, where the 'quitting' each of the other rises to a height. So too Marvell's Damon answers Clorinda, or Thyrsis responds to Dorinda; his Thestylis animadverts upon Ametas, his Cynthia upon Endymion (*Two Songs at the Marriage of the Lord Fauconberg and the Lady Mary Cromwell*). These Marvellian rejoinders can be so vigorous that in *Upon Appleton House, To My Lord Fairfax*, one of the figures within the poem wittily comes to correct her own narrator's earlier figure of speech, this 'bloody Thestylis' thus stepping out from the frame of the picture as if a stage character breaking the fourth wall (lines 401–8). The contest that emerges here is more challenging than critical consensus used to allow in emphasizing that with Marvell every point of view 'bears with it also, in true metaphysical fashion, the implication of its own opposite'.[12]

Moreover, such self-answering in Marvell's poetry is matched by its answering of others' poems. Modern scholarship has done much to reveal the myriad 'pre-texts' on which Marvell bases his poems, not least in his lyric responses to other poets' publications of the late 1640s (notably Abraham Cowley's *The Mistress*, 1647) and early 1650s (notably William Davenant's *Gondibert*, 1651). Marvell's long fascination with Milton's 'Lycidas', for example, resulted in often positive recollections of that work in his own poetry. But with other poets, especially Edmund Waller, he enjoyed a more agonistic relationship, whether in his lyrics, as when Marvell's *Bermudas* comments on Waller's newly republished *Battle of the Summer Islands*, or in his satires, as when Marvell's 'advice to a painter' poetry mocks the heroic pretensions of Waller's *Instructions to a Painter* (1665–6).[13] Even with the last, however, Marvell in some part responds also to his own prior engagement – notably in his *First Anniversary of the Government under His Highness the Lord Protector* (1655) celebrating Cromwell's government – with the heroic style he now puts to scorn.[14]

The resulting intricacy of Marvell's works sets the arresting sophistication of the witty moment against the rhetorical or narrative impetus of the work as a coherent whole. The balance between these in his longer verse satires seems lost at first in his prose animadversions; hence the modern critical preference for the episodic energies of the former over the restless argumentation of the latter. The incessant wit of Marvell's *Character of Holland* (1653) is by the mid 1660s much leavened by the mock-heroic narration in his Advices to a Painter. Though Marvell's satires operate as animadversions of a kind, commenting adversely on Waller's and other misrepresentations of English fortunes in the Second Anglo-Dutch War, they come to gain an increasing independence of any one specific source. This liberty favours these satires' imaginative elaborations of story and of voice beyond animadversion, famously in the Archibald Douglas passage in *The Last Instructions to a Painter* (lines 649–96), but also in the Duchess of Albemarle's compelling rant in *The Third Advice to a Painter* (lines 201–434). There are still some notably self-correcting couplets – for example, *The Second Advice to a Painter*, lines 183–8, and *Last Instructions*, lines 91–6, 561–2 – but these satires now gain much more of their energy from the skilful manipulation of episode. In the 1670s, such re-narrations of events on the national stage eventually gave way to his anecdotal, secret history of *An Account of the Growth of Popery and Arbitrary Government* (1677),[15] where the story, often heavily inflected with observations but still with much narrative energy, encompassed disparate materials: a hostile 'character of popery', narratives of parliamentary sessions including summaries of debates, royal speeches and parliamentary addresses, the full text of a failed (and in Marvell's view scandalous) bill (*PW*, II:207–14). Here the critically charged narration includes much witty disputation of particular claims or misrepresentations, but in the main subordinated to Marvell's evocation of the larger plot that he denounces.

This animadverting style of narration in the *Account* had been anticipated in Marvell's correspondence, especially his more private letters. The impulse thus to comment on events does not much appear in his almost 300 extant constituency letters (1660–78). The very first is the exception proving the rule (*Letters*, 1–3); it airs critical views with a freedom Marvell avoids already in his second such letter a few days later, which self-control he largely maintains in such correspondence thereafter, if still capable of much silent irony. That MP's persona and the stricter news and business it retails are distinct from Marvell's self-revelation in his more private letters to other correspondents, especially to his beloved nephew William Popple in Bordeaux. In writing these letters to France, or another to a friend in Persia, Marvell was safe from government interference with the mails. Moreover, in Popple he had a correspondent whom he loved and trusted, and for whom he liked to perform. The result is a private correspondence that often works as if it is animadversion on his more public correspondence. Privately, Marvell can react openly to events that his letters to the Hull Corporation handle instead with a parliamentarian's discipline in exploiting the decorum of addresses to the crown, a constraint that deepens the often bitter ironies in his *Account* (*PW*, II:195–6).[16] If irony is the distance between expectation and experience, Marvell's letters show him again and again setting things as they should be against things as they are, explicitly in letters to his friends, implicitly in those to his constituency.

Marvell and his friends could mock the passion for debate in the heroic drama of the Restoration, but they themselves aspired to a more nonchalant version of the same flair in conversation or debate. Marvell himself seems to have attained it only with difficulty on that great stage the floor of the House of Commons, where he conceded in one of his rare interventions that 'He is not used to speak here, and therefore speaks with abruptness' (*Chronology*, 185). The same speech shows what difficulties he faced when addressing with such convoluted wit what was no friendly assembly. But on the page he was a much more confident operator. He was of the Duke of Buckingham's circle, from which stemmed *The Rehearsal* (1670), that great parody of especially John Dryden's excesses as a dramatist, which Marvell would adapt for his own purposes in animadversion; in the 1670s he also drew on George Etherege's *Man of Mode* for further animadversions in *Mr Smirke*, and admired as a satirist the Earl of Rochester, who himself admired Marvell's satire (*Chronology*, 149–50, 185, 218). Marvell relished their genius for witty exchange. Such self-possession amid the fierce tensions of court culture he loved to report, as when, for example, his friend the Lord Wharton, a political prisoner, successfully petitioned to Charles II for his release. The better to reflect the theatricality of this fraught moment, it is worth reprinting the passage from Marvell's letter as if from a playbook:

[*CHARLES II*] The King jested with him and said he would teach him a text of scripture.

WHARTON It will be very acceptable from your Majesty.

CHARLES II Sinne no more.

WHARTON Your Majesty has that from *my* quotation of it to my Lord Arlin[g]ton when he had been before the house of Commons!

CHARLES II   Well my Lord you and I are both old men and we should love
   quietnesse.
WHARTON   Beside all other obligations I haue reason to desire it having some
   1500 pounds a yeare to lose . . .
CHARLES II   Ay my lord but you haue an aking tooth still.
WHARTON   No indeed, mine are all faln out.

(Letters, 354)

Wharton parries each royal thrust stroke by stroke, and where Charles finally
goes to the sore point of Wharton's political ambition – 'you haue an aking
tooth still' – Wharton brilliantly recalls Charles's emollient emphasis that
they are 'both old men' and offers that he himself is now toothless.

In the 1660s, by which time Marvell had become a Member of Parliament,
the genre of animadversion itself was temporarily in eclipse, although Marvell
in his verse satires, especially his Advices to a Painter, offered mordant
comment on the heroic poetry of the day and the court it had sought to
celebrate. At the end of the 1660s, however, the attempts of the restored
Church of England to enlarge its gains met with the revived aspirations of
English Presbyterians and Independents. Fresh print controversy followed.
Some churchmen knew enough to worry about any renewal of such hostili-
ties, since worse might be feared from the likes of Marchamont Nedham and
'Milton, with their Junto'.[17] But it was the unheralded Marvell who soon
entered the breach and who, in the words of the same fulminating observer,
now 'deservs to be brought on his Knees in that house where he sits; and from
thence to be sent to O[liver] C[romwell]s quarters, since apparently he justi-
fyes that foule cause. And, if the Universityes would nowe bestirre themselves,
as they ought to do, I doubt not, but they might make Mervell an Example, for
a terror to others.'[18] The offending work was that tour de force of animadversion The Rehearsal Transpros'd (1672).

Victorious animadversion

The rapid republication of The Rehearsal Transpros'd in 1672–3 and also its
Second Part (1673–4) attests to their initial popularity. Even some readers
hostile to Marvell's cause might concede his triumph over his adversary
Samuel Parker: 'Your Book's the talk of all the Town, | And hath begot you
great renown'.[19] In later years it won praise from no less a satirist than
Jonathan Swift, who on this point admired Marvell's 'great Genius' – 'so we
still read Marvel's Answer to Parker with Pleasure, tho' the book it answers be
sunk long ago' – and who through imitation flattered it further, seeming to
recall it in his own A Tale of a Tub, in his Houyhnhnms, and in the Scriblerians'
satire on the art of sinking.[20] The success stemmed from Marvell's flair in

displacing theological and political discussion into the language of the theatre and coffee house.[21] Parker himself had elaborated his polemics with a 'raillery' meant to enliven his very long works of controversy. Marvell seized the opportunity to display his own mastery of the joco-serious, a mode with classical antecedents which had thrived in especially the journalism of the 1640s and become a staple of mid-seventeenth-century pamphleteering.[22] When Marvell promises 'I shall treat him betwixt Jest and Earnest' (*PW*, 1:268), it is to shift ground nimbly as occasion merits, whether to lament Parker's jests as laborious and unbefitting a clergyman, or to bring Parker up short for joking about matters of great significance, or to mock Parker's own attempts to be serious or to stand on his dignity. In keeping with Marvell's bitter attacks on clerical presumption, some of his cruellest ironies scoff at Parker's dignity, not least where Marvell sexualizes Parker's more innocent reference to his 'comfortable importance', which term then for wife or mistress became a standing joke well into the eighteenth century.[23]

Marvell's nimbleness also lies in his skilful manoeuvring through the mass of Parker's publications, of whose length and frequency he sometimes complains. In 1670 Parker had published the 374-page *Discourse of Ecclesiastical Politie*; in 1671, the 766-page *Defence and Continuation of the Ecclesiastical Politie*; in 1672, the 100-page 'Preface' to *Bishop Bramhall's Vindication*. These came on the heels of some not short works by Parker in the 1660s, including the 440 Latin pages of his *Tentamina Physico-Theologica de Deo* (1665). His *Reproof* to Marvell (1673) came to another 536 pages and the other like attacks on the *Rehearsal Transpros'd* in 1673 came to many hundreds of pages more.

Marvell wisely decided that the part must stand for the whole. He was not the first animadverter to decline the straitjacket of point-by-point refutation, page by page, in favour of some much more tactical or synthetic organization of his response. There was still some expectation that animadversion should dutifully work through the text animadverted upon, as appears from Marvell's faulting Parker for having begun the *Reproof* (1673) *in medias res* and from Marvell's grudging promise that he 'will not decline the pursuit, but plod on after him in his own way, thorow thick and thin, hill or dale, over hedge and ditch wherever he leads' (*PW*, 1:268). But this requirement he observes in the breach.

In both the *Rehearsal Transpros'd* and its *Second Part*, Marvell skips back and forth through their multiple pretexts so that he can boldly arrange their materials to his advantage. The effect is most striking in the *Rehearsal Transpros'd*, where the first quarter and the last half comment on Parker's 'Preface', while the second quarter addresses Parker's *Discourse of Ecclesiastical Politie* and its *Defence and Continuation* (*PW*, 1:11ff.). In a formidable show of skill, Marvell summarizes the over 1,100 pages of the *Discourse* and its *Defence* under six headings, even though this is 'but collateral to my work of examining the Preface'; each of these headings he turns into a stinging rebuke of Parker's Hobbesian ecclesiology and politics, or so Marvell describes them, ranging from the dangers of 'The Unlimited Magistrate' to 'Pushpin-Divinity' (*PW*, 1:95–6, 99, 101, 102, 104, 109).[24] With the 'Preface' itself he is no more patient, even as he attacks it in more detail. His handling of Parker's *Reproof* in the *Second Part* of the *Rehearsal Transpros'd* shows how much he had learned in controversy. It more fluently subordinates the many sources with which Marvell works, including the *Reproof* first of all, but also earlier of Parker's works going back to his first publications in the mid 1660s. By contrast, Marvell has only a 70-page text on which to animadvert in his later *Mr Smirke* (1676) and works through it more nearly in order, if still very selectively; in his *Remarks* (1678), he also comes nearer to following the order of the 140-page tract he impugns, if with renewed freedom and in still narrow selection.

Marvell's principle of selection is first of all ethical. He puts Parker's character into question as a way of attacking his arguments, but he also attacks his arguments as a way of putting his character into question. In part this was the lasting legacy of classical rhetoric, famously in Cicero's crushing *ad hominem* assaults on Catiline or other of the victims of his orations. Especially if Marvell did assist Milton with *Defensio secunda*, he had first-hand experience of how to deploy vicious personal calumnies, whether justified or not, in long philippics destroying the credibility of his adversary. The balance shifts between the *Rehearsal Transpros'd* and its *Second Part* from dwelling on ethical faults evident from Parker's writings to Marvell's aggravation of those faults with reference to what he knows about Parker himself. Marvell was fighting fire with fire. He describes how Parker and his 'Posse Archidiaconatus' had sought incriminating details about Marvell's own life (*PW*, 1:249). Parker's *Reproof* infers much about Marvell's failings from details in the *Rehearsal Transpros'd* but he and others in the 'Posse' were eager to add more, not least about Marvell's possible sexual incapacity.[25] Marvell was able already to read the *Reproof* as it went through the press and found it 'the rudest book, one or other, that ever was publisht (I may say), since the invention of printing' (*Letters*, 328). He seems briefly, at least, to have wondered how ever to respond 'to so scurrilous' a publication. But there was 'a noble and high argument' at stake, and those greater issues, chiefly of religious toleration, made all the more pressing his ethical arguments against Parker and for himself.

Key to Marvell's attack on Parker is the characterization of a man driven by private interest, whatever the clergyman's pretence to any higher calling. As

Marvell delves into the psychology of such clerical vanity, Parker's self-promotion proves a form of anti-social madness. A dark comedy of relentless material forces follows. As if a monster propelled by Hobbesian mechanism, Parker is driven by impulse, which turns his head, maddening him. Marvell sexualizes Parker's rapture 'of Ecclesiastical Felicity', mocking such 'growing' enthusiasm 'when a man's Phancy is up, and his Breeches are down' (*PW*, 1:47–8). Or that chaplain becomes 'like a raging Indian' who runs amok, 'stabbing every man he meets, till himself he be knockt on the head'; or a 'howling, yelling, and barking' werewolf, scratching even after corpses in their graves. Worse, 'Nothing now would serve him but he must be a madman in print', when 'his whole discourse, as proceeding from a Man in the confines of two so contrary distempers, partakes all thorow equally of Stupidity and Raving' (*PW*, 1:73, 78, 77, 145, 227, 243). All logic is lost in the wilderness of 'infinite Tautology'. As Parker's vanities proliferate, Marvell frolics amid them, only from time to time to break off abruptly as if impatient of such folly: 'But enough of this Trash' (*PW*, 1:199, 55).

Against Parker's consuming self-interest, Marvell proposes a rival ethical standard of more gentlemanly disinterest. Here some of his key terms are *candid*, *ingenuous*, *generous*. His self-representation is of a modest but sporting man about town, with his gaming talk helping to develop this persona (nor was he put off by Parker's and the Posse's dark inferences from his gambler's terms of art, *PW*, 1:43–4, 182, 252, 255). But that is a feint, in keeping with the languages also of duelling and military service that Marvell deploys (*PW*, 1:136, 142, 148–9, 175–6, 267). In his main assault, Marvell promotes his own ethos through his performance of literary authority, set emphatically against the ecclesiastical authority claimed by Parker. Here he could triumph especially over Parker's defects as a would-be master of humanist disputation. Parker's works, in Marvell's view, had fallen between the two stools of pulpit and coffee house. And the Restoration coffee house he depicts as his own natural habitat, whence he reports the banter of 'some critical People' faulting Parker, only for Marvell to defend him, only for 'the mirth' to rise to the point 'It was grown almost as good as a Play among us' (*PW*, 1:69–70; see also II.41–2). The attacks on Marvell by turns appeal to the same audience and seek to discredit coffeehouse culture as disreputable at best (*PW*, 1:3–4). But Marvell had an unrivalled grasp of the literary idiom appropriate to such informal disputation. Where Milton had in his *Defensio* and *Defensio secunda* trumpeted his own Latinity against the barbarism of his antagonists, Marvell achieves a like effect in the vernacular, in part through denunciation but also through his bravura display of wide-ranging cultural references. So often did he play this suit that he left himself susceptible to the sneer that his was only commonplace-book learning, as if his tropes were drawn from some ungentlemanly hoard of others' *aperçus* rather than any truer wit, spontaneously generated out of more active magnanimity. Such derision is heard in the hostile *Common-place-Book Out of the Rehearsal Transpros'd* (1673) but also in friendlier quarters, where his flair as writer might nonetheless be set against his failings as a public speaker.[26] On this point, Marvell had sought to beat Parker to the punch, mocking the 'flowers' in his rhetorical garden – thus playing on the Greek root of 'anthology' (Latin *florilegium*) – which criticism may carry a special charge in view of our familiarity with Marvell as a supreme garden-poet (*PW*, 1:135–43).

But the variety of literary reference at Marvell's disposal is never in question. He can dispute points of the Bible in earnest and in jest, or burlesque the high style of Guarini's *Il Pastor Fido* or Davenant's *Gondibert*, or recall his schooling in Ovid, or readily improve on Parker's use of *Don Quixote* (*PW*, 1:43, 101; 1:50, 200–1; 1:85, 11:45, 101; 1:74, 140, 145, 172, 175, 360). At the other end of the spectrum, he can predict Parker will come 'to endite Tickets for the Bear-garden', or that his treatises will likely prove waste paper for 'the more judicious Oylmen and Grocers' (*PW*, 1:44, 66). And in this cultural fairground there are still simpler entertainments, as when Parker's exaggerations recall 'those frightfull Looking-glasses, made for sport' or 'a St Christopher in the Popish Porches, as big as ten Porters' (*PW*, 1:56, 57). Between high and low are found myriad further allusions, to works ranging from the still well-known to the long forgotten. Sometimes Marvell's literary associations are obvious, as when he springs to the defence of Milton, who had been brought into this controversy because his infamy as a monarchomach writer suggested Marvell's guilt by association. Sometimes his gestures are more private, as when, also with reference to Milton, he echoes that poet's Satan, pausing on the edge of Chaos – '. . . Into this wild abyss the wary fiend I Stood on the brink of hell and looked awhile, I Pondering his voyage' (*Paradise Lost*, 11:910–19) – by himself pausing, confronted by Parker's chaos, 'before I commit my self to the dangerous depths of his Discourse, which I am now upon the brink of' (*PW*, 1:51).

Marvell's style of writing, as well as the burden of his argument, led as far as royal approval of the work as well as some support for him in the Privy Council. The difficulty remained that his literary riches could be transmuted into only some social capital. That Marvell may have too much depended on them appears from others' criticism and also from his own adjustment of his subsequent animadversions. The extravagance of *The Rehearsal Transpros'd* he brings under some restraint already in its *Second Part*, published a year later.[27] There is still vivid variety but the latter work features more fluent running commentary on Parker's *Reproof* and other of his works. Now the flashing strokes of local wit are further subordinated to Marvell's larger stratagem in argument. Moreover, having been faulted for his lack of citations in *Rehearsal Transpros'd*, Marvell in the *Second Part* supplies them thick and fast, however miscellaneous they sometimes prove. There are further contests implicit in Marvell's disputing of Parker's scholarship, with Marvell fighting at once a rearguard action and seeking also to advance his position.[28] A still more bitter seriousness of purpose shows in Marvell's biting references to Parker's father's interregnal writing against the crown: 'It befitted our Author to have wash'd off the blood from his own Threshold before he had accused others' (*PW*, 1:291–2, 418). In the *Second Part*, Andrew Marvell, Esquire, the Member of Parliament who had been widely identified as the author of the *Rehearsal Transpros'd*, projects a sometimes pained sobriety, a worthier rectitude that permits him only here and there to show his coffee-cultural claws. Now Marvell increasingly deploys a weapon somewhat at odds with the *ad hoc* quality of animadversion: the majestic reasonableness of an ingenuous, right-thinking if sometimes sceptical, Restoration man of the town.

Beyond animadversion

For Marvell's last great move as an animadverter was to turn on animadversion itself. In both *Mr Smirke: Or, the Divine in Mode* (1676) and *Remarks Upon a Late Disingenuous Discourse* (1678), his quarrel begins to be with quarrelling *per se*.[29] He makes the move ostentatiously to model 'a piece of due Civility from one of the Laitie' (*PW*, 11:37) by contrast with the combative excesses whether of High Church or of too rigid Presbyterianism. His titles for his own efforts suggest Marvell's change of tack: the main part of *Mr Smirke* he styles 'annotations'; its companion piece is an 'essay', and he later supplies *Remarks* on Danson's animadversions (*PW*, 11:401–2). He aligns himself and his readers with 'all sober men', 'the sober and serious', 'in good sober earnest', which 'Laity are commonly more temperate and merciful (I might say more discreet) in the exercising of any Authority they are intrusted with' than the clergy (*PW*, 11:41, 44, 104, 52). In the 1670s, Marvell repeatedly sets the polite moderation of the citizen against clerical 'cruelty' also in his poetry – notably *The Loyal Scot*, his related *Epigram: Upon Blood's attempt to steal the Crown*, and *Scaevola Scoto-Brittannus*.

Marvell anticipates Enlightenment manners in a way revealing of 'something very English: the need of a swiftly changing gentlemanly class to disarm the clerisies by themselves taking over letters and philosophy'.[30] He does so especially in his companion to *Mr Smirke*, his *Short Historical Essay* unmasking the councils and creeds of the early church. That mocking history shows how bracing the encounter may prove when a sceptical classicist explores the history of the early church.[31] Moreover, closer to home, he threatens that one could write a like essay on the venality of the Savoy Conference, where episcopal resistance had put paid to any broader settlement of the Church of England after the Restoration. The tactic is again to align the gentleman with the crown. Years before, Marvell had extolled as good councillors to the king those 'born to virtue and to wealth' and of 'gen'rous conscience' (*Last Instructions*, lines 983–90). Now he muses that someone with just such a generous conscience, that is 'A man disinterested either way', could 'make a pleasant story of the *Anecdota* of that [Savoy] Meeting, and manifest how well his Majesties Gracious Declaration [of toleration] before his Return, and his Broad-Seal afterward were pursued' (*PW*, II:95). This might have been material too hot to handle, though Marvell did not shun the fire when he next turned to writing his *Account of the Growth of Popery and Arbitrary Government*.

Marvell is of course at the top of his game where it comes to disparaging the clergy's 'new Books of ridiculous and facetious argument' (*PW*, II:38). For the eponymous Mr Smirke, he again turns to the drama, now the recent production of George Etherege's scintillating *Man of Mode* (première 11 March 1676). But in keeping with his new mood, he does not long dwell on that victim of fashion. Instead, he presents his adversary first and foremost as 'the Animadverter', which title he gives ever more pejorative weight, adding the Swiftian observation that it is 'An Animal which hath nothing Humane in it but a Malicious Grinne'. Saint Paul himself had denounced animadverters (*PW*, II:53–6, 92; Acts 17:5–6). Marvell too, piously insisting on 'the ordinary rules of civility, or ... the sober way of arguing Controversy', decries 'the utmost extremity of Jeer, Disdain, and Indignation'. The problem, he knows, stems as ever from 'the false and secular interest of some of the clergy', and also from the universities' failure sufficiently to support 'the modest Skirmish of Reason', however lavish their building funds (*PW*, II:41, 52, 68). Privately, he can raise an eyebrow when a thank-you note from Bishop Croft, to whose defence he had sprung in *Mr Smirke* lest that 'most judicious Author ... enter'd the Pit with so Scurrilous an Animadverter', itself betrays the good bishop's unbecoming bitterness against 'yᵉ dirty language of foule mouthed beasts' arrayed against him (*PW*, II:37; *Letters*, 347).

Marvell's critique is both general and specific. In a memorable passage he describes a whole system of distribution in which the crabbed writings especially of ambitious chaplains find promotion through universities and church, in town and in country (*PW*, II:85–8). His analysis may have been the sharper since Marvell himself seems to have benefited from an analogous Presbyterian system of dissemination (*Chronology*, 170, 173, 191). He also generates an ethos argument against the anonymous animadverter by describing him as the very type of such an upwardly mobile churchman. Again madness is a problem (*PW*, II:45). Worse is the 'disingenuity' of the animadverter's resorting 'disingenuously' to 'all disingenuous methods' (*PW*, II:77, 70, 57). The ethos-driven argument shows in Marvell's lengthy handling of the early pages in the work he confutes, only then to move very rapidly through the main text (*PW*, II:106ff.). In the end he breaks off with a vivid evocation of the hectic circumstances of his own clandestine publication, even as he himself seems to rise above the situation: 'The Printer calls: the Press is in Danger. I am weary of such stuff, both mine and his. I will rather give [Turner] this following Essay of mine to busie him . . .' (*PW*, II:113).

But the man in question, Francis Turner, was no ineffectual opponent. Marvell's chief tactic against him is to identify his methods in order to discredit them. Overall, he pits 'his Levity' against 'his Argument', but he also faults each of those (*PW*, II:69). As for levity: there is no apostolic succession where it comes to wit, Marvell avers, yielding his cold-eyed observation that 'It is not every man that is qualified to sustain the Dignity of the Churches Jester' (*PW*, II:38, 40). He mocks the clergyman's excess of effort when he 'wretchedly' hunts 'for an University Quibble' or strains 'to hale in an ill-favor'd Jeer at the Author' (*PW*, II:45, 46). As for argument: Marvell very insistently faults Turner's logic, whether it be his feigning or frustrating any 'Rational Deduction', offering a false *reductio ad absurdum*, inferring 'a whole Cargo of Consequences' so remote from Croft's work that they are rather the animadverter's own 'Inconsequences and Inanimadversions', losing all coherence in comment prone to 'hacking and vain repetition', or supplying a 'division' that is 'all fooling' (*PW*, II:75, 80–3; 76; 59; 45–6; 44). Or, 'civilly', Marvell can give Turner the lie almost direct: 'I do not believe him' (*PW*, II:96).

Behind his turn against animadversion, however incomplete, lies Marvell's fresh investment in the language and politics of moderation, an ever more frequent theme in these late works. Marvell's ideals for the clergy, whether in *Mr Smirke* or *Remarks*, are deliberation, modesty and more patient study of the Bible, beyond which scripture they are discouraged from much venturing. Many of the same reservations apply both to the Athanasian excesses of High Churchmen seeking to impose their creeds and to the Calvinist overcertainties of any too rigid Presbyterian hostile to the voice of moderation. It is unlikely that Marvell needed much help with the biblical and theological arguments he ventured in these works. As he had done with Parker, he again delights in quoting scripture improvingly to the clergymen under his correction (for example, *PW*, II:57, 63–4, 73, 84). But this seems more than just mischievous sanctimony. Marvell is here responsive to fresh currents in Restoration churchmanship, especially the latitudinarian thinking associated with the more rational religion of John Tillotson, cautious friend of Nonconformity. Marvell's defence of the moderate Bishop Croft, friend of a more comprehensive national church, praises that bishop's emphasis on the simpler rudiments of Christianity because so 'seasonable' in divided times: 'When the sickly nation had been so long indisposed and knew not the Remedy, but (having taken so many things that rather did it harm then good), only longed for some Moderation, and as soon as it had tasted this, seemed to itself sensibly to recover' (*PW*, II:41). But if Marvell's assertion of these simplicities takes him nearer to the simpler style of Tillotson, the habits of a lifetime were not so easily overcome.

The magnificent openings of *A Short Historical Essay* and of *Remarks* display a magnanimous rationality in affirming principles of toleration. But Marvell's exalted style cannot long stay free of irony or more immediate polemical inflection:

> The Christian Religion, as first instituted by our Blessed Saviour, was the greatest security to Magistrates by the Obedience which it taught, and was fitted to enjoy no less security under them by a Practice conformable to that Doctrine. For our Saviour himself, not pretending to an Earthly Kingdom took such care therefore to instruct his Followers in the due subjection to Governours ... [though] he thought it good reason to retain his Religion under his own Cognizance, and exempt its Authority from their Jurisdiction.   (*PW*, II:115)

Where is animadversion here? Nowhere, and everywhere. In stating such general principles, Marvell easily implies rebuke to those in breach of them, whether in the early or the modern church. Or again, beginning his *Remarks*:

> Of all Vocations to which men addict themselves, or are dedicated, I have alwaies esteemed that of the Ministry to be the most noble and happy Imployment; as being more peculiarly directed to those two great Ends, the advancement of God's Glory, and the promoting of Man's Salvation. It hath seemed to me as if they who have chosen, and are set apart for that Work, did, by the continual opportunity of conversing with their Maker, enjoy a state like that of Paradise; and in this superiour, that they are not also, as Adam, put in *to dress and keep a Garden*; but are, or ought to be, exempt from the necessity of all worldly avocations. Yet ...   (*PW*, II:415)

Marvell's high-minded air of unconcern soon yields, of course, to the present polemical necessity, as he sees it, of defending a moderate against an extreme Presbyterian. What has a reasonable gentleman to do here? Again in the conclusion Marvell reverts to his expectation in

> this litigious Age, that some or other will Sue me for having Trespassed thus far of Theological Ground: But I have this for my plea, that I stepped over on no

other Reason than (which any man legally may do) to hinder one Divine from offering violence to another. And, if I should be molested on that account, I doubt not but some of the Protestant Clergy will be ready therefore to give me the like Assistance. (*PW*, II:482)

The question remains whether this very resistance to adversarial language is not itself adversarial, or whether, in the words of one of Marvell's enemies, 'the Poyson has not eaten quite thorough the Vernish' (*PW*, II:196).

The deeper issue is Marvell's insinuation of himself into clerical controversy, as if disputes in religion must not be left to the parties immediately interested, but rather invited lay arbitration. A like issue arises in the praises for Marvell from later writers in the Enlightenment, as when John Toland in the 1690s applauds that 'great man', 'my old Lay-Friend, the most ingenious Mr Andrew Marvell', 'who by his Parts and Probity made himself so much known ... in England' (*Chronology*, 248, 252). Toland can draw on Marvell with and without acknowledgement, but whatever the attractions of Marvell's bravura animadversions against Parker, it is his intrusion into the professional fold of the clergy that seems as lastingly to have made an impression. Toland was less sure of touch but in another reader of Marvell we find a like note, not least in defence of religious toleration, namely John Locke (himself no mean animadverter). Their voices can seem peculiarly melded where Marvell's beloved nephew, William Popple, supplied the first English translation of Locke's *Letter Concerning Toleration* (1689). In Marvellian fashion, it is Popple who faults 'partiality' and those who proceed 'upon narrow principles, suited only to the interests of their own sects'. Marvellian too is his call for 'more generous remedies than what have yet been made use of in our distemper'; Marvellian too is his note when he breaks off, 'But the thing itself is so short, that it will not bear a longer preface.'[32] But Marvellian in a still deeper sense is the forceful impartiality with which this Englished Locke achieves adversarial aims in no openly adversarial style.

NOTES

1. *The Complete Prose Works of John Milton*, ed. Don M. Wolfe *et al.*, 8 vols. (New Haven, 1953–82), I:717ff., 726.
2. T. S. Eliot, 'Andrew Marvell', in *Selected Essays* (London, 1951), 302–4; see also A. J. Smith, 'Marvell's Metaphysical Wit', in C. A. Patrides, ed., *Approaches to Marvell: The York Tercentenary Lectures* (London, 1978), 57, 63; Harold Toliver, *Marvell's Ironic Vision* (New Haven, 1963), 3; Toliver, 'The Critical Reprocessing of Andrew Marvell', *English Literary History* 47 (1980), 192.
3. See Allan Pritchard, 'Marvell's "The Garden": A Restoration Poem?', *Studies in English Literature* 23 (1983), 371–88; Smith, in *Poems*, 85–6; von Maltzahn, 'Andrew Marvell and the Prehistory of Whiggism', in David Womersley, ed.,

assisted by Paddy Bullard and Abigail Williams, '*Cultures of Whiggism*': *New Essays on English Literature and Culture in the Long Eighteenth Century* (Newark, NJ, 2005), 31–61; Paul Hammond, 'The Date of Marvell's "The Mower against Gardens"', *Notes and Queries* 251 (2006), 178–81.

4. Quoted in Mordechai Feingold, 'The Humanities', in Nicholas Tyacke, ed., *The History of the University of Oxford*, Vol. IV: *Seventeenth-Century Oxford* (Oxford, 2001), 226.

5. Hull City Archives (HCA), Borough Letters 247–247b.

6. Derek Hirst and Steven N. Zwicker, 'Andrew Marvell and the Toils of Patriarchy: Fatherhood, Longing, and the Body Politic', *English Literary History* 66 (1999), 629–54; Walter Ong, *Fighting for Life: Contest, Sexuality, and Consciousness* (Ithaca, NY, 1981), 24.

7. Blair Worden, *Literature and Politics in Cromwellian England* (Oxford, 2007), esp. 63ff., 131ff.

8. Von Maltzahn, 'Liberalism or Apocalypse: John Milton and Andrew Marvell', in Marianne Thormählen, ed., *English Now* (Lund, Sweden, 2008), 44–58; cf. Louis L. Martz, *The Poetry of Meditation*, 2nd edn (New Haven, 1962).

9. Worden, *Literature and Politics*, 82ff., 130, 138.

10. Christopher Ricks, 'Its Own Resemblance', in Patrides, ed., *Approaches to Marvell*, 109; John Carey, 'Reversals Transposed: An Aspect of Marvell's Imagination', in Patrides, ed., *Approaches to Marvell*, 143.

11. David Norbrook, 'Marvell's *Scaevola Scoto-Britannus* and Political Violence', in Marshall Grossman, ed., *Reading Renaissance Ethics* (New York, 2007), 176.

12. Peter Schwenger, ' "To Make his Saying True": Deceit in *Upon Appleton House*', *Studies in Philology* 7 (1980), 84.

13. See Timothy Raylor, 'Moseley, Walkley, and the 1645 Editions of Waller', *The Library* 7th ser. 2 (2001), 236–65; and Smith, *Poems*, 321–96.

14. Discussed in Annabel Patterson, 'Lady State's First Two Sittings: Marvell's Satiric Canon', *Studies in English Literature* 40 (200), 405–6.

15. See Annabel Patterson, 'Marvell and Secret History', in Warren Chernaik and Martin Dzelzainis, eds., *Marvell and Liberty* (Basingstoke, 1999), 23–49.

16. See N. H. Keeble, ' "I would not tell you any tales": Marvell's Constituency Letters', in Conal Condren and A. D. Cousins, eds., *The Political Identity of Andrew Marvell* (Aldershot, 1990), 124–9.

17. See von Maltzahn, 'Laureate, Republican, Calvinist: An Early Response to Milton and *Paradise Lost* (1667)', *Milton Studies* 29 (1992), 181–98.

18. Quoted in William Poole, 'Two Early Readers of Milton', *Milton Quarterly* 38 (2004), 82.

19. Royal Society (London), MS 32, 41; see also *PW*, I:20–2.

20. *PW*, I:281, 308, 137, 261; Pritchard, 'The Houyhnhnms: Swift, Suetonius, and Marvell', *Notes & Queries* 235 (1990), 350–6.

21. For further discussion of this point see Keeble, 'Why Transprose the *Rehearsal?*', in Chernaik and Dzelzainis, eds., *Marvell and Liberty*, 249–68.

22. See Blair Worden, ' "Wit in a Roundhead": The Dilemma of Marchamont Nedham', in Susan D. Amussen and Mark A. Kishlansky, eds., *Political Culture and Cultural Politics* (Manchester, 1995), 301–37; and also Peter W. Thomas, *Sir John Berkenhead, 1617–79: A Royalist Career in Politics and Polemics* (Oxford, 1969).

23. *Irish Miscellany, or Teague-land Jests* (London, 1746); Francis Grose, *A Classical Dictionary of the Vulgar Tongue* (London, 1785), s.v. 'comfortable importance'.
24. This exchange is examined more fully by Jon Parkin, 'Liberty Transpos'd: Andrew Marvell and Samuel Parker', in Chernaik and Dzelzainis, eds., *Marvell and Liberty*, 269–89.
25. On the sexual libels directed against Marvell see Paul Hammond, 'Marvell's Sexuality', *The Seventeenth Century* 11 (1996), 87–123.
26. See *Plays, Poems, and Miscellaneous Writings Associated with George Villiers, Second Duke of Buckingham*, ed. Robert D. Hume and Harold Love, 2 vols. (Oxford, 2007), II:166, 466.
27. Annabel Patterson discusses the comparative restraint of the *Second Part* of the *Rehearsal Transpros'd*, also of Marvell's later works, in *Marvell: The Writer in Public Life* (Harlow, 2000), 118–28.
28. See Jason P. Rosenblatt, *Renaissance England's Chief Rabbi* (Oxford, 2006), 112–34.
29. As noted by Patterson, *Marvell*, 128; *PW*, II:397–9.
30. J. G. A. Pocock, *Barbarism and Religion*, Vol. I: *The Enlightenments of Edward Gibbon, 1737–1764* (Cambridge, 1999), 262.
31. Cf. Edward Gibbon, *The History of the Decline and Fall of the Roman Empire*, ed. David Womersley (Harmondsworth, 1995); also Neal McLynn, *Ambrose of Milan: Church and Court in a Christian Capital* (Berkeley, 1994).
32. John Locke, *A Letter Concerning Toleration*, ed. John Horton and Susan Mendus (London, 1991), 12–13.

Further reading

Anne Dunan-Page and Beth Lynch, eds., *Roger L'Estrange and the Making of Restoration Culture* (London, 2008).
N. H. Keeble, 'Why Transprose the *Rehearsal*?', in Warren Chernaik and Martin Dzelzainis, eds., *Marvell and Liberty* (Basingstoke, 1999), 249–68.
Harold Love, *English Clandestine Satire, 1660–1702* (Oxford, 2004).
Annabel Patterson, *Marvell: The Writer in Public Life* (Harlow, 2000).
John Spurr, *England in the 1670s: 'This Masquerading Age'* (Oxford, 2000).
Peter W. Thomas, *Sir John Berkenhead, 1617–1679: A Royalist Career in Politics and Polemics* (Oxford, 1969).
Nicholas von Maltzahn, 'Milton, Marvell, and Toleration', in Sharon Achinstein and Elizabeth Sauer, eds., *Milton and Toleration* (Oxford, 2007), 86–104.
Blair Worden, *Literature and Politics in Cromwellian England* (Oxford, 2007).

12

NIGEL SMITH

How to make a biography of Andrew Marvell

A more elusive, non-recorded character is hardly to be found. We know
all about him, but very little of him ... the man Andrew Marvell
remains undiscovered. He rarely comes to the surface.
Augustine Birrell, *Andrew Marvell* (1905)

I ... who haue no imployment but idlenesse and who am so oblivious that
I should forget mine own name did I not see it sometimes
in a friends superscription.
Marvell to Sir Henry Thompson (January 1674/5)

Evidence

Authors from the past leave behind their literary works, but biographers need
to construct their lives from other pieces of their life history evidence, apart
from their poems, plays, novels or other kinds of writing. Works do of course
function as life evidence, but without that other evidence, usually called
documentary evidence because it is found in various types of historical document (records of birth, baptism, marriage, burial, property transactions,
taxation accounts, and so on), the picture of a 'real life' would be impoverished. Letters, diaries and personal notebooks have an additional special
status, because they are in a sense literary works too, and because they also
record how the subject of a biography sees the world, or interacts with it. To
have a large cache of letters is a gift for a biographer; it might be said that to
engage in writing a life without such a collection is folly.

As with the documentary evidence for most early modern biography, in
Andrew Marvell's case a very great deal is missing. It is not as bad a case as
Shakespeare's: because Marvell was an MP there survive a series of constitu-
ency and related letters, and Marvell's activities as an MP are traceable in
parliamentary records. These largely document political events in
Westminster, and tell us little about the man himself and not a great deal

more about his own activities. Nonetheless, they deliver a regular account of one aspect of his life during the Restoration, and thus supplement the much smaller body of miscellaneous letters most of which are far more revealing in telling us what he personally thought and felt (see *Letters*, 304–57). Yet Marvell was prone for a number of reasons to be secretive, and several of his 'personal letters' (such as the single letter to Oliver Cromwell, dated 28 July 1653) performed a specific function of communicating information as part of one of Marvell's official roles (in this case as a household tutor): they tell us little about what he really thought (*Letters*, 304–5). Thus he wrote to Cromwell: 'the onely Ciuility which it is proper for me to practise with so eminent a Person is to obey you' (*Letters*, 304). Much of the non-Hull correspondence was concerned with news, suggesting that he may have been in the pay of some (Lord Wharton, Sir Henry Thompson) to provide professional newsletters. Only his letters to his nephew William Popple written in the last decade of his life (and where the initial formality of 'Dearest Cousin' quickly modifies to 'Dearest Will'), and perhaps also the letters of the same period to his friends Richard and Edward Thompson, and his political associate Sir Edward Harley, give us candid viewpoints, uninflected by the protocols of employment or the need for guardedness (for at this time Marvell was with good reason concerned that his correspondence would be intercepted and read by his political enemies).

We know extremely little about Marvell's life, especially the early parts in Holderness, Hull, Cambridge, continental Europe and London before he joined the Fairfax household in 1650. These are, unfortunately, the areas that we would like to know most about, because some of these periods correspond with the writing of much of his most famous verse, in so far as we know with certainty in a minority of cases and in so far as we conjecture in all the rest. There has been much critical lament over these gaps, so that anything resembling a faithful rendering of Marvell's life records as a biographical narrative necessarily focuses upon events after September 1657, when Marvell was appointed to work in the Office of Foreign Tongues for the Cromwellian Protectorate. Thomas Cooke's 1726 biography exhausted itself of life records after fifteen small octavo pages and turned to the works. So many gaps have provided licence for novelists to create a fictional life for Marvell often by means of a conjuring up of colourful invented episodes set against a backdrop of the momentous events of Marvell's own lifetime. Hence Will Davenport's *The Painter* (New York, 2003), a fanciful account of Marvell and Rembrandt meeting up as competing lovers in a trip to east Yorkshire during the 1660s, or Christopher Peachment's *The Green and the Gold* (London, 2003), a tale of Marvell's secret life as spy and lover of coy mistresses.

Marvell's early biographers were not faced with the problem of missing evidence since they regarded him primarily as a political figure, and they were not trying to match the standards of modern biography. These biographers, Thomas Cooke and Edward Thompson, were both editors of Marvell's works, and they were developing Marvell's reputation as Whig champion that had grown in heated polemical exchange during the years following his death in August 1678. Their lives of Marvell were conditioned by the myth of Andrew Marvell the patriot that had developed in this time. Before Marvell had a biography he had an afterlife, a construction of his identity that was a consequence of his involvement in his last two years in a constitutional dilemma that reached crisis proportions immediately after his death.

Afterlife

The unfolding of political events in the months after Marvell's death reads like the prophecy of the popish conspiracy in church and state that Marvell had made in *An Account of the Growth of Popery and Arbitrary Government* (1677) come true. The evidence of a widespread conspiracy of Roman Catholics – indigenous and foreign, and designed to ensure a Catholic succession of the monarchy and future for England – was widely believed and caused a massive crisis in church and state. Titus Oates made his allegations of a 'Popish plot' in late September 1678, and on 12 October Sir Edmond Berry Godfrey went missing: his body was discovered one week later, and the murder was widely suspected to be the work of Catholic agents. The immediate outcome was the fall of the Earl of Danby, the king's chief minister, and, at long last, the summoning of a new parliament – the dissolution of the old, which had been elected in 1661, came on 24 January 1679. In the medium term, the huge political battle known as the Exclusion Crisis took its three-year course. In it the Whig and Tory parties formed themselves as the issue of the Protestant succession of the monarchy was debated.

Perhaps early in 1679, John Ayloffe wrote the powerful verse satire 'Marvell's Ghost'. No longer was Marvell a composer of surreptitiously circulated poetry on affairs of state, he was now a subject of the poetry itself and a hero to boot, denouncing Stuart oppression ever more strongly. Four more separate poems of this kind are known to exist, one from 1687, one from 1690, another from 1691 also entitled 'Marvell's Ghost', and yet one more from 1697 perhaps deliberately designed to be published with a collection of Marvell's state poems.[1] Marvell's political verse began to have a greater impact too: John Oldham's 'Satyr II' bore particular traces of Marvell's *The Loyal Scot* and his epigram on Thomas Blood; other works showed that Oldham had read Marvell's prose. Other echoes still of poetry and prose appeared in other poems. The attributions of opposition poetry to Marvell grew although many of these would prove to be incorrect: Marvell's reputation and association with a certain kind of poem (for instance, the 'advice to a painter' poem) was the cause. Even a Whig, nonconformist poet might occasionally resist the 'desire to be deified after Marvell's manner'.[2] Dryden began his decidedly negative allusions to Marvell at this time, and Tory poetry further railed at Marvell's associations with Whig grandees such as Buckingham and Shaftesbury. This added to the names that Marvell would be called by his enemies, and indeed even by impartial judges: 'sneering', 'untowardly'. To read a Marvell pamphlet became a Tory byword for a credulous Whig, and Marvell's *An Account of the Growth of Popery and Arbitrary Government* (1677) was regarded as fuel, among other writings, for the Rye House Plot of 1683 against the lives of the King and the Duke of York. Roger L'Estrange, Charles II's Surveyor of the Press, regarded *An Account* as part of a larger plot to exclude James from the succession. He even claimed that Marvell 'dreamed' the idea of the Popish plot and complained that Marvell had been canonized 'if not for Saint, yet for a Prophet, in shewing how pat the Popish Plot falls out to his conjecture'.[3] In L'Estrange's view, Marvell's tract was evidence of a republican conspiracy that had its roots in a culture of lewd tavern dwellers, led by the Earl of Shaftesbury, in his view the supreme aristocratic turncoat. This was all part of a hero's afterlife: Marvell's biography began with this posthumous reputation as Whig patriot, hero of political liberty and religious toleration. In this literature, little reference was made to Marvell as political, religious or love poet, but the reality, as future biography would discover, was rather different.

Yet Marvell was never entirely forgotten as a poet during the course of the eighteenth century in which his reputation as a patriot flourished. In addition to the limited appearance of some of the lyrics in anthologies, Cooke and Thompson readily recognized him as a poet (Cooke only presents the poetry, a small selection of letters and no controversial prose, and judges Marvell's poetry to have 'the Effect of a lively Genius, and manly Sense, but at the same Time seem[s] to want that Correctness he was capable of making'), and played a crucial role in the development of Marvell's poetic reputation. Thompson considered Marvell original, and a significant force of innovation in English poetry. *Flecknoe, an English Priest at Rome* was thus in his view the inspiration for the title and perhaps also the pattern of Dryden's *Macflecknoe*.[4] Nonetheless, Cooke and Thompson thought of Marvell primarily as the patriot MP ('a Man, who always thought for the Good of his Country and the Glory of Religion')[5] and devoted such materials as they had to the tracing of an essentially political life. It is not hard to see why. Cooke's entire career as man of letters was associated with Whig causes. Thompson was from Hull, and decidedly a Whig; his seminal three-volume edition of Marvell's works, with life, was published in 1776, the year of the outbreak of the American Revolutionary War. His biography of Marvell, 'The Life of that Most Excellent Citizen, and Uncorrupted Member of Parliament, Andrew Marvell' appeared on pages 433–93 of the third volume of the works, between the central body of poetry and the addenda of recently recovered Cromwell poems. In this particular book, Marvell appeared as a hero of liberty in pro-American propaganda.

A third life appeared in the same year as Cooke's, 1726, in Latin, and then in English translation in 1727 and 1728. This was of an entirely different order: fourteen pages and some further references, all of a hostile nature, in Samuel Parker's *De Rebus Sui Temporis Commentariorum Libri Quatuor* (*Bishop Parker's History of his Own Time* as it appeared in English). Parker had in fact written this in 1686 and was intent on settling scores with Marvell after the *Rehearsal Transpros'd* controversy of 1672–3, in which literary fracas he had generally been thought to have been Marvell's inferior. Marvell is judged by Parker to be a slanderer and malign rebel, like Milton, and also a member of the radical Whig Green Ribbon Club; before that, claimed Parker, he had joined the conspiratorial sixty MPs in the Cavalier Parliament who had attempted to maintain Commonwealth and/or Protectorate principles; when Marvell was, in Parker's view, silenced by vocal opposition to his voice in the Commons, he resorted to malign, clandestine activity outside Parliament.

Parker joined the tradition, to which Samuel Butler had already contributed, of regarding Marvell as innately wicked, impudent and sour (as opposed to witty). Abandoned by his father and cast out of college, claimed Parker, Marvell scraped a living as a penniless poetaster until at Milton's pleadings he was employed as a Cromwellian undersecretary, and published *The First Anniversary of the Government under His Highness the Lord Protector*. Marvell was also a hypocrite because he had defended the Declaration of Indulgence in 1672 but argued against it in 1677.

Yet the sense of Marvell as author if not poet was nonetheless very important. For Thompson, Marvell's writings were seamlessly connected to the life of a new kind of public figure, one of the 'first patriots that this, or any other country hath produced': 'he hath given us so pure and perfect an image of his own mind in the immortal monuments of his wit and writings, and in the incorruptibility of his life and actions' (435–6). The anonymous author of the account of Marvell published in the *Retrospective Review* in 1824–5 thought that the writings, with their 'poetical genius' and sense of 'irreproachable' character were quite enough as a life record: biographical material in family history was simply 'dull'.[6] At this time, however, Marvell's reputation as a poet took considerable steps forward. Hartley Coleridge thought that Marvell would have been more famous as a poet had he not been important as a politician (1832), and surely the principles of assessment had changed when John Ormsby, writing in the *Cornhill Magazine* in 1869, opined that with five editions of his poetry extant since his death, Marvell had a poetic popularity only exceeded by Milton, Dryden and Samuel Butler. Ormsby also stressed that Marvell put poetry to the service of his attack on corruption during the Restoration, a view that had not generally been accepted.[7] It is in this context that we should read Marvell's own plea for the power of political art since it stimulates the imaginations of the powerful: 'the Pillars to add Strength, the Medalls Weight, and the Pictures Colour to their Reasons' (*PW*, II:260).

Cooke's intention in his 1726 life was to fashion patriots with Marvell's example: 'to draw a Pattern for all free-born *English-men,* in the Life of a worthy Patriot, whose very Action has truely merited to him, with *Aristides,* the Sirname of the *Just'* (3). In these pages, Cooke assembled or reshuffled the myths that made Marvell a Whig hero of liberty, not all of which have been accepted. First came the temptation of the Jesuits during Marvell's under-graduate days, then the temptation by Danby to take a bribe in return for his vote – rejected despite pressing poverty; this was deemed an example of a 'true *Roman* spirit'. The manifest mistakes in Cooke's biography, of course unknown at the time of publication, are that Marvell was secretary to the Turkish as opposed to the Russian embassy, and that Marvell was friendly with the Duke of Devonshire, for which no contemporary evidence exists, although the friendship with Prince Rupert (Marvell was allegedly his 'tutor', Rupert always voted with Marvell and for political reasons always visited Marvell in disguise), no less poorly grounded in evidence, has found more acceptance. Cooke was sure that Marvell was also Charles II's drinking companion, and that Marvell was fatally poisoned in 1678. At least he used Marvell's own words to dispel some other false views by quoting liberally from Marvell's autobiographical statements in *The Rehearsal Transpros'd* in respect of the friendship with Milton. Cooke's interest was also in showing that Marvell was often quoted or at least read as a guide by many influential authors of his day, such as Ambrose Philips, who edited and wrote for *The Freethinker.*[8] That Marvell was attacked as much as he was during the Restoration by his enemies is taken by Cooke as a confirmation of his virtues, being against the grain in an age 'when Flattery was esteemed a Virtue'.[9] But that Marvell revealed his own opinions in his constituency letters, as is alleged by Cooke, has not been accepted over time. As N. H. Keeble puts it: 'Omission was as important to the construction of this persona as inclusion: he is defined by the tales he did not, or could not, tell'; Keeble then regards Marvell's partisan Restoration satires as the other half of the 'truth' told by the apparently non-partisan letters.[10]

Thompson assumed that anecdotes of Marvell's life were relatively reliable and were a genuine window onto Marvell's character. He connected some of them to trustworthy evidence such as the books of admission and conclusion at Trinity College, Cambridge ('Life', 441–2). We might question the reliability of many of these stories but we still use reliable ones in this way, such as the instance in 1663–5 of the quick-tempered Marvell pistol-whipping the wagon driver outside Bremen in a dispute during the return journey of the Moscow embassy when Marvell was the Earl of Carlisle's secretary, and having to be rescued by the other members of the party from an angry mob of affronted peasants.[11] Thompson is happy to rely on an anecdote reported in May 1761 by Caleb Fleming in a letter to the republican Thomas Hollis: here Marvell had tripped up Parker during an encounter in London when the chaplain had disrespectfully demanded the wall of the MP. Marvell had called Parker the 'son of a whore', and in an ensuing interview with the Bishop of London had explained that he meant Parker's mother to be the Church of England, which, by Parker's own earlier expression had given birth to two 'bastards', the Presbyterians and the Congregationalists and hence was a 'whore'.[12] The anecdote is now almost entirely disregarded. More prosaic was the legend that Marvell was the last MP to receive the parliamentary stipend of 6s. 8d., whereas in fact he was paid steadily if modestly (the stipend was never meant to be a living wage) by the Corporation of Hull.

Speculative, foundationless stories continued to abound in the brief lives of Marvell attached to editions of his poetry. The Boston edition of 1857, with a prefatory notice based on the *Edinburgh Review* notice of Henry Rogers, assumed that Milton and Marvell probably met for the first time in 1640s Rome (in this Rogers follows Thompson), and went to the Vatican to discuss the shortcomings of the Roman church.[13] But Rogers also makes much of running mere rumour to ground: and it is humbling for any biographer to see someone so exposed to posterity's greater hindsight even as they seek to be scrupulous with the truth, and to root out 'those fictions which have gained extensive circulation only because they have been felt to be not intrinsically improbable'.[14] The other strategy in these biographies, like the earlier Whig hagiography, is to devote considerable space to identifying Marvell's impeccable moral qualities and to praising them. Dating should also be mentioned: there is a tendency in the early biographies to date poems at the earliest possible moment. Thompson assumed that the poem on Maniban was written during Marvell's first visit to France in the 1640s, whereas correspondence now suggests a more probable and much later date of 1676.[15] Finally there is plagiarism. With sparse available details, earlier biographers were left to repeat each other in a very absolute way. Rogers thus noticed that John Dove, the author of the first biography of the poet that was not part of an edition, had taken without acknowledgement parts of Isaac D'Israeli's 1814 account of the quarrel between Marvell and Parker and the unsigned essay of 1824–5 in the *Retrospective Review*.[16]

Lives of the poet

The modern era of Marvell biography, the era that begins with the assumption that at the least Marvell was a major poet as well as a politician and therefore should have a poet's life, and that that life should be as detailed and impartial as possible, starts with Pierre Legouis's remarkable *thèse* of 1928: a painstaking gathering together of very many different materials. It used a variety of documentary materials, and is a very impressive achievement for someone writing abroad and outside English-language culture at that point in time (although Legouis did visit English libraries and archives, and met and corresponded with several experts). It was fashioned considerably before modern literary biography had attained the standards of competence to which we are now used, although it looked to the example of Masson's monumental study of Milton.[17] Its impact has to be seen in the light of T. S. Eliot's widely influential essay of 1921, commemorating Marvell's birthday but also sealing his reputation as a major poet in the English and European traditions.[18] Even so, much of the life was still hard to write: in 1965 Legouis published in English a condensed, updated version of his study. That Marvell's father's death happens on page 7 of this version (p. 17 in the original) underlines Legouis's own claim that his book was rather poetry commentary than biography. By page 20, Marvell has arrived at Nun Appleton, but his life was more than half over. Of the original 449 pages of French text, just 144 were devoted to the life.

This brings us to work of the last few years. Nicholas Murray is a professional biographer who numbers Matthew Arnold, Aldous Huxley, Bruce Chatwin and Franz Kafka among his subjects. His 1999 *World Enough and Time: The Life of Andrew Marvell* aimed to bring together the poet and the politician and to show his 'dedicated avocation, . . . energy, imagination, moral commitment and literary skill' all at work at once inside one personality (4). No early modern scholar, Murray constructed his life from readily available sources, and treats Marvell very much as if he were a modern man of letters, comparable to Matthew Arnold or to T. S. Eliot (Arnold actually appears in these pages to help define Marvell as a moral reformer: 38). A good deal of skill is invested in conjuring the atmosphere of Marvell's world, especially his early days in Hull and his undergraduate days in Cambridge, but despite his judiciousness with sources, Murray is not attuned to the resonances of seventeenth-century politics, and we are left with a picture of a commonsense, right-headed man of good judgement, immune to the dangerous energies of seventeenth-century political culture and possessed of a 'certain kind of English liberal outlook'.[19] This hardly does justice to the complexity or significance of the ideas and causes with which Marvell struggled. There is a general reliance on older secondary material instead of reinvestigating primary evidence. Not only is the complexity of republican, Protectoral and Restoration politics absent, we simply do not see a Marvell engaged in this complex world, or indeed a Marvell of any complex or deep personality at all, despite the acknowledged difficulty of coming to know the man. Nor do we have much of judgement on the poems; certainly none at the level practised by the current generation of critics on Marvell. This leaves unexplained the connection (or apparent disjunction) between some of the poems (famously that the apparently pro-Commonwealth *An Horatian Ode* should be followed by the royalist *Tom May's Death*). Where Murray considers more intriguing questions, such as Marvell's sexuality, and the charge of homosexuality, he is very willing to close the book on the grounds that evidence does not exist to probe the question very far (250). To any expert of the period's history, Murray's analysis appears wanting, although he himself rests his biographical findings in the 'unique voice' in the poetry: 'delicate, enigmatic, yet passionate as the man himself' (261). His biography appeared four years before the modern edition of the prose works: these and their contexts he largely ignores.

In truth, and as Murray is the first to admit, new life records concerning Marvell require much extremely careful and laborious searching in national and local record offices and other archives. An up-to-date edition of the letters, including those addressed to as well as those written by Marvell, is now needed: several remain uncollected.[20] A true biography, and one that finally escapes from the myths that have been present in Marvell biographies, is only possible after a new foundation of the documentary knowledge of Marvell's life has been laid. After Legouis, the most valuable work in making the conditions possible for a comprehensive life of Marvell has been conducted on this level; in respect of genealogy by Pauline Burdon and more generally by Hilton Kelliher. Kelliher's most impressive earlier achievement was an exhibition at the British Library of documents that went to make up Marvell's life, accompanied by an exhibition catalogue.[21] The intention was not to provide a complete biography but to give a detailed representation of the documents that did exist; to give each one enough space for considered interpretation. Biographical evidence is replaced by a 'map' of evidence, with microscopic attention paid to the 'dots' themselves, rather than to the narrative that joins them up, and this tendency has been brought latterly to a magnificent fullness with Nicholas von Maltzahn's 2005 *Chronology* of Marvell's life records, a detailed descriptive and evaluative list of the different types of evidence. It seems a more honest way to proceed: for the time being and until we have better tools to work with, the 'map' provides us with a series of departure points in which Marvell's views and attitudes might be addressed in forensic detail. There is no doubt too that the recent annotated editions of Marvell's poetry and prose have added more detail to this picture through their findings with regard to the composition, circulation and publication details of many of the works. In this respect Kelliher's recent extensive discussion of the manuscript circulation of the *Last Instructions to a Painter* explains Marvell's connections with the Harley family in more detail than previous scholarship, and overcomes the inevitable effects of compression in a shorter life, such as that published by Kelliher himself in the Oxford *Dictionary of National Biography*.[22]

Criticism has played its role in improving Marvell's biography too. One important area of criticism that has contributed greatly to the possibility of writing an informed life of Marvell is the scholarly attention paid to the public poetry. It is from the contextual understanding of the Cromwell poems and the Restoration verse satires in the publications of John M. Wallace, Annabel Patterson, Blair Worden, Derek Hirst, Steven N. Zwicker and David Norbrook that a picture of Marvell as political creature and political thinker was able to emerge.[23] The poetry was shown to be the work of an arch political observer, enforced by an informed knowledge of advanced contemporary political theory, and to be part of the historical process itself. It is here that we see emerging Marvell the follower of Machiavelli, user of Hobbes, inheritor of interest theory. Marvell suddenly had a serious political life before as well as after 1660. The same might be said in respect of Marvell's knowledge of visual art in John Dixon Hunt's *Andrew Marvell: His Life and Writings* (London: 1978), which is particularly valuable in evoking the Europe through which Marvell travelled and the England in which he spent the early 1650s. In the public poetry and the commentary it has accrued, two significant debates remain somewhat unresolved. The first is the nature or degree of Marvell's apparent royalism in the late 1640s, as judged by his elegies on Villiers and Hastings and his verse letter to Lovelace.[24] The second is the degree to which Marvell might be seen to be being underhandedly critical of his patrons Fairfax and Cromwell.

Bare facts and safe extrapolations

Yet there are some concrete facts concerning Marvell's life and reasonably solid extrapolations that we can make from them. He was born in east

Yorkshire to a clergyman father who was making his way from humbler origins: Andrew Marvell's grandfather was a yeoman farmer from Cambridgeshire. Andrew was educated in classic fashion at Hull Grammar School, and within a Protestant household whose head, his father, was open to the full range of difference fermenting in the English church, having himself come from the Puritan environment of Emmanuel College, Cambridge. Andrew continued to be educated in humanist Protestant fashion at Trinity College, Cambridge, and by all accounts he proved the worth of his meagre funding by performing as a good scholar. Elected to a scholarship he had every expectation that he would pursue a profitable career in the church and possibly the university.

Everything was changed with the loss of his father and the deprivation of his scholarship. His lifeline was cut off and he had to find a new means of subsistence. This meant, perhaps disagreeably to him for much of the time, seeking the patronage of greater men for a living. A short period trying to find a way in early 1640s London, perhaps in the London households of important northern families, perhaps in search of a teaching appointment, gave way to a resolve to mortgage his property inheritance and to spend the sum he realized travelling in Europe in order to gain a thorough knowledge of other languages and cultures. He was aiming at being a secretary, and perhaps beyond it there might be a career in a higher diplomatic appointment.

But this took a long time to happen. He had to settle for life as a far more humble kind of educated servant: a tutor in a noble household – a tutor in a gentleman's household to the heir of a very rich gentleman. He spent some time probably in London at the end of the 1640s, probably at first in royalist company, and certainly writing in a poetry circle some of his very best poetry. Perhaps in pursuit of patronage, perhaps genuinely as an address to a new age, he wrote his first poem on Oliver Cromwell. Some further poems in praise of the republican ethos betoken yet more gestures towards employment by writing the right sort of poem for England's new leaders, and perhaps already Marvell was functioning as an intelligence agent in this period, that is, as a spy. But then came the tours of duty first at Nun Appleton as tutor to Lord Fairfax's daughter Mary and then in Eton and associated environs as tutor to William Dutton, the ward of Oliver Cromwell. This latter period, of four to five years, included a further trip to France with Dutton, and indirect participation in the embassy to Queen Christina's court in Sweden. It was in part as a Baltic expert that Marvell's services were finally recognized when he was appointed assistant secretary of foreign tongues in the office of John Thurloe, Cromwell's spymaster, and under John Milton.[25] He was by all accounts an agreeable and solicitous diplomat, translating letters and treaties from Latin and French into English and vice versa, including one long piece pleading Sweden's cause against Holland and Spain, occasionally writing himself to English ambassadors on behalf of Thurloe, seeking permission for passports from the Council of State, delivering messages to residents from foreign powers in London, and sometimes hosting foreign diplomats in Westminster.[26] At one point in October 1659 Marvell was appointed as secretary of a committee summoned by the Council of State to negotiate with the Portuguese ambassador.

From this point onwards (he was first elected to Parliament as MP for Hull in January 1659), Marvell's life as civil servant and MP can be written with a confidence based on relatively full records of correspondence and rich parliamentary and other political sources for the time. We are given in a diplomatic letter of 11 February 1658 to George Downing, the Protectorate's resident in the United Provinces, a clear preference for the Protector and against the republican opposition in the Protectoral parliament (*Letters*, 307–8). Marvell's life, with its subject paying assiduous detail to the committee work of the House of Commons, was marked by a reluctance and very probably an inhibition to speak in the Commons: only a very few speeches are recorded. These are in places tortuous: oral eloquence was not Marvell's forte, and he may well have found public speaking difficult. But he did not avoid controversy: physical collisions or exchanges of blows with other MPs threatened to ruin his career as a representative on at least two occasions. Nonetheless his work as a political operator is evident and was impressive for its serious application. In addition to keeping the Mayor and Aldermen of Hull abreast of affairs in Westminster, we know that he operated in favour of religious toleration. This seems to have been to do in part with the fact that he was a client of several powerful pro-toleration aristocrats and gentlemen, such as Lord Wharton, the Earl of Anglesey and Sir Edward Harley. He therefore spent time in their service or at least at their behest in a role more like that of a secretary, sometimes also helping them with their private affairs. It was in the role of secretary that he attended Carlisle and Downing in Holland in the early 1660s (where his career as a spy was probably reactivated), and he accompanied Carlisle on the embassy to Russia in 1663–5, tasks that would take him away from his place in the Commons for long periods of time. But his involvement in the production and circulation of the 'advice to a painter' poems, which attacked Clarendon's administration, and the six prose works of the 1670s, five of them markedly controversial and in different ways sharply *ad hominem*, give plenty of evidence that he was prepared to exploit political opportunities outside as well as within the walls of Parliament, even as toleration had been joined as a concern by the need to combat widespread bribery (the means by which Danby, the King's minister, was able to control the House of Commons), prorogation (the means by which the king ruled through his prerogative without Parliament), and fears of French influence, risking the unfortunate evolution of an absolutist monarchy. All of this is to be considered alongside Marvell's functioning as an agent for the Corporation of Hull in the capital, and his further advocacy on behalf of Trinity House in Hull, with the prolonged dispute over the prospective ownership of the lighthouse that was to stand on Spurn Point at the entrance to the Humber estuary.

The self in poetry

Perhaps under the influence of Romantic lyric convention, there has been an interest in seeing Marvell's lyrics speak a truth about the nature of Marvell the person. The most sustained and notable attempt here has been a series of recently published work by Derek Hirst and Steven N. Zwicker. This approach uses categories that fuse social history with the terms of psychology, psychoanalysis and sociology.[27] Hirst and Zwicker might be seen to be historicizing an earlier psychological tradition of reading the poetry, notably the pastorals, but also making use of the hints in earlier hostile accounts such as Parker's *History of his own Time*.[28] Psychoanalysis meets history in the narrative of family life. Thus Marvell is seen as suffering, and registering this suffering in his verse, from a denial of what he might have expected as a patriarch: children and the possibility of inheritance. Marvell's verse, in Hirst and Zwicker's view, also registers a trauma of loss: as an adolescent and a very young man, and in relatively quick succession, he lost both his mother and his father; 'a wish to preserve unsullied innocence, an acknowledgement of the guilty pleasures of aberrant desire, anger against and yearning for what should have been the sheltering arms of patriarchy, and, finally and consequentially, an incapacity in face of the demands of sexual maturity'.[29] Hirst and Zwicker then move to other instances where the alleged homosexual predilections of some schoolmasters (and other frank acknowledgements of the habits of adolescent boys such as masturbation) are apparent. The result is a series of representations in the poetry, on the one hand of the poet, and on the other of figures of denial and aversion: markers of the Marvellian psyche. Thus the stock doves in *Upon Appleton House, To My Lord Fairfax* stand for the absence of marital union. Marvell's poetic projections amount to a demand for 'another and intermediating category for the dramas and dialectics of selfhood: the imagined life. That term fuses the historical person – living in the body and in the turmoil of events – with a self rooted in the psyche and performed in and felt through textual production.'[30] The danger is of course that it threatens to reduce the subtlety of such a richly complicated life to a series of stereotypes, and all such lives might become part of an undifferentiated psychoanalytic jungle. One might be troubled too by the absence of discussion of the kind of methodology applied here.

The severance of ties with the past and no certain direction in the future helps in large part explain the sense of the isolation and apartness of Marvell's lyric speaking voices, and his willingness to entertain in his imagination sexual connections and encounters that lay outside the patriarchal, heterosexual pale. In this respect Hirst and Zwicker seek to answer the argument, most notably in the important work of Paul Hammond, that if Marvell was not revealing himself to be homosexual in his verse, he was certainly expressing various kinds of homosocial bonding, part of a burgeoning and highly unusual interest in non-'orthodox', non-heterosexual identity and relationships, a view that has raised significant interest and that has persuaded many.[31] Social historians have provided suggestive corollary evidence concerned with the structure of the household: Marvell's marriage, the nature of which, if it indeed existed, is still a matter for debate, need not after all have required him to sleep in the same bed as his wife.[32]

It was also known to the earlier biographers that Marvell, like other poets such as Jonson and Cowley, died poor, even though they were each 'incomparable' poets. Elsewhere, Marvell was considered alongside Milton, Cowley and Spenser as a flower of Cambridge.[33] Two significant perspectives branch from this point. One is to underline the fact that Marvell was compelled to be a servant for his entire adult life: such anxieties, expressed in his letters and poems, over his personal and social status and identity as we can infer were no doubt a consequence of this indubitable fact. He was sharply aware of his non-elite status. He wrote to Sir Henry Thompson of 'that duty of those in our station to doe right to any gentleman' (*Letters*, 321). He lived modestly, and Sir Henry Thompson for one was keen to help him by identifying a rich Puritan widow who would have given him substance. The other line is the simple evidence that Marvell was acknowledged at an early stage, within five years of his death, as one of the great ('incomparable') poets. From this point of view, the assumption that he had no reputation as a significant poet until much later is one more myth.

As for personal character, the evidence that stands out as among the most solid is that he liked being alone – in the Highgate cottage that he acquired in 1671, or in the Maiden Lane garret that he used in 1677–8. He had few friends and generally did not trust people. He liked drinking but would not drink in company. It was form to express thanks for gifts of ale from Hull, but talk of 'meddling' with a barrel of beer (some of which had suspiciously disappeared in transit from Yorkshire to London) suggests a more dedicated interest. In his last years he conducted his business in a purely private place: the lodging in Maiden Lane. These facts are borne out by the woman who would claim after his death to be his wife.[34] Privacy and in some sense invisibility were requirements for most of his professional duties. Being an MP and a secretary required discretion, and sometimes operating behind the scenes so as to deny detection. This was necessary because of the surveillance systems operating at the time, and in particular the ability of government agents to open letters. Being a spy always required secrecy, and we suppose that Marvell was employed in secretarial intelligence work (in respect of relations with the United Provinces c. 1651 and 1662–3; perhaps again in 1674–5): another arena where discretion was utterly necessary.[35] Most of these spheres required the development of a professional, public or civic persona, a sense of self, that was entirely in denial of oneself as a person, even indeed as a late Renaissance 'self-fashioned' man of letters, or a humanist advisor to a prince. One's identity was part of someone else's or one did not have an identity: one was a blank. Marvell's poetry is full of the confession of this erasure, impossibility or insufficiency of expressed identity, as in *The First Anniversary of the Government under His Highness the Lord Protector*, lines 125–6: 'my muse shall hollow far behind | Angelic Cromwell who outwings the wind'. The poet is always a shadow of the object of praise, be it the hero Oliver Cromwell or Mary Fairfax. The poet is the invisible opposite of these centres of charisma, and often Marvell confesses that it is the hero who is the real poet, the real source of energy. In this sense, the poetry expresses accurately and sensitively the patronage relationships upon which Marvell was dependent, from Lord Fairfax and Lord Wharton to the Corporation of Hull and Trinity House.[36] From this point follow a long series of insights in Marvell's writing with regard to how this poet's art is a kind of negation: it is an imitation of someone else's art even to the extent of gathering so many fragments of others' verse together that they return as the final integrated fulfilment of so many clichés.[37] Marvell found his poetic identity in this negative way, a shadow presence in the pastoral landscape, helping to make it, but barely perceptible in it. Indeed, this circumstance is sometimes represented as a sacrifice of the poet: witness the witty martyring by drowning of the speaker in *Upon Appleton House* (lines 623–4). The drowning is in one of its senses a matter of being overwhelmed by so much other poetry and painting, to the extent that the poet 'chokes' on it: witness too the mockery of aesthetic pretension, such as that of Davenant, as Marvell saw it, again in *Upon Appleton House*. The sense of being overwhelmed was also a figure of the patron's presence and 'interest', and is precisely not 'disinterested': 'His decorum, or courtesy, which [T. S.] Eliot struggled to define as wit, rises to the challenge of interestedness. But this is exactly not disinterest or that much-vaunted impersonality celebrated by Eliot and by much subsequent criticism indebted to him.'[38] In the poem on *Paradise Lost*

Marvell seems able to hold his own with Milton, confessing his own measured appreciation and awe for his friend's achievement, appreciating Milton's sublimity but in his own verse implicitly stating his own poetry's merits.

In this evidence we can see Marvell suffering a good deal of repression: we do not need psychoanalysis to pick it up. There are serious signs of a frequently frustrated and disappointed person. The outbursts of anger, especially when not being understood or when unable to communicate optimally (for instance when speaking publicly), are striking. The peevish 'sneer' so hated by Parker and his supporters was a related feature: he resented those who enjoyed a better position in public life through merit or placement, but whom he felt were his inferiors. The description of Marvell as a sneering wit suggests someone permanently jealous of others and that may be too strong; the perspective of an outsider and someone slightly outcast, still looking to the days of Richard Cromwell's Protectorate, is more convincing. It is someone who was let down repeatedly by causes and sources of protection (Andrew Marvell Sr, the royalists, the Protectorate, Charles II, the Church of England), and who was compelled to respond. It was someone whose mental powers were ahead of his ability to communicate them; someone who could write fluently, translate from and manipulate other languages with excellence, but who frequently failed when it came to speaking in public. Coupled with this has to be the matter of Marvell's lethargy, expressed several times, of being unable to find the will to address a situation, and this may perhaps have been connected with drinking (*Letters*, 348).

It also suggests someone in some kind of suppressed pain. We have already encountered the significance of Marvell's father's death. It is no surprise that the sea and Milton's elegy for a drowned acquaintance, *Lycidas*, figure significantly in Marvell's imagination.[39] His father had not finished providing a framework, discipline and means for his son when he drowned in the Humber. Biographical reference courses through the prose tracts: the motif of drowning recurs as a comparison of the persecution of Herbert Croft to medieval trial by water: guilty if you float, innocent if you sink and drown (*PW*, II.63). The lasting sense of trauma in Marvell is well explored in the reading of *The Unfortunate Lover* provided by Zwicker and Hirst.[40] Does the Caesarian section that brings Marvell's lover into the world figure an unpleasant premature birth into maturity? We should also mention the pain at loss expressed by the *Nymph Complaining for the Death of her Fawn*. Was there something more to hide? Was Marvell not merely without means but also damaged or defective, not only psychologically but also physically, as Samuel Butler seems to suggest: 'Nature, or Sinister Accident has rendred some of the Alteration-strokes useless and unnecessary. This expression of mine may be somewhat uncouth, and the fitter therefore (instead of Figleaves, or White Linnen) to obscure what ought to be conceal'd in Shadow'?[41] Certainly it is the case that Marvell seems as a person to have been unable to experience fatherhood, and yet greatly treasured his role as uncle and mentor to William Popple. The letter to Sir John Trott of August 1667 is particularly sensitive to the issue of the failure of patrilineal descent.[42] Marvell was told of a likely wife by Sir Henry Thompson who clearly understood his need for a proper-tied partner. Nothing came of it. The 'love' that he could express in his writing, highly sublimated as it was, was a further rendering of the variety of desires driven by his dependencies – the attachments of patronage he needed to make his life livable. The opposite perception in Marvell's writing, but intimately attached to this understanding of 'love', is the passion-driven portraits of the lustful courtiers in the verse satires and the clerics in the prose satires.

In so far as we can construct a picture of Marvell's life, poetry was a welcome refuge, and was associated by contemporaries with Marvell's love of retirement:

> after he has carv'd his Mistresses Name with many Love-knots and flourishes in all the Bushes and Brambles; and interwoven those sacred Characters with many an Enigmatical Devise in Posies and Garlands of Flowers, lolling sometimes upon the Bank and sunning himself, and then on a sudden (varying his Postures with his Passion) raising himself up, and speaking all the fine things which Lovers us'd to do.[43]

Poetry was a place where one could escape and where strife would disappear. So, much of the poetry avoids the passionate clash of opposites, of lovers harmonious or disharmonious, in order to seek solitary enlightenment and fulfilment. Take for instance *The Garden*. The lover loves himself or himself through his environment. Marvell's mower appears to be a miserable fru-strated poet is some places, but in others he is a figure fulfilled by his true connection with nature. The world of women to the mower is figured as unnatural (*The Mower against Gardens*), and some of Marvell's women are unattractive witchlike crones (*Upon Appleton House*), elderly, overweight engastrimyths (*The Third Advice to a Painter*) or lustful aristocratic ladies sexually excited by horses and who make the Wife of Bath seem frigid (*The Last Instructions to a Painter*). The speaker poet is more interested in the mower than in Julia. Where women are goddesses in Marvell, and hence unapproachable, they are also unknowable. The great moment of sexual passion in Marvell, in *To His Coy Mistress*, is not so much personal as a brilliant feat of poetic appropriation, imitation and reorganization. The poem is exciting because of this, and the limits of the speaker's epicurean persona, through partially hidden dramatic ironies, are evident. Neither is it at all personal, in the way we see real people flit through the poetry of, for instance, Petrarch, Surrey and Donne. Intimacy in Marvell's lyric verse is absent. There is certainly sexual intercourse: in *To His Coy Mistress* and *The Match* stylized and glorious, an end to literary inventiveness. All the same, it is a performance rather than a means to intimacy.

From a biographical viewpoint, Marvell's poetry is one of fulfilment of a kind of self-love. The object of desire is finally a reflection of a subject identified as oneself, self-enclosed like the drop of dew. It is therefore no surprise that the straitened world of Puritan behaviour, of the 'reformation of the household', with its rules of denial and its concealing of body parts, could be attractive for Marvell. Hence the delicately observed assessment in the epitaph on Frances Jones, which nonetheless is also a poem of distance, remote from its subject and recording its pious subject's remoteness in the profane 1670s from the pious past. *Clorinda and Damon* is a surprising rejection of pastoral dalliance for the sake of rigorous piety. Other poems are accounts of the mutual binding of disparate aspects of a single person to each other: *A Dialogue between the Soul and Body* is a document of closure. Hence also the remarkable poems on the life of the soul, in Latin as well as English, which manage to set the balance between earth and heaven, soul and body, with perfect poise. The soul for Marvell is admirable on account of its enclosure from the temptations of the world, as in *Ros*, lines 29–32.

Young Love suggested a world of sanitized older man/young women relations, but one devoid of either identities or feelings. We never quite see who the young love is, although there is a hint in the third stanza that it is female; this sense then disappears, and the poem remains a highly abstract expression of mutuality. The conclusion of *Mourning* suggests that women are as difficult to understand as the poet himself: access to the full array of feminine deliberation is not granted. Neither do we see the male lover's intentions except by sly inference in *Daphnis and Chloe*. What is clear is that Marvell's collection of lyric poems contains markedly alternative and even deviant versions of heterosexual love. First there is the *senex* and the younger lover, as we have seen, in *Young Love*, and the related scenario of a voyeuristic older man and a young girl in *The Picture of Little T. C. in a Prospect of Flowers* This is not exactly paedophilic poetry, certainly not in terms of the ancient tradition from which it comes, but it does nonetheless challenge a norm. There is also the presence of homosocial and perhaps also homoerotic verse: in the Villiers elegy, in *Last Instructions to a Painter* and, in terms of the manipulation of source poems, in *To His Coy Mistress* and *Damon the Mower*.[44] In other words, and to say the very least, the lyric poems offer collectively a dispersal or dissolution of the sexual energies we are meant to find in a lyric verse collection of this period. A good deal of the energy of the verse goes in these sexually heterodox directions: this was where his imagination went. Marvell may not have been as frank as Rochester in his libertine verse (Rochester's verse was beginning to circulate in Marvell's lifetime and was read by him) but it is arresting and disturbing. The level of control or restraint in these portrayals also suggests more denial or repression, deliberate or not. The portrayal by both Parker and Butler of Marvell as a pervert, a man who chose to go in disguise to public places, and to gratify himself with male or female prostitutes, might be part of ecclesiastical satire, but it is also not to be entirely dismissed.[45] It certainly has to be put alongside the stereotype of Marvell as incorruptible, right-headed patriot hero, and a poet who could live above the passions he described. The charges of deviancy were made and threaten to stick in part because Marvell was so private: how could his private virtue be publicly judged? In this light the accomplishment of the poetry looks like a brilliant sublimation of a set of social and sexual confusions and frustrations or incapacities. The hours of musing and the love of solitariness is the place where that sublimation occurred, allegedly often through the power of wine.

Yet it is precisely because that musing occurred that Marvell was able to make a leap between his personal perceptions and his political assertion of liberty: it was his own particular version of achieving what his hero Ben Jonson had urged in fighting forsaken virtue's cause. For it is in the satires, especially the verse satires, that we see a full and alarming human portrait. Through the veil of satire's need to ridicule, the portrait of the courtly and other actors is not without sympathy or pity, repellent though the frank portrayals of courtly sexual appetites can be. It is here that tyranny and sexuality are seen to connect, however partial Marvell's picture of events is. There does not seem a great deal of distance here between the Countess of Castlemaine and the hero-martyrs of virtuous behaviour: Archibald Douglas and James Mitchell. He may not have been aware of it, but the sum of his writing in poetry and prose was 'a program that deconstructs the very bases of heterosexuality and patriarchalism alike'.[46] Marvell's notions of liberty in the escape from political and spiritual tyranny were inherently linked to this acknowledgement of alterity. The eighteenth, nineteenth and twentieth centuries might have had little use for the full dimensions of Marvell's revelations in this respect, the teachings of his life. That is something for us and our future, an appreciation that might seek to answer those many disappointments and denials that produced his vision.

For someone who was consciously aware of the way in which others around him and just before him had sounded their own trumpets, proclaiming themselves latter-day Virgils, Ovids or Lucans, Marvell is remarkable for the degree to which he is able in his verse and his prose to speculate on his own career as a poet even while refusing the terms of aggrandizement claimed by his contemporaries. This is another dimension of his biographical self-consciousness. Jonson, Milton, Herrick, Cowley, Davenant, Katherine Philips all took pains to make their voices major, distinctive and above or beyond the tradition that had formed them. Marvell is a poet who denied this sense of poetic egotism by a form of studied imitation (echoing all of the people named above and many more) but who nonetheless made a virtue and indeed a highly creative resource of being other men's (and women's) mirrors. Interestingly Thompson saw this, although he chose to relate it to Marvell's ethical excellence: 'as men are more or less mirrours to each other, such was Mr. Marvel to the world, that all men might so clearly discern perfection in him, as to dress, and even ornament themselves, by so compleat a pattern'.[47]

This pursuit of reflective doubleness is at the heart of Marvell's understanding of literary activity, and it is an element in the consciousnesses of his characters. Thus, the Villiers elegy is concerned not with a loyal subject but with a lover; it is 'a poem attempting to mediate between modes of representing its dead'. 'There is a narcissistic, self-enclosing movement about [Villiers's] gaze which is directed at himself, and which finds other masculine objects – even the eyes of an enemy soldier – to reflect it back, rather than the eyes of his mistress. Marvell's conceit labours to preserve, in this case, the all-male circuit of vision.'[48] More famously, we have the gaze of the coy mistress, textually drawn from Ovid's Narcissus and its English translations, engaged in mutual reflection with the poet (in the position of Ovid's Echo), who can only promise to the future his 'echoing voice': 'Thy beauty shall no more be found; | Nor, in thy marble vault, shall sound | My echoing song' (lines 25–7).[49]

These qualities of self-enclosure, self-reference, and perception or argument by doubles, are related to the chiming effect of Marvell's rhymes where the power of the rhyme throughout and not merely at the ends of lines suspends our ability to make distinct judgements of who is speaking and what is happening:

> Oh let our voice His praise exalt,
> Till it arrive at heaven's vault:
> Which thence (perhaps) rebounding, may
> Echo beyond the Mexique Bay.   (*Bermudas*, lines 33–6).

The other or echoing voice speaks when you have spoken, and in a rhyming poem is always there, a fraction of a second behind the lead voice: the rhyme, the mirror of the maker. Some of these qualities have been identified and venerated by critics for a long time: 'reversals transposed' and 'its own resemblance'.[50] But the point is not merely that these are formal qualities of the poetry and the prose. They are ways for Marvell to structure his own sense of career as a poet, his own sense of performance, despite seemingly having missed all the boats that guaranteed esteem. Not for the first time in this period, the reference back to Ovid's verse and the idea of Ovidian perception is telling. In the poem on *Paradise Lost*, Marvell 'commends' *Paradise Lost* into praise (because praise will not rhyme with 'offend'), even as he lets Milton's blank verse largely stand, and mocks Dryden's own attempts to rhyme *Paradise Lost* for the stage. In this prefatory verse, the mirror of rhyme is subversive both of Miltonic authority (even as the poem offers deep respect to Milton) and once again also of those who would have regular literary rules in authoritarian monarchies. In Marvell's last poem, in Latin, an (in his view) unjustly tortured Scottish Presbyterian and assassin is given a victory because the verbs suggest that it is the executioner administering the torture who is more the sufferer. One cannot help but feel that the arrest induced by Marvell's rhyme was as subversive of orthodox perspectives as his panegyrics are notable for articulating the contrary energies that make up polities. Marvell's doubles are inherently subversive entities, making verse do its arresting or troubling work in a disturbing career when the sublime was neither regularly available nor appropriate.

There is something scandalously Ovidian about *The Rehearsal Transpros'd* that broaches on the biographical. If Bramhall is made effeminate by Marvell, Parker is subjected to a sexual travesty. His energies in respect of his verbal superabundance are complicit with a sexual intemperance, so Marvell suggests: Parker is the slave of a mistress as well as a bookseller, the child of his invention inseparable from the work of his loins. Later on, his overblown rhetoric makes him a lover of Bishop Bramhall ('he should make a dead Bishop his Mistress'). Parker's love of uncontrolled discourse makes him an enthusiast, the very kind of Puritan he wishes to attack, and the climax of his pleasure is not to be hidden from public view. Indeed, in a parody of Aretino, Marvell has Parker running naked and erect down the street, a phallic travesty of Archimedes, perhaps with more water to displace: 'But there was no holding him. Thus it must be and no better, when a man's Phancy is up, and his Breeches are down; when the Mind and the Body make contrary Assignations, and he hath both a Bookseller at once and a Mistris to satisfie; Like *Archimedes,* into the Street he runs out naked with his Invention' (*PW*, 1:48). Picking up on a common Restoration theme, heroic boasts are indicative of unbounded priapic energy. Elsewhere, we glimpse Parker as a sexual deviant, a sadist deriving sexual pleasure from the punishment he wreaks on Nonconformists: 'down with their breeches as oft as wants the prospect of a more pleasing *Nudity*'. Taking this pathology further, Marvell sees that this attitude may have an educational root. Parker had formerly been under John Owen's sway when the latter was Vice-Chancellor of Oxford. Now in the driving seat in the Restoration, Parker can transfer his abuse to Owen, to say nothing of the spy networks that Marvell associates with this persecutory attitude. No less than with the emaciated Richard Flecknoe, presented by Marvell as a Catholic poetaster, the overwhelmingly important point to note is that Parker is a mirror for Marvell, with their shared Puritan roots and associations with Milton. But this time the figure in the mirror is grotesque, terrifying and violent.

None of this should be divorced from the serious intellectual biography to which we can submit Marvell's life. It is not merely that both poetry and prose share obliqueness in method, or that the wit of *The Rehearsal Transpros'd* and *Mr Smirke* involve commentary on poetry and employ poetic method. The inversionary qualities that we have seen in the poetry are also reflected in key associations that Marvell made and which were then reflected in his developing prose arguments. The most important aspect here would be his acquaintance with John Hales, the keenly royalist Vice-Provost of Eton College who was nonetheless a defender of personal religious liberty, and who maintained that religious schisms and sects were the consequences of the policies of intolerant rulers. It is from this starting point that we can begin to glimpse the development of a fully fledged Marvellian theory of toleration in church and state, one that encompasses both efficient government and liberty of belief. The presence in Marvell's father's library of his own translation of the Socinian Racovian Catechism, and the serious encounters of Marvell with Machiavellian and reason of state or 'interest' theory suggest an eminently pragmatic thinker who, unlike his friend Milton, did not think that the best government was tied to a particular form (such as republicanism) but rather that the 'balance' of powers in church and state should be wrought to maximize the interests of both prince, parliament and people. Privately, we may be sure he was the holder of advanced religious views involving the power of reason against the excesses of enthusiasm on the one hand, and persecuting tyranny on the other.[51] He was after all a longtime friend of James Harrington. Such a perspective undermines any simple picture of Marvell as a 'Protestant poet'.[52]

Like that of many early modern figures, the biography of Andrew Marvell is not finished and has not reached a significant point at which it will be evident that nothing much more can be said for some time. New documentary evidence will from time to time appear: it is very hard to dislodge from archives but it is there, and we become ever better at knowing archives. This body of growing knowledge meets the ongoing interpretation of the writing, which itself seems ever able, almost deliberately so, to suggest a code to decipher its author's secret self. But in this meeting of archival excavation and interpretation we must be wary of replacing the mere myth of the Whig patriot hero with another: the myth of the post-Freudian victim-poet agonizing at or bemused by his avoidance of a patriarchal destiny. The testing subtlety of Andrew Marvell's writing demands more than that.

NOTES

1. These texts are discussed by Nicholas von Maltzahn in 'Marvell's Ghost', in Warren Chernaik and Martin Dzelzainis, eds., *Marvell and Liberty* (Basingstoke, 1999), 50–74.
2. [Thomas Brown], *The Reasons of the New Convert's taking the Oaths to the Present Government* (1691), sig. A2$^{r–v}$.
3. Roger L'Estrange, *The Parallel or, An Account of the Growth of Knavery* (1679), sig. A2$^{r–v}$.
4. Edward Thompson, 'The Life of that Most Excellent Citizen, and Uncorrupted Member of Parliament, Andrew Marvell' (hereafter 'Life'), in *The Works of Andrew Marvell, Esq.*, ed. Thompson, 3 vols. (London, 1776), III:442.
5. Thomas Cooke, 'The Life of Andrew Marvell Esq.' (hereafter 'Life'), in *The Works of Andrew Marvell*, ed. Cooke, 2 vols. (1726), I:2.
6. In Elizabeth Story Donno, ed., *Andrew Marvell: The Critical Heritage* (London, 1978), 143.
7. Hartley Coleridge, *The Worthies of Yorkshire and Lancashire* (London, 1832), 61–4, reprinted in Donno, ed., *Andrew Marvell: The Critical Heritage*, 158–9; John Ormsby, *Cornhill Magazine* 20 (July 1869), in Donno, ed., *Andrew Marvell: The Critical Heritage*, 221.
8. See Ambrose Philips, *The Free-Thinker* 253 (22 August 1720); *Chronology*, 262. This specific connection is erroneously denied by Thompson: 'Life', 443.
9. Cooke, 'Life', I:8.
10. N.H. Keeble, ' "I would not tell you any tales": Marvell's Constituency Letters', in Conal Condren and A.D. Cousins, eds., *The Political Identity of Andrew Marvell* (Aldershot, 1990), 129.
11. As recounted by Guy Miège, *A Relation of Three Embassies from his Sacred Majestie Charles II to the Great Duke of Muscovie ...* (1669), 427–33.
12. Thompson, 'Life', III:473–5.
13. 'Notice of the Author', in *The Poetical Works of Andrew Marvell* (Boston, 1857), xliii; Thompson, 'Life', III:442–3.
14. 'Notice of the Author', xxii.
15. Thompson, 'Life', III:443; *Chronology*, 171.
16. See Donno, ed., *Andrew Marvell: The Critical Heritage*, 141, 169; see also 188–96.
17. Pierre Legouis, *André Marvell, Poète, Puritain, Patriote, 1621–1678* (Paris, 1928); see David Masson, *The Life of John Milton: Narrated in Connexion with the Political, Ecclesiastical, and Literary History of his Time*, 7 vols. (London, 1859–94).
18. T.S. Eliot, 'Andrew Marvell', *Times Literary Supplement*, 31 March 1921; reprinted in T.S. Eliot, *Selected Essays* (London and New York, 1932).
19. For Murray on 1650s politics, see Blair Worden, *Times Literary Supplement*, 14 July 2000, 25, and ensuing correspondence.

20. Nicholas von Maltzahn will produce the next edition of Marvell's letters.
21. Hilton Kelliher, compiler, *Andrew Marvell, Poet & Politician, 1621–78: An Exhibition to Commemorate the Tercentenary of His Death* (London, 1978).
22. Kelliher, 'Marvell's *Last Instructions to a Painter*: From Manuscript to Print', *English Manuscript Studies* 13 (2007), 296–343; and his 'Andrew Marvell', *Oxford Dictionary of National Biography*, online edn.
23. John M. Wallace, *Destiny His Choice: The Loyalism of Andrew Marvell* (Cambridge, 1968); Annabel Patterson, *Marvell and the Civic Crown* (Princeton, 1978), rev. as *Marvell: The Writer in Public Life* (Harlow, 2000); Derek Hirst, ' "That Sober Liberty": Marvell's Cromwell in 1654', in John M. Wallace, ed., *The Golden and the Brazen World: Papers in Literature and History, 1650–1800* (Berkeley, 1985), 17–53; Derek Hirst and Steven N. Zwicker, 'High Summer at Nun Appleton, 1651: Andrew Marvell and the Lord Fairfax's Occasions', *Historical Journal* 36 (1993), 247–69; David Norbrook, *Writing the English Republic: Poetry, Rhetoric and Politics, 1627–1660* (Cambridge, 1999), 158–82, Chapter 6, 337–57; Blair Worden, *Literature and Politics in Cromwellian England: John Milton, Andrew Marvell, Marchamont Nedham* (Oxford, 2007), chapters 3–6. See also now Edward Holberton, *Poetry and the Cromwellian Protectorate: Culture, Politics and Institutions* (Oxford, 2008), and Nicholas McDowell, *Poetry and Allegiance in the English Civil Wars: Marvell and the Cause of Wit* (Oxford, 2008).
24. Cf. Patterson, *Marvell: The Writer in Public Life*, 14–15; James Loxley, 'Prepar'd at Last to Strike in with the Tyde? Andrew Marvell and Royalist Verse', *The Seventeenth Century* 10 (1995), 39–62; Blair Worden, *Literature and Politics*, 58–63.
25. See von Maltzahn, 'Liberalism or Apocalypse? John Milton and Andrew Marvell', in Marianne Thormählen, ed., *English Now* (Lund, Sweden, 2008), 44–58.
26. For these, see *Chronology*, 47–59; *PW*, vol. 1, Appendix A.
27. Derek Hirst and Steven N. Zwicker, 'Andrew Marvell and the Toils of Patriarchy: Fatherhood, Longing and the Body Politic', *English Literary History* 66 (1999), 629–54; and their 'Eros and Abuse: Imagining Andrew Marvell', *English Literary History* 74 (2007), 371–95.
28. Barbara L. Estrin, *Laura: Uncovering Gender and Genre in Wyatt, Donne, and Marvell* (Durham, NC, 1994); Lynn Enterline, *The Tears of Narcissus: Melancholia and Masculinity in Early Modern Writing* (Stanford, 1999).
29. Hirst and Zwicker, 'Eros and Abuse', 383–4.
30. *Ibid.*, 390.
31. Paul Hammond, 'Marvell's Sexuality', *The Seventeenth Century* 11 (1996), 87–123, and *Figuring Sex between Men from Shakespeare to Rochester* (Oxford, 2002), Chapter 4.
32. Phil Withington, *The Politics of Commonwealth: Citizens and Freemen in Early Modern England* (Cambridge, 2005), 224–7.
33. J[ohn] A[dams], 'To Mr Creech on his Translation of Lucretius', in *T. Lucretius Carus, the Epicurean Philosopher: his six books, De natura rerum, done into English Verse with Notes* (2nd edn, 1683), sig. C2^{v}.
34. For the matter of whether or not Marvell was married, see *Chronology*, 11–12.

35. See Worden, *Literature and Politics*, 'Appendix A: Marvell and the Embassy of 1651'; Nigel Smith, *Andrew Marvell: The Chameleon* (New Haven and London, 2010), 94, 281–2.

36. As discussed by von Maltzahn, 'Andrew Marvell and the Prehistory of Whiggism', in David Womersley, ed., assisted by Paddy Bullard and Abigail Williams, *'Cultures of Whiggism': New Essays on English Literature and Culture in the Long Eighteenth Century* (Newark, NJ, 2005), 47–53.

37. See, e.g., *Poems*, 75–84.

38. Von Maltzahn, 'Andrew Marvell and the Prehistory of Whiggism', 33. See also Nigel Smith, ' "Courtesie is Fatal": The Civil and Visionary Poetics of Andrew Marvell', Chatterton Lecture 1998, *Proceedings of the British Academy 101* (1999), 173–89.

39. Von Maltzahn, 'Death by Drowning: Marvell's "Lycidas" ', *Milton Studies* 48 (2008), 38–52.

40. Hirst and Zwicker, 'Eros and Abuse'.

41. [Samuel Butler], *The Transproser Rehears'd* (London, 1673), 135.

42. See Hirst and Zwicker, 'Andrew Marvell and the Toils of Patriarchy'.

43. [Butler], *The Transproser Rehears'd*, 137–8.

44. See Hammond, 'Marvell's Sexuality'.

45. [Butler], *The Transproser Rehears'd*, 137–8.

46. Hirst and Zwicker, 'Andrew Marvell and the Toils of Patriarchy', 631.

47. Thompson, 'Life', III:435.

48. Hammond, 'Marvell's Sexuality', 107–9.

49. Ovid, *Metamorphoses*, III.419ff. Marvell also echoes in several significant places in his poem the translations of Golding and Sandys: see Marvell, *To His Coy Mistress*, in *Poems*, pp. 82–3, nn. 26, 27, 33–6, 36, 39–40.

50. From the titles of essays respectively by John Carey and Christopher Ricks in C. A. Patrides, ed., *Approaches to Marvell: The York Tercentenary Lectures* (London, 1978).

51. See von Maltzahn, 'Milton, Marvell, and Toleration', in Sharon Achinstein and Elizabeth Sauer, eds., *Milton and Toleration* (Oxford, 2007), 86–104.

52. See Gary Kuchar, *The Poetry of Religious Sorrow in Early Modern England* (Cambridge, 2008), Chapter 3.

Further reading

Primary material

John Ayloffe, 'Marvell's Ghost', in *Poems on Affairs of State: Augustan Satirical Verse, 1660–1714, Vol. I, 1660–1678*, ed. George de F. Lord (New Haven, 1963), 285–6.

[Samuel Butler], *The Transproser Rehears'd* (London, 1673).

Thomas Cooke, 'The Life of Andrew Marvell, Esq.', in *The Works of Andrew Marvell*, ed. Cooke, 2 vols. (London, 1726), vol. I.

Guy Miège, *A Relation of Three Embassies from his Sacred Majestie Charles II to the Great Duke of Muscovie* (London, 1669).

Edward Thompson, 'The Life of that Most Excellent Citizen, and Uncorrupted Member of Parliament, Andrew Marvell', in *The Works of Andrew Marvell, Esq.*, ed. Thompson, 3 vols. (London, 1776), III: 433–93.

Secondary material

Pauline Burdon, 'Marvell and His Kindred', *Notes & Queries*, 229 (1984), 379–85.

Elizabeth Story Donno, ed., *Andrew Marvell: The Critical Heritage* (London, 1978).

Paul Hammond, 'Marvell's Sexuality', *The Seventeenth Century* 11 (1996), 87–123.

Derek Hirst, '"That Sober Liberty": Marvell's Cromwell in 1654', in John M. Wallace, ed., *The Golden and the Brazen World: Papers in Literature and History, 1650–1800* (Berkeley, 1985), 17–53.

and Steven N. Zwicker, 'High Summer at Nun Appleton, 1651: Andrew Marvell and Lord Fairfax's Occasions', *Historical Journal* 36 (1993), 247–69.

'Andrew Marvell and the Toils of Patriarchy: Fatherhood, Longing, and the Body Politic', *English Literary History* 66 (1999), 629–54.

'Eros and Abuse: Imagining Andrew Marvell', *English Literary History* 74 (2007), 371–95.

John Dixon Hunt, *Andrew Marvell: His Life and Writings* (London, 1978).

N. H. Keeble, '"I would not tell you any tales": Marvell's Constituency Letters', in Conal Condren and A. D. Cousins, eds., *The Political Identity of Andrew Marvell* (Aldershot, 1990), 111–34.

Hilton Kelliher, compiler, *Andrew Marvell, Poet & Politician, 1621–78: An Exhibition to Commemorate the Tercentenary of His Death* (London, 1978).

'Marvell's *Last Instructions to a Painter*: From Manuscript to Print', *English Manuscript Studies* 13 (2007), 296–343.

Pierre Legouis, *André Marvell: Poète, Puritain, Patriote, 1621–1678* (Paris, 1928); translated and abridged as *Andrew Marvell: Poet, Puritan, Patriot, 1621–1678* (Oxford, 1965).

Nicholas McDowell, *Poetry and Allegiance in the English Civil Wars: Marvell and the Cause of Wit* (Oxford, 2008).

Nicholas Murray, *World Enough and Time: The Life of Andrew Marvell* (London, 1999).

David Norbrook, *Writing the English Republic: Poetry, Rhetoric and Politics, 1627–1660* (Cambridge, 1999).

Annabel Patterson, *Marvell and the Civic Crown* (Princeton, 1978).

Marvell: The Writer in Public Life (Harlow, 2000).

Nigel Smith, *Andrew Marvell: The Chameleon* (New Haven and London, 2010).

Nicholas von Maltzahn, 'Marvell's Ghost', in Warren Chernaik and Martin Dzelzainis, eds., *Marvell and Liberty* (Basingstoke, 1999), 50–74.

An Andrew Marvell Chronology (Basingstoke, 2005).

'Andrew Marvell and the Prehistory of Whiggism', in David Womersley, ed., assisted by Paddy Bullard and Abigail Williams, *Cultures of Whiggism: New Essays on English Literature and Culture in the Long Eighteenth Century* (Newark, NJ, 2005), 31–61.

'Death by Drowning: Marvell's "Lycidas"', *Milton Studies* 48 (2008), 38–52.

John M. Wallace, *Destiny His Choice: The Loyalism of Andrew Marvell* (Cambridge, 1968).

Blair Worden, *Literature and Politics in Cromwellian England: John Milton, Andrew Marvell, Marchamont Nedham* (Oxford, 2007), chapters 3–6.

INDEX

INDEX

militia, 112–13, 115
Milton, John, 3, 19, 42, 68, 115, 179, 186, 209, 214
Monk, General George, Duke of Albemarle, 65
More, Thomas, 106, 125
Moseley, Humphrey, 15, 16
Murray, Nicholas, 202

Narcissus, 20
natural world, 3–4, 122–39
Nedham, Marchamont, 13, 150–4, 178
Nelthorpe, Edward, 118
New Criticism, 142
Nicene, 170. *See* Marvell, Andrew: creeds
Nonconformists, 40, 103, 115, 163, 170
Norbrook, David, 142
Nun Appleton, 46, 135

Overton, Robert, 115
Ovid, 19, 21, 78
Oxenbridge family, 159
Oxenbridge, John, 161

Parker, Samuel, 40, 164, 167, 177, 182–7, 200, 214–15
pastoralism, 38, 126–7, 131–2, 160
patronage, 11
Patterson, Annabel, 41, 142
Peachment, Christopher, 195
Pepys, Samuel, 104, 152, 167
Petrarch, 2, 58
Philips, Katherine, 12, 43
Platonism, 13
Pocock, John G. A., 104
Polito, Robert, 51
Popple, Edmond, 102, 103, 116, 117
Popple, William, 111, 117, 181, 191, 195, 210
praise poems, 15
print culture, 16, 177, 189
Protectorate, 10, 17, 62–3, 119, 140, 144–7, 148
Protestantism, 68, 105, 106, 165–6

Ramsden, John, 110, 114
Restoration, 40, 41, 99, 102–3, 111, 112–19, 163
Ricks, Christopher, 178

Rochester, 212 John Wilmot, 2nd Earl of
roses, 80
royalists, 15–16
Rubens, Peter Paul, 99
Rupert, Prince, of the Rhine, 199

Sandys, George, 20
Schwyzer, Philip, 69
Seneca, 34
Shadwell, Thomas, 42
Shakespeare, William, 19, 108, 125
Shell, Alison, 69
Sherburne, Edward, 12
Shirley, James, 13, 19
Smith, Nigel, 21, 71, 74
Spenser, Edmund, 69
Stanley, Thomas, 13, 14, 20
Stillingfleet, Edward
Stocker, Margarita, 59
Swift, Jonathan, 182

Taylor, Jeremy, 12
Thompson family, 117, 118
Thompson, Edward, 141, 197, 213
Toland, John, 191
Touchstone, 174, 175
Trott, Sir John, 8, 105
Turner, Francis, 188–9

Villiers family, 9, 11
Virgil, 14
Virgin Mary, 69
von Maltzahn, Nicholas, 171

Wallace, John M., 9, 142
Waller, Edmund, 29, 98, 148, 180
Wayne, Don E., 124
Wharton, Philip Lord, 159, 163, 166, 181–2
Whiggery, 3, 118, 141, 158, 163, 196–7, 199
Wilcher, Robert, 59, 60, 142
Williams, Raymond, 134
Witty, Robert, 9, 34
Worden, Blair, 142

York, 115, 117–18

Zwicker, Steven N., 206–7

Cambridge Companions to. . .

AUTHORS

TOPICS